GOING YARD

The Everything Home Run Book

Lew Freedman

Foreword and Commentary by Frank Thomas

TRIUMPH
BOOKS

Library of Congress Cataloging-in-Publication Data

Freedman, Lew.
   Going yard : the everything home run book / Lew Freedman ; foreword and commentary by Frank Thomas.
      p. cm.
   ISBN 978-1-60078-535-1
   1. Home runs (Baseball) 2. Baseball—United States—History. 3. Baseball players—United States. I. Title.
   GV868.4.F74 2011
   796.357'26—dc22

                              2010051214

This book is available in quantity at special discounts for your group or organization. For further information, contact:

Triumph Books
542 South Dearborn Street
Suite 750
Chicago, Illinois 60605
(312) 939-3330
Fax (312) 663-3557
www.triumphbooks.com

Printed in U.S.A.
ISBN: 978-1-60078-535-1
Design by Wagner Donovan Design

Frank Thomas headshot courtesy of AP Images

CONTENTS

Foreword

A home run is always something special, a game changer, a momentum-changing hit. A lot of things have got to happen before you hit a home run. You've got to be focused. The pitcher's got to throw the right pitch. You've got an area with your bat that you can control, and you have a swing line.

I never really went to the plate thinking about hitting a home run. I was always taught that the home run happens. You should focus on hitting the ball hard, and good things happen. That was my goal throughout my whole career. Just to hit the ball hard.

I started playing baseball when I was 11 or 12 years old in Little League, and I was a home run hitter right away. I'm a big guy, but I wasn't that big for my age group. I had great hand-eye coordination as a kid. I followed the usual path in baseball, from Little League to Babe Ruth League to high school. And at Auburn University I played football as well as baseball.

My sophomore year in high school at Columbus High School in Columbus, Georgia, I hit a home run to win the state championship. I hit .400 that year. My high school coach was driven, and he made you want to play baseball. We had a very good team and I was around some special players. That's when I knew I wanted to be a professional baseball player.

When I was playing football for Auburn, that was the first time in my life I had a trainer force me to work out hard. The trainer was strict, so when I got back to the baseball field in the spring, the ball was really jumping off my bat like I had never seen. I had been a good hitter, but after that first year of football training and weightlifting for the football team, man, I had extra strength. I put on 15 pounds of muscle going from a boy to a man, and I could see the difference that first year.

I was 6'4½" when I got to Auburn and I had a natural swing. Don't get me wrong. I was a big home run hitter in high school, but when I put on that 15 pounds of muscle, man. I went from 240 to 255. Later, I was about 265 pounds with the White Sox. Actually, when I first got to the White Sox I was 255, but in spring training in Sarasota, Florida, there was a trainer who made us run, run, run. I'd never run so much in my life. I was 255 when I got there, but I went down to 240. I was in the best shape of my life.

Football was always my favorite sport, but baseball was always my No. 1 sport to play. Realistically, I knew I couldn't play football for a long time. Those careers just don't last that long. I always thought if I made it in baseball it would last for a while because I would have an advantage of being bigger and stronger than everybody else. It was true.

My goal was always to be an all-around hitter. But my size created an image for some people who felt I should be mainly a home run hitter. That shocked them. I never cared about hitting home runs as much as some other people did. I would drive the ball into the gap between the bases, hit those doubles, try to score runs, just do whatever I could to help the team win. I am perfectly okay with making contact.

Growing up in Columbus, Georgia, I used to watch Hank Aaron and Dale Murphy with the Atlanta Braves. I was never just a home run hitter. I was not a guy who would go up to the plate and just try to crush one. I always felt that scoring runs for the team, to drive one in or taking a walk to score one, was important. The outcome was just to get on base and make something happen. One of my favorites to watch was Dave Winfield. He was so big, like 6'6", his hitting just didn't make sense. This guy was huge. He could be in the NBA if he wanted to, playing basketball. It was special to watch him hit because it's really hard for a guy that big to have the kind of hand-eye coordination he had and to shorten his swing to make great contact.

Most people think because you're big it should be easy to hit a baseball. It's not. When you're big and tall there are a lot of other things going on. It's the short, stocky guys who have won in baseball. Being tall changes the strike zone. There haven't been many really tall guys who have done that well in baseball. You've got to be short and sweet to play baseball and cover the strike zone. The strike zone is different for every guy, and it's bigger for big guys.

I became a student of the game and a student of hitting when I first went to the White Sox in 1990 and it was my hitting coach, Walt Hriniak, who really changed my life as a hitter. He taught mechanics and the consistency of mechanics in your swing. To be successful, you have to do the same thing day in and day out. He was correct. I profited from that.

Walt just broke things down. He said, "To be successful, you've got to work the same way. You've got to take the same approach every day. You've got to do the same routine. I don't care if you're 10-for-10 or you're 0-for-10, you've got to have the same pattern every day." He was so right about that.

There were some people who looked at me and my physique and said, "He's a big guy and he should be able to hit the ball 500'." They thought I should hit home runs all of the time. A lot of people might hit 25 home runs or more, but only bat .250. I remember that happening. I wanted to be one of those guys who won a batting title. And I did win one. It's hard for a guy my size to win a batting title, because I didn't get many infield hits. I had to hit my way and walk my way to a batting title.

Some people felt that big guys like me should be able to hit the ball a country mile. Some days I could hit the ball a long way. Sure, I thought about that, but I never lost focus on hitting the ball where it's pitched. I took what the pitcher gave me.

It can be exciting to hit a home run at a big moment and feel the ballpark erupt because that's what the team needed. It's what the fans needed. It's the ultimate feeling running around those bases because a lot had to happen for that home run to occur. It's not just by accident. You had to be focused. You had to have the perfect swing, and the pitcher had to throw the perfect pitch.

I played in an era when an awful lot of home runs were hit. I guess it goes in cycles. Before Babe Ruth, nobody hit home runs. I played in a real home run era.

When I came into the league, hitting 30 home runs was the standard for a good season. If you hit 40, you were a special player. If you hit 50, you were a major superstar. I consistently hit 40. That's a good testament to hard work, and it spoke of ability and having the right hitting coach who had me doing the same thing every day. I was blessed. When I lost Walt Hriniak, I lost a lot. I told people that. I had a rough couple of years after I lost Walt Hriniak. People said, "Oh, you have this all figured out." You don't have it all figured out. Walt Hriniak was one of those coaches I believed in. There was no B.S. going on. In my mind I felt like I was a robot, in a great way.

I could repeat everything we talked about. I knew we were going to get through a slump one way or another. His advice would carry me through the bad times and the good times with the same work ethic. I got a lot of unfair criticism because I didn't hit more home runs. I was a 40-home run guy. My whole career, my best years were 40, 41, 42. That's me. I knew what my role was. Hitting 40, 41 home runs was my goal every year.

Fans got caught up in the idea that home run hitters had to hit 50 or 60. I just never lost focus on what I was doing. I didn't focus on what everybody else was doing. It was kind of sad when things unfolded and we started hearing about guys taking steroids and performance-enhancing drugs. I played within the system, and I'm proud of my career because I was able to play at a high level against guys who were loaded. I had no idea how many guys were using. When it unfolded, I was like, "Are you kidding me? How could I be so blind?" I'm kind of glad that I was blind to a lot of stuff. I just kept doing stuff with my bat that I was taught as a rookie.

Just play hard and work hard every day. That's what I did throughout my whole career. I think for a three- or four-year period in the late 1990s or so all people wanted to see was home runs. There wasn't as much respect for being a consistent hitter and driving in runs. Consistency is what wins a ballgame. Home

runs do happen, but they don't happen every day. I think people got caught up in, "Who's going to hit a home run today?"

My favorite year was 1994, the strike year. I really think that year would have been my biggest home run year ever. I think I could have gotten 50 that year. I had 38 home runs when we shut down for the strike (in early August). That was my best year, and I only got to finish half of it, basically. The strike year I felt I could have approached Roger Maris' 61 homers.

That's a huge amount of home runs. It's amazing. You have to have that perfect year and that year I was dialing everything. I hit some home runs, got walks, everything was working. Everything I hit well seemed to leave the park. Some years are just great years. You feel it.

There were times when the situation made you think about trying to hit a home run. I'd say it was probably only 10 percent of the time during my career that I ever thought about hitting home runs, which is interesting for a guy who hit so many. And only a few times did it happen. Just a few times that I remember going out and trying to hit one that I did hit one.

But I didn't go up to the plate like Babe Ruth and point to center field or anything like that. You really just can't call the shot. Sometimes I told my teammates I was going to hit a home run. They believed me. They didn't think I was only kidding. When I didn't hit one after saying something they would go, "Oh, whatever." But if I hit one after I said I was going to they were all like, "Holy cow!" You've got to be lucky, and believe me you're not going to be doing it all of the time. There's really no reason to think it's ever going to happen.

I ended up with 521 home runs. That's a lot of home runs. It was the same number Ted Williams got. Ted Williams was a great hitter, but I like to think I was the same kind of hitter. I had a lot of power, but I hit for a good average and I got a lot of walks. Getting a lot of walks showed that I was a disciplined hitter. I didn't just walk up to the plate swinging away. And, of course, Ted Williams was known for that. He got more walks than just about anybody.

I hit a lot of home runs and I got a lot of walks, and it worked for me.

—*Frank Thomas*

Introduction

The home run is the big bang. No single play in baseball has the power to electrify more than a sudden swat that sends a ball into orbit. The home run is baseball's nuclear weapon, the great equalizer. Home runs demoralize opponents and uplift teams that benefit from the runs scored.

Home runs are game changers. Home runs are game deciders. Home runs make fans leap from their seats as if they had sat on a pin cushion. Home runs awe. Home runs leave jaws agape.

Home runs make spectators laugh. Home runs make hearts pound. Home runs elicit shouts. Home runs provoke wild applause.

When launched, home runs fly in an uncontrollable pattern, a punctuation mark for a pitcher's mistake. Sometimes the batter has two strikes and is about to strike out. Fans can be somnambulant one minute, ebullient the next.

Baseball is beloved for its idiosyncrasies, its quirks, its lexicon, its lack of a clock, its subtleties, its strategy, its marathon season, its esoteric nature, its long history. But home run hitters put people in the seats, make good teams great, put the swagger in the game, and create heroes for all ages. Home run hitters are household names.

In the war between power pitchers and power hitters, home run hitters represent the offense and each time they knock a ball into the bleachers or out of the park, the blow symbolizes the triumph of beating the odds. In a sport where batting safely three out of 10 times makes for an All-Star, hitting a home run one out of 15 times at bat makes one a millionaire.

Baseball fans love home runs. It is indisputable. The same fan may appreciate great catches, smart hit-and-run plays, or that southpaw pitching a shutout, but his guilty pleasure—just like munching on thousands of calories worth of chocolate—is cheering for home runs.

Baseball fans root for home runs to rescue their favorite team in the bottom of the ninth inning. They root for someone to hit 50 in a season. They root for someone to hit 500 in a career. Those are magical numbers, and fans admire anyone who can reach the milestones, especially if, in an era of steroid suspicion, a player's career is beyond reproach.

One reason home runs are so popular is because not everyone can hit them. Most of the fans who attend major league baseball games have played or studied the sport. They know how hard it is to hit a pitched ball. They know how difficult it is to hit a pitched ball over the fence. The majority of players on major league rosters don't hit home runs very frequently.

So when a slugger comes along who can belt the ball out of play, seemingly at will, he occasions comment. People go home from the park talking about how far Mickey Mantle, Mike Schmidt, or Mark McGwire hit one. The image sticks in their minds in the way a base hit to right field that wins a game never will. A home run hitter is a Hollywood A-list celebrity. A singles hitter not only never gets lead billing, but he may also be killed off in the opening scene.

Onetime Pittsburgh Pirates basher Ralph Kiner is attributed with a saying that summarizes the difference between a home run clouter and a high-average man without power: "Home run hitters drive Cadillacs, and singles hitters drive Fords."

The home run was once a forgotten weapon, in the rulebook but an afterthought part of the game plan. When the ball was dead, the sport was measured step by step, inch by inch, one base gained at a time like the infantry advancing slowly to claim fresh territory. When the ball came alive, so did the game.

From the moment Babe Ruth took over the sport in the 1920s, American society has bowed down to the slugger. The home run hitter is king. There is something about big muscles and pop in the bat that folks admire more than the precision of taking two and hitting to right. The free seizing of all four bases seems just reward for the batter who hits the ball so far he cannot be put out. The man who hits the most home runs is roughly the baseball equivalent of the heavyweight champion of the world.

The record for the most home runs in a single major league season is 73 by Barry Bonds, surpassing Mark McGwire's 70, who surpassed Roger Maris' 61.

The record for the most home runs in a major league career is 762 by Barry Bonds. He passed Hank Aaron's record of 755, who passed Ruth's record of 714.

Since 1876, when the National League was founded, 25 men have hit at least 500 home runs in their careers. It is an exclusive club of big boppers, and one member is Frank Thomas, who spent most of his career with the Chicago White Sox and after 19 seasons retired with 521 homers.

As the story of the home run unfolds in these pages, Thomas offers his comments about unique and famous moments in home run history, his thoughts on his own home run ability, his memorable and favorite home runs, and his opinions on how steroids have tainted the feats of some who took drugs to enhance their performance.

The 6'5", 270-pound Thomas, a former football player at Auburn University where he was a teammate of Bo Jackson's, is tied with Ted Williams and Willie McCovey on the all-time home run list. He also drove in 1,704 runs and batted .301 with 1,667 walks and a .419 on-base percentage. A two-time American League Most Valuable Player Award-winner and a five-time All-Star, Thomas also won the 1997 AL batting championship.

Thomas may have hit a lot of home runs, but he didn't take them for granted.

"It's the hardest thing to do in pro sports," Thomas said. "There's a lot that goes into hitting a home run. I think a lot of people don't understand. You watch guys taking batting practice, and even then a lot of guys are trying to hit home runs and they don't hit a home run. It's harder than people think. You've got guys throwing the ball in the mid-90s and they throw to a certain spot. If you crack one and hit a home run, it's a special thing."

Babe Ruth did not invent the home run. He did popularize it and revolutionize baseball with his timing and gargantuan feats. Completely overshadowed by Ruth and the next generation of home run sluggers, the early home run hitters seem like a quaint bunch, with home run totals that leave the modern-day reader chuckling and with nicknames all out of proportion to the numbers produced. But they are part of the lore.

We all know who hit the most home runs in a major league season, but who hit the most in the minors? In the movie *Bull Durham*, Kevin Costner's character Crash Davis breaks the minor league record for the most homers. Who is the real-life Crash?

For discussion: Does having the most home runs make you the greatest home run hitter of all-time? Does being the greatest home run hitter of all time make you the greatest baseball player of all time? What is the most famous home run in baseball history? What is the most important home run in baseball history? They are not automatically the same thing.

Included in the following pages are home run lists and anecdotes of the larger than life and the most unlikely, of the famous and the obscure. The numbers may settle arguments, but the opinions will only fuel debate.

Every baseball fan knows what a home run is when he sees it. Goodbye, Mr. Spalding. But sitting in the stands with someone who has never seen a baseball game, what words would be used to define a homer? Try this: A hit driving the ball safely beyond the reach of the opponent fielders and permitting the batter to make a circuit of the bases to score a run.

Or this: A home run occurs when the ball is hit in such a way that the batter is able to circle the bases in one play without any errors being committed by the defensive team.

Those thoughts cover smacking the ball onto Waveland Avenue at Wrigley Field, hitting it over the Green Monster at Fenway Park, or an inside-the-park home run.

The only thing left to say is, "Play ball!"

Note. The author would like to thank the National Baseball Hall of Fame Research Library, director Tim Wiles, Freddy Borowski, and Bill Francis. And thanks to former Chicago White Sox slugger Frank Thomas.

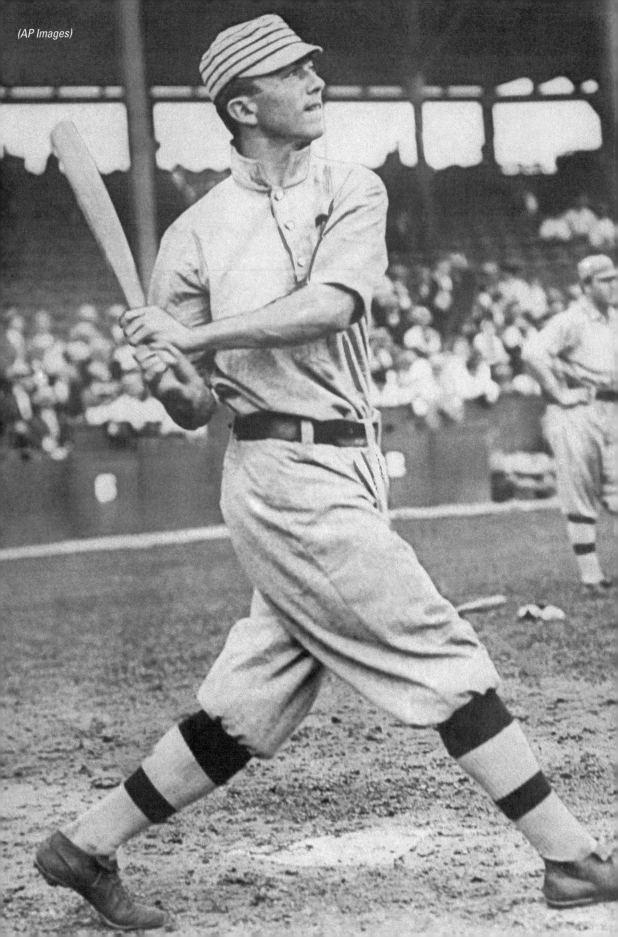

CHAPTER 1

THE DEAD-BALL ERA

450
440
430
420
410
400
390
380
370
360
350
340
330
320
310
300
290
280
270
260

When Ross Barnes of the Chicago White Stockings stepped into the batter's box on May 2, 1876, he was about to make history and become the answer to a trivia question that would stump even the best *Jeopardy* players.

In the first season of National League play, Barnes was the leading batsman, hitting .429, but for those who seek out his name and background, Barnes represents something else. The 5'8", 145-pound second baseman from Mount Morris, New York, did not have a very long career, but in this game, facing the Cincinnati Red Stockings' pitcher Cherokee Fisher in the fifth inning, Barnes did something special.

He hit a home run.

It was the only home run that Barnes hit in the 66 games he played that season. However, it was notable because his swat was the first home run ever hit in major league play.

Roscoe Charles Barnes (or as was also referred to in print, Roscoe Conkling Barnes) is not a name mentioned when great sluggers are listed. Nor was he a slugger by any stretch of the definition. Barnes was the speedy leadoff hitter type who was known for beating out infield hits.

Never has there been a case of making a home run count more. Barnes, who played just four major league seasons and won a batting title but hit just two home runs total in his career.

Given how insignificant the home run was as a play during Barnes' time and how few he hit, the wavy-haired infielder who died in 1915 probably would laugh to hear his name associated with the feat.

Home runs were always part of the rules package in major league play. But it's just that they were nothing special in the early days of the sport as a profession.

There were several obstacles to an individual hitting many home runs in a season in the early days of baseball. There was no emphasis on the home run as a strategy for bringing runners in to score—the entire approach was advancing one base at a time to home plate. Ballparks were not symmetrical, with peculiar and

Baseballs, like many politicians, were not wrapped too tight. They were sometimes lopsided, with threads in danger of unraveling and stitches coming loose. They were not as hard at the center. For decades, it was expected and demanded that foul balls be returned to umpires to keep them in use. They were kept in play for pitch after pitch and hit after hit until after they softened up.

Thus was born the phrase "Dead-Ball Era" to describe the period of time in Major League Baseball between the founding of the National League in 1876 and 1920. Historians consider this a pitcher's period of dominance. Ty Cobb, perhaps the greatest player of all time, who batted .366 mainly for the Detroit Tigers over 24 seasons, termed the style of play "the scientific game."

THE GEORGIA PEACH

The swashbuckling Cobb exhibited a take-no-prisoners type of baseball. He scratched for every hit, relished turning bunts into singles, stole bases with abandon, and was so hard-nosed taking the extra base that he always seemed poised for a fight. Cobb ruled the game when hitting a home run was a rarity, yet he belted 117 homers in his career. He hit as many as 12 in a season and actually won the American League home run title in 1909 with nine.

In Cobb's view, however, hitting home runs was less than sporting. A ballplayer wasn't earning a run if he just knocked the ball into the stands with one swing. Cobb was no fool, either. He could see how a proliferation of home run hitting would undercut what he did best. He

Ross Barnes, who played for the National Association's Boston Red Stockings in the early 1870s, hit the first home run in major league history while playing for the Chicago White Stockings on May 2, 1876.
(Mark Rucker/Transcendental Graphics/Getty Images)

lengthy dimensions to various fields, the high average hitter was the best rewarded player in salary, and above all there was the dead ball.

Detroit's Ty Cobb slides around Philadelphia Athletics third baseman Frank "Home Run" Baker during a game at Detroit's Navin Field. Cobb, who collected 4,189 hits and stole 897 bases in his career, was critical of the proliferation of home run hitting in the 1920s.
(Mark Rucker/Transcendental Graphics/Getty Images)

took great pride in his game and being the all-around best player.

For most of his career, which began in 1905, Cobb gave little thought to home runs. They were part of the game but not plays that excited the crowd as much as stealing home might. Still, years after the game was played, Cobb cited a home run he hit against the Philadelphia Athletics in

a 17-inning contest in 1907 as his greatest thrill in baseball.

Cobb first began to speak out against the home run in the 1920s, when he was still active and when Babe Ruth was battering down fences and smiting mighty blows beyond outfield walls at unprecedented rates. Dismayed by the attention Ruth received for his long-

4

distance pokes and with the way fans responded to the homers, Cobb could see his own legacy being tarnished before he even retired.

In 1952, after the home run had transformed the game and after Ruth's death, Cobb penned a two-part series for *Life* magazine that was called "They Don't Play Baseball Any More."

"There are only two players in the major leagues today who can be mentioned in the same breath with the old-time greats," Cobb said. "Most players don't learn the fundamentals. Most of them don't practice. They don't even train. The sole object, encouraged by the lively ball and the shortened fences, is to make home runs.

"One of the few scientific hitters left in baseball today is Phil Rizzuto. Pound for pound he is the best baseball player alive." What Cobb admired most about the one-time New York Yankees shortstop was his ability to bunt. Being a superb bunter was more important in Cobb's eyes than being a home run hitter. The other player of the time Cobb admired unequivocally was Stan Musial. Cobb considered Ted Williams a great natural hitter but one who pulled the ball too often.

The irascible but highly intelligent Cobb also raised some what-ifs in making comparisons between eras. He wondered how the Musials, Williamses, and Joe DiMaggios would fare against pitchers with an arsenal that could legally include spitballs, balls slit by razor blades, emery balls, and other trick pitches of a soggy nature.

"There were lots of ways of tampering with balls in the old days," Cobb told *Life*. "The greatest disgrace of modern

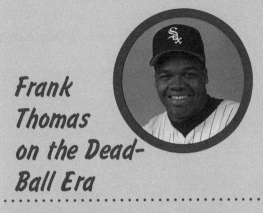

Frank Thomas on the Dead-Ball Era

"Boy, the dead-ball era had to be tough. They had to be big strong guys to hit home runs then. It's amazing how big some of the ballparks were. That park in Boston with 635' to center field. That's amazing to think about. No wonder nobody hit many home runs. You would need a bazooka to hit one out. It was just different times."

baseball is that few batters even know how to lay down a good bunt. Modern baseball puts a premium on the freak, on the man who will hit the ball over the fence if he hits it at all."

And Cobb never saw Dave Kingman play.

Did Cobb make some good points? Yes. Was Cobb more jealous than anything else?

Probably.

AN EVOLVING SPORT

The standard baseball of the 2000s weighs between five and five and one quarter ounces. Manufactured from the inside out, the center of a hard ball under baseball rules must be cork, rubber, or a substance that is similar to those, be covered by yarn, then horsehide or cowhide.

When professional baseball was just beginning in the latter half of the 1800s,

"Big Dan" Brouthers, pictured with Philadelphia in 1896, slugged 106 home runs between 1879 and 1896. *(Mark Rucker/ Transcendental Graphics/Getty Images)*

the center of a ball might be made from a walnut, a rock, or a bullet, according to data unearthed by Tim Wiles, director of the National Baseball Hall of Fame Research Library. Covers were made of horsehide or cowhide, and the weight

of the ball was considerably less precise, weighing between three and six ounces.

The ball became more uniform and standardized over time, but in 1910, Wiles noted, George Reach, known throughout the sport as publisher of his own baseball annual and operator of a line of sporting goods, discovered that a cork center made for a baseball that took off more readily when clubbed. The so-called "lively" ball was introduced for regular season play in 1911, but full-time usage of the ball and adaptation in strategy to change hitting approaches did not take root immediately.

The year 1920 marked a major change in major league baseball rules. The spitball and other pitches that relied on artificial stimulants were outlawed. Although a select number of active spitball pitchers were grandfathered in, the sea change benefited hitters. Knowing that they would not have to hit crazily floating pitches, hitters became more relaxed at the plate. Also, the decision to permit fans in the stands to keep foul balls as souvenirs was a boon to batters. More and more new, fresh baseballs were put into play replacing bruised or softened balls.

Although Babe Ruth hit 29 home runs for the Boston Red Sox in 1919, he was a solo phenomenon until the 1920s. With Ruth's flamboyance, popularity, and dramatic style dominating the headlines of newspaper sports pages and fans swooning over his air-clearing swings even when he missed, other players tried to focus on hitting home runs, too.

That attitude represented a whole new way of thinking, akin to the switch from silent movies to talkies. The home run hitter of the past would not be the home run hitter of the future. The dead-ball era kings of home runs were eclipsed quickly but, like Barnes, left a mark.

EARLY HOME RUN KINGS

George William Hall was born in England in 1849 and was a member of the Philadelphia club of the National League during that circuit's first season of play in 1876. A .345 hitter in two National League seasons, Hall's claim to home run fame is being the first season's home run champ. Hall hit five homers that year.

Later, when with the Louisville Grays, Hall was implicated in a scandal and confessed to throwing games. He was out of organized baseball by 1881. Despite only his handful of homers, Hall's record stood for three seasons because the next two major league home run champs, Lip Pike and Paul Hines, hit just four apiece.

Although not even the most devoted of baseball fans have likely heard of Ross Barnes or George Hall, one early season home run champion is far better known. In 1881, Dan Brouthers won the first of his two home run crowns with eight blows. Nicknamed "Big Dan," Brouthers capped his 19-year career with a .342 average and 106 home runs. Brouthers clouted a high of 12 homers in 1887, a year after he led the league with 11.

Brouthers also won four National League batting championships and another in the American Association. A wavy-haired dude with a thick, dashing mustache and plenty of pop in his bat, Brouthers was a free swinger who could practically start a hurricane with a whiff at strike one.

"Brouthers really was a great hitter, one of the most powerful batters of all time," said legendary New York Giants manager John McGraw. "The first time I ever ran across Brouthers, he was with the Red Sox. He had a great reputation as a slugger, and our pitchers did their best to keep from feeding him a low ball. He not only hit low balls hard, but he hit them where nobody could get them."

In a story in the 1960s, Boston sportswriter Harry Grayson called Brouthers "the Babe Ruth of the '80s and '90s" because he too began as a pitcher and then uncovered his latent talent as a hitter. Brouthers was elected to the Hall of Fame in 1945.

A player who has a little bit more long-term notoriety—in Philadelphia annals, anyway—is Sam Thompson, who led the National League in home runs with 20 in 1889 and did so again with 18 in 1895.

Thompson hit .331 lifetime, and in 1894 he was part of the Phillies' outfield that was the only one to ever send out three .400 hitters in the same year. Thompson batted .415 that season, and Ed Delahanty complemented him at .404 and Billy Hamilton at .403. Thompson hit 126 career home runs, the National League record until Rogers Hornsby surpassed him in 1924, two years after Thompson's death.

One of Thompson's old teammates, a catcher named Charlie Bennett, reminisced about the player when he died. Thompson, Bennett said, hit the ball so hard "infielders used to blow on their fingers" to assuage the pain from his line drives. Thompson sounds as if he was much like the power-hitting sluggers who followed him in the game.

BIG ED

One of the true greats of the early days of baseball, whose life ended

7

> "[Dan] Brouthers had a great reputation as a slugger, and our pitchers did their best to keep from feeding him a low ball. He not only hit low balls hard, but he hit them where nobody could get them."
>
> —*New York Giants manager John McGraw*

mysteriously while he was still active, is Big Ed Delahanty, the best of five major league brothers.

Big Ed was born in 1867 in Cleveland and broke into the majors in 1888. He was eventually joined by brothers Frank, James, Joseph, and Thomas. Together they comprise the largest contingent of brothers ever in the majors. Ed Delahanty was the best in the family with a lifetime average of .346 and 455 stolen bases. Delahanty led the National League in homers with 19 in 1893 and with 13 in 1896. Lord knows what Delahanty would have batted if he would have been a disciplined hitter.

"If I could only hold myself like that old crab Cap Anson," Delahanty said, "I would bat better than he ever did. But I can't. When the ball seems to me to be coming to my liking, I am going to belt it. I don't care where it comes. I'll either hit it or miss it, and when I miss it, God knows I'll miss it by a mile."

A story in the *Sporting News* in 1943 was headlined "Mighty Mauler Delahanty Put Life in Dead Ball." Delahanty

Sam Thompson, whose likeness was captured in this 1887 lithograph as a member of the Detroit Wolverines, totaled 126 career home runs. *(Transcendental Graphics/Getty Images)*

possessed speed and power. According to the *Baseball Encyclopedia*, Delahanty measured 6'1" and 170 pounds. But period newspaper accounts variously refer to him as weighing 190 pounds or even 210 pounds. Maybe they didn't want to suggest that small guys could hit homers.

Delahanty recorded one of the greatest single days by any home run hitter. Boston's Bobby Lowe established the record of four home runs in one game on May 30, 1894. It has been tied several times since but never broken. On July 13, 1896, Delahanty captured his share of the record with four homers in one game. But Delahanty also cracked a single, giving him 17 total bases, another record. In the 115 years since Delahanty accomplished his feat, there have been arguments about just how many of his homers actually left the park.

Delahanty, who batted .410 in 1899, won two batting titles, too. He didn't seem to appreciate that smashing four home runs in a game would be long-remembered. He seemed to care more about garnering a high average, typical of his time. When Delahanty slugged one of his homers he was congratulated upon return to the dugout by a teammate. But Delahanty said, "If I could have cut up that hit into singles, I'd lead the whole damn league."

In a strange way, Delahanty is best recalled for the end of his life instead of the greatest day of his life. No foul play was ever proved, and suicide was surmised, but Delahanty plunged to his death from a railroad bridge over the Niagara River on July 2, 1903, in the middle of the baseball season. Some thought he was pushed. Some thought he jumped.

Hall of Famer Ed Delehanty, pictured as a member of the Washington Senators in 1903, slugged 101 home runs over 16 seasons before his mysterious death on July 2, 1903. *(Chicago History Museum/Getty Images)*

At the time, Delahanty was jumping teams from Washington to the Giants. Known as a heavy drinker, some reports indicated Delahanty was ousted from the train for his drunken belligerence, and other stories say he fought with a railroad employee on the tracks. No one knew for sure, and it was a week before his body was discovered.

Delahanty hit 101 home runs over 16 years and was just a few months shy of his 35th birthday when he perished.

Dead-Ball Era Home Run Champions

NATIONAL LEAGUE				AMERICAN LEAGUE		
1876	George Hall	5		1908	Tim Jordan	12
1877	Lip Pike	4		1909	Red Murray	7
1878	Paul Hines	4		1910	Fred Beck and	
1879	Charley Jones	9			Wildfire Schulte	10
1880	Jim O'Rourke and			1911	Wildfire Schulte	21
	Harry Stovey	6		1912	Heinie Zimmerman	14
1881	Dan Brouthers	8		1913	Gavvy Cravath	19
1882	George Wood	7		1914	Gavvy Cravath	19
1883	Buck Ewing	10		1915	Gavvy Cravath	24
1884	Ned Williamson	27		1916	Dave Robertson and	
1885	Abner Dalrymple	11			Cy Williams	12
1886	Dan Brouthers and			1917	Gavvy Cravath and	
	Hardy Richardson	11			Dave Robertson	12
1887	Billy O'Brien	19		1918	Gavvy Cravath	8
1888	Jimmy Ryan	16		1919	Gavvy Cravath	12
1889	Sam Thompson	20				
1890	Osyter Burns,					
	Mike Tiernan, and					
	Walt Wilmot	13		AMERICAN LEAGUE		
1891	Harry Stovey and			1901	Nap Lajoie	14
	Mike Tiernan	16		1902	Socks Seybold	16
1892	Bug Holliday	13		1903	Buck Freeman	13
1893	Ed Delahanty	19		1904	Harry Davis	10
1894	Hugh Duffy	18		1905	Harry Davis	8
1895	Sam Thompson	18		1906	Harry Davis	12
1896	Ed Delahanty and			1907	Harry Davis	8
	Bill Joyce	13		1908	Sam Crawford	8
1897	Hugh Duffy	11		1909	Ty Cobb	9
1898	Jimmy Collins	15		1910	Jake Stahl	10
1899	Buck Freeman	25		1911	Frank Baker	11
1900	Herman Long	12		1912	Frank Baker and	
1901	Sam Crawford	16			Tris Speaker	10
1902	Tommy Leach	6		1913	Frank Baker	12
1903	Jimmy Sheckard	9		1914	Frank Baker	9
1904	Harry Lumley	9		1915	Braggo Roth	7
1905	Fred Odwell	9		1916	Wally Pipp	12
1906	Tim Jordan	12		1917	Wally Pipp	9
1907	Dave Brain	10		1918	Babe Ruth and	
					Tilly Waker	11
				1919	Babe Ruth	29

"When the ball seems to me to be coming to my liking, I am going to belt it. I don't care where it comes. I'll either hit it or miss it, and when I miss it, God knows I'll miss it by a mile."

—1890s slugger Ed Delahanty

HOME RUN HARRY

The kings of baseball in the 2000s are the big guns, the home run hitters who carry teams on their shoulders to the pennant. The biggest sluggers become familiar names because they either win the home run crown or contend for it each year. Those big boppers endorse automobiles, cereal, you name it.

Maybe Harry Davis got to endorse cigarettes after leading the American League in homers in 1904, 1905, 1906, and 1907, four years in a row for the Philadelphia Athletics. Barely remembered, Davis was the preeminent slugger of the fledgling league although he hit just 10, eight, 12, and eight homers, respectively, in his heyday.

The numerical totals are miniscule by today's standards, right around the type of numbers a fair-hitting second baseman might put up now. But yes, Harry Davis was called "Home Run Harry." Davis was unusual in another way. At Girard College he studied to be a stenographer. However, A's owner and manager Connie Mack recognized that Davis had other talents. He signed him and put him at first base. Davis became captain of Athletics championship teams in the early part of the century. After he died of a stroke, one part of the headline on Davis' 1947 obituary in the *Sporting News* read, "Homer King."

THE BUCK STOPS NOWHERE

Illustrating how being even the best home run hitter in the league was not akin to a get-rich-quick scheme around 1900, John "Buck" Freeman was paid $1,500 when he bashed the unheard of total of 25 in 1899 for the Washington Nationals. In 1903, Freeman recorded the rare accomplishment of leading a second league in homers when he slugged 13 for the American League Boston Red Sox. Freeman also played in the first World Series in 1903 for the Red Sox against the Pittsburgh Pirates.

"That was a great team, that old Red Sox outfit," Freeman said.

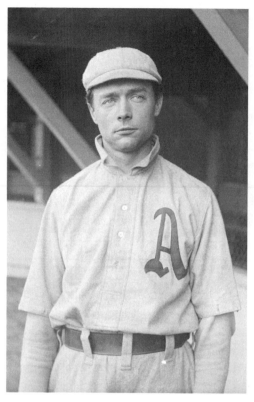

Harry Davis of the Philadelphia Athletics led the American League in home runs four years in a row from 1904 to 1907. *(Chicago History Museum/Getty Images)*

Freeman's run to 25 home runs was not watched with the same enthusiastic perseverance as Babe Ruth's march to 60 in 1927, Roger Maris' pursuit of 61 in 1961, or the Sammy Sosa–Mark McGwire summer of love in 1998. Still, Ira Thomas, a Yankees and Athletics player, said, "Freeman was the greatest home run hitter of all time." It was not clear if Thomas was drunk or sober when making the comment, joking, or truly believed it. "Freeman hit a ball that was hard to make go far."

He did that, but Freeman's emergence as special in his time will have to suffice in terms of all-time ratings.

SETTING THE TABLE FOR RUTH: NED WILLIAMSON AND ROGER CONNOR

Another early basher who hit home runs in bunches before it became fashionable—at least for one year—was Ned Williamson, then playing for the Chicago White Stockings, who in 1884 smacked 27. That was a stupendous total for the time, and Williamson's mark lasted until 1919. Williamson's outbreak of homers was notable for another reason. On May 30 of that 1884 season he mashed three home runs in one game. That made Williamson the first player to record three homers in a single game.

Williamson, who wore a fashionable mustache common to the era, broke into the majors in 1878 with the little-known Indianapolis Blues, a major league team for only that season. A prolific doubles hitter, Williamson totaled just 64 homers in his major league career, nearly half of them in a single season.

Williamson was a member of the crew of players sporting goods magnate Albert Spalding took on baseball's first world tour that included stops in Australia, Ceylon, Egypt, and France, among other countries. Williamson suffered a severe knee injury in Paris. The injury ruined the rest of his career and led to his downfall. Williamson died of tuberculosis and edema at age 36.

If Ross Barnes is an obscure answer to a trivia question, then Roger Connor has him beat, though not by much. Connor hit Major League Baseball's first-ever grand-slam homer. Connor was born in Connecticut in 1857 and broke into the majors in 1880 with the Troy, New York,

Buck Freeman led both the American League and National League in home runs, slugging 25 for Washington in 1899 and 13 for Boston in 1903. *(Chicago History Museum/Getty Images)*

team that was part of the top echelon of the game at the time.

Connor hit baseball's first grand slam on September 10, 1881, in a game against Worcester. Proving he had a sense for the dramatic, Connor's blow came with two outs in the bottom of the ninth inning to win the game 7–4.

The most legendary shot off of Connor's bat occurred at a game in New York in 1886 when he smacked a ball that traveled so far, so quickly, spectators were in awe. Charles Radbourn, the Hall of Fame pitcher, surrendered the hit and said it "sped upward with the speed of a carrier pigeon." However fast that was, Radbourn, better known as "Old Hoss," was duly impressed. There happened to be a crowd of fans from the New York Stock Exchange on hand that was even more impressed.

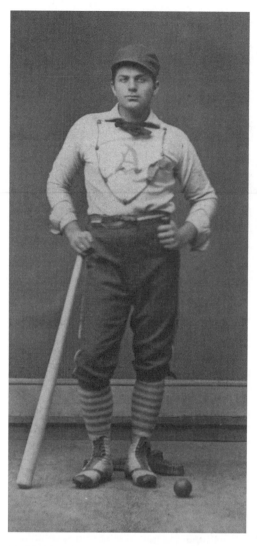

Ned Williamson, pictured in 1887, hit 27 home runs for the Chicago White Stockings in 1884—a major league record that stood until Babe Ruth slugged 29 for the Boston Red Sox in 1919. *(Mark Rucker/Transcendental Graphics/Getty Images)*

They passed the hat to reward Connor for the thrill and collected $500, indeed a princely sum at the time. They took the cash and bought Connor a gold watch to commemorate the occasion.

It was no wonder that Connor could say of his home run hitting prowess, "I used to nail the horsehide over the fence into the tall grass and that would tickle some of the old New York stockbrokers."

Connor was a large man for an athlete of his era, standing 6'3" and weighing 220 pounds. He mostly played first base. Although almost everyone seemed to wear a mustache, Connor's was longer and broader than most. In 1883, Connor, who seemed born for the role of showman in what even then was the nation's most hectic and electrifying city, moved on to play ball in New York.

Connor played 18 seasons. Unusual for the period, he slammed more than 10 homers seven times. He hit three home runs in one game. In his best season he belted 17 and concluded his career with 138 homers, the most until Babe Ruth broke the mark in 1921. His lifetime average was .316 when he retired in 1897. Long after his death, Connor was elected to the Hall of Fame in 1976.

BIGGER PARKS THAN YOSEMITE

Park dimensions discouraged home runs in many cities. When Pittsburgh's Forbes Field opened in 1909, the deepest spot in the park from home plate was 462' away, although it was in a quirky corner, not center field. Center was far enough away at 442'. Center field at New York's Polo Grounds was 483'.

One reason home runs were on the back burner for many teams—besides the fact that the baseball that flew with all of the velocity of a wiffle ball—was the dimensions of some ballparks. Shibe Park, built in Philadelphia in 1909, was the first concrete and steel major league baseball stadium. It also measured 515' to dead center field, an invitation to Paul Bunyan, perhaps but not many mortal human baseball players. It was also 360' down the left-field line, the strong field for right-handed hitters. No cheap home runs at Shibe.

The home of the Boston Red Sox from 1901–11 was the Huntington Avenue Grounds. Center field was 530' from home plate—at first. Then it was expanded to 635' in 1908, a heroically ridiculous distance that ensured no one would ever hit a home run to straightaway center unless his name was Samson.

Huntington Avenue's park was torn down after Fenway Park opened in 1912, but if it had been the Red Sox's home park when Babe Ruth came up a few years later he would have hitch-hiked to New York and not waited to be traded. There may never have been a Babe Ruth as we know him if the Sox had still been at Huntington Avenue. Ruth might have remained a pitcher.

"HOME RUN" BAKER

Babe Ruth had many nicknames, from "Bambino" to "Sultan of Swat," but the irony is that the most appropriate one was taken before he came on the scene, so he was not called "Home Run" Ruth. Frank Baker, a first-class third baseman for the Philadelphia Athletics was called "Home Run" Baker, and he was nowhere near as prolific a home run hitter as The Babe or any of hundreds of other players who came along after Baker's 1908–22 career.

Roger Connor, pictured in 1894, hit the major leagues' first grand slam in 1881. *(Mark Rucker/Transcendental Graphics/Getty Images)*

"Home Run" Baker did lead the American League in homers four times in a row, with 11 in 1911, 10 in 1912, 12 in 1913, and nine in 1914. He was out of control compared to others at that time, but that shows the comparative insignificance of the home run if Baker was highlighted as a slugger extraordinaire. These days he would be moved to shortstop or second base because third is a power position, and Baker's light-hitting credentials wouldn't get him into the starting lineup there.

Though it was possible this comparison has never been made by anyone else, Baker earned his nickname by performing like Reggie Jackson in the postseason. If Jackson was "Mr. October" for his long-distance blasts during the playoffs and

500-Home Run Club

1.	Barry Bonds	762
2.	Hank Aaron	755
3.	Babe Ruth	714
4.	Willie Mays	660
5.	Ken Griffey Jr.	630
6.	Alex Rodriguez	613
7.	Sammy Sosa	609
8.	Jim Thome	589
9.	Frank Robinson	586
10.	Mark McGwire	583
11.	Harmon Killebrew	573
12.	Rafael Palmeiro	569
13.	Reggie Jackson	563
14.	Manny Ramirez	555
15.	Mike Schmidt	548
16.	Mickey Mantle	536
17.	Jimmie Foxx	534
18.	Frank Thomas, Ted Williams, and Willie McCovey	521
21.	Ernie Banks and Eddie Mathews	512
23.	Mel Ott	511
24.	Gary Sheffield	509
25.	Eddie Murray	504

World Series with the Oakland A's and New York Yankees, Baker was "Mr. End Of Season," at least, in an era that had no division playoffs or league championship series.

Baker's time to shine was the World Series, which, way back when, didn't always extend very far into October, never mind courting November. Baker was a member of Connie Mack's $100,000 infield (Alex Rodriguez's late-night snack money) in the early 20th century, and when his Philadelphia A's went up against John McGraw's New York Giants in the Series in 1911, Baker won two straight games with home runs. He took Rube Marquard deep in the first one and went yard on Christy Mathewson in the next game. The A's won the Series, four games to two.

Two years later Baker hit another home run during the World Series against the Giants. Baker grew up in a tiny town in Maryland and retired to it as well. In 1955, he was selected for the Baseball Hall of Fame, the frosting on the cake of his career. Baker did envision himself making game-winning hits but not ever being voted into the sport's hall.

"I could see myself in a big-league uniform," Baker said of his younger days. "I dreamed of playing before big crowds. I dreamed of being a hero. But never, never, never did I dream that I would ever be in the Hall of Fame."

It is actually a wonder that Baker ever hit a home run because at times—including against Mathewson and Marquard for the big blows—he swung a 52-ounce bat. That's not a bat; that's a maple tree. Some major leaguers might not have been able to lift it, never mind swing it levelly at a fastball. Baker called it using "a man's size

bat. You had to hit that ball fair and square and with some weight and back of it to make it go over the fence."

Baker's career overlapped the prime time of the spitter and unexamined goofy pitches, followed by baseball's ban of them.

"I'm certainly glad that the spitball, emery ball, and the paraffin [wax] ball were ruled out," Baker said. "These pitches gave hurlers an unfair advantage over the batters. I would be opposed to legalizing them again. The spitter was tough to hit. The emery ball handcuffed everybody. I'd have to say that the spitter was the most effective of all trick pitches."

A few years before his death in 1963, Baker, who hit 96 homers in all, compared dead-ball slugging against modern lively ball slugging.

"Baseball is just a different game than when I played it," Baker said. "Home runs were much rarer, but I used to get a big bang out of hitting one and so did the Philadelphia fans. Now they hit as many home runs in a day as we sometimes hit in a month, but the present game is a good spectacle and the crowds certainly do enjoy it."

Frank Baker's nickname pretty much made him the best-known home run

"It's a great thing to stand up at the plate, knock a home run, leisurely trot around the bases, and listen to the wild ravings of the howling fans. A guy who knocks the ball out of the lot is a hero in these modern times."

—*1910s National League slugger Gavvy Cravath, years after he retired*

hitter of the dead-ball era, and the appellation gives him a certain cachet with baseball fans that might not otherwise have heard of him. However, it doesn't automatically make him the best home run hitter of the dead-ball era. Roger Connor is in the running, but another, lesser-known figure only dimly remembered outside of Philadelphia was Gavvy Cravath, who was ahead of his time smashing home runs.

A HOME RUN FINED: GAVVY CRAVATH

Cravath, the onetime Phillies outfielder, won six National League home run crowns between 1913 and 1919 with the first three coming in a row. Cravath hit 19 dingers in 1913, 19 in 1914, and blasted 24 in 1915.

Cravath was born in Poway, California, in 1881. After five seasons in the Pacific Coast League where he never hit more than 13 homers, Cravath reached the majors with the Boston Red Sox in

1908 and played for the Chicago White Sox and Washington Senators in 1909. But soon he was back in the minors in Minneapolis. Cravath got his real chance to perform with the Phils in 1912 when he was already past 30. He promptly reached double figures in homers eight times and totaled 119.

If more evidence was needed that Cravath and the handful of sluggers like him in the dead-ball era were ahead of their time, Cravath had a story stashed in his hip pocket that he loved to pull out in his later years when the home run had become more popular.

After his first trip to the majors ended in 1909, Cravath hooked up with the Minneapolis Millers, then a Double A minor league team. He found his stroke and began bashing the ball out of the park so often that the Federal Aviation Administration was about to start classifying him as his own airline.

Most of Cravath's home runs flew over the right-field wall. Trying to prove he belonged in the majors again, the player was loving the show he put on, until one day when his manager angrily confronted Cravath and ordered him to stop hitting the ball over the fence or face a $50 fine.

"Can you beat that?" Cravath said. "Fined $50 for making a home run instead of getting patted on the back. I couldn't make it out and thought Joe [Cantillon] had lost his mind until I learned the true facts of the case."

The story behind the story was that a men's clothing store was located across the street from right field at Nicollet Park, and Cravath's shots were crashing through the owner's large plate-glass window. The owner was not a baseball fan, and each time a ball either bounced off the street through his window or a ball shattered it on the fly, he raced across the street to complain. He demanded $50 each time to replace the window.

Cravath was told to cease and desist because he was costing a money-losing operation too much money. Still, he ended up bashing 29 homers that summer, and it earned him his fresh chance with the Phillies. It was worth the aggravation.

Even if Cravath's home run prowess peaked before the lively ball became part of everyday play, he remained a home run fan throughout his life and gained some satisfaction from the benefits future sluggers earned. Years later he reflected on how the home run hitter had evolved into a player accorded great respect and fame. He did refer to the lively ball as "the jackrabbit ball" and lighter bats as "whiplash, thin-handled bats which they can swing faster and pull the ball."

He begrudged none of them their due.

Gavvy Cravath, center, poses with Philadelphia Phillies teammates including Casey Stengel, left, before a game in 1919. Cravath won six National League home run crowns between 1913 and 1919. *(Mark Rucker/ Transcendental Graphics/Getty Images)*

"It's a great thing to stand up at the plate, knock a home run, leisurely trot around the bases, and listen to the wild ravings of the howling fans," Cravath said years after his own career ended. "A guy who knocks the ball out of the lot is a hero in these modern times."

Cravath would have been happy to be one of them, a slugger swinging at the lively ball, but he was 40 when the lively ball change came.

"I merely submit that the good hitters of my time were unfortunate in that they didn't put the jackrabbit in the ball soon enough," Cravath said. "We were born too soon."

CHAPTER 2

THE
BABE

450
440
430
420
410
400
390
380
370
360
350
340
330
320
310
300
290
280
270
260

> "Fame is a spotlight one minute and a bull's-eye the next. The people who cheer loudest when you succeed are those who throw pop bottles when you fall. The crowd begins by overrating you. When you don't live up to its exaggerated opinion of you, it underrates you. Nobody would be famous if people didn't go to such extremes. Loud cheers make heroes. Pop bottles make martyrs."
>
> *—Babe Ruth*

George Herman Ruth was a man for his times. The product of a Baltimore orphanage whose prodigious feats transformed the way baseball was played, he came to adulthood as a poor man yet become the icon of an era and acquired riches.

As much as Babe Ruth's singular ability to smash a baseball into the stratosphere electrified, enthralled, and entertained fans, he was as much a symbol of America's wildest decade, the Roaring '20s, as he was of America's national pastime. Ruth was the ultimate example of living large at a time when everyone either did so—or wished he could.

The two sides of Ruth, on the field and off, went hand in hand. Ruth was sent to the orphanage, abandoned by his parents because he was supposedly incorrigible. When he departed St. Mary's Industrial School, he was trained not only as a shirt-maker but as a ballplayer, too.

Ruth was paid $600 for the 1914 season to play for the old minor-league Baltimore Orioles. The money, he said, "seemed to be all the wealth in the world."

Soon enough, Ruth was in the lineup for the Boston Red Sox and, after being swapped to the New York Yankees in one of baseball's most foolish trades, Ruth's jaw-dropping hitting accomplishments became an ideal match for Broadway. He was a true celebrity athlete, long before television made sports figures household names, a player beloved by children long before they so avidly collected baseball cards, and he backed up his flashy, glitzy, partying with performances so far beyond what had come before him that Ruth practically reinvented baseball.

REINVENTING THE GAME

At the least, according to many, Ruth saved it. Baseball was at low ebb after the

A young Babe Ruth poses for a Providence Grays team photograph in 1914. *(Mark Rucker/ Transcendental Graphics/Getty Images)*

Chicago White Sox fell to the Cincinnati Reds and were accused of fixing the 1919 World Series. The Black Sox Scandal shook trust in the game to its foundation, ruining its reputation as an on-the-up-and-up game. Fans were disillusioned, disappointed, and distrusting. The image of the fallen heroes was summed up in the phrase, perhaps apocryphal, of a little boy outside a Chicago courtroom pleadingly asking "Shoeless" Joe Jackson, "Say it ain't so, Joe." Joe couldn't.

New commissioner Kenesaw Mountain Landis acted swiftly and harshly to re-establish baseball's credibility when he banned eight White Sox players from the sport for life and implemented strict rules for the future. The punitive approach may have stanched the bleeding, but winning back fans with doubts called for something else.

Baseball has always been resilient. In a game that has been part of the American professional sports scene for about 135 years, it has not surprisingly had its ups and downs. Landis could provide answers for specific problems, but just as many a frustrated young man has learned, he couldn't make the country fall in love again.

That task fell to Ruth. Ruth broke into the majors in 1914 as a pitcher for the Red Sox, and for most of his first five seasons was a dominating southpaw, who even set World Series records with his arm. Like any other pitcher, on the days when it wasn't his turn to throw, he watched games from the dugout. Slowly, he eased into pinch-hitting roles. Then Ruth began playing the outfield on his days off. He argued loudly that he would be of more value to the team if he played the field every day and gave up pitching. The problem was that Ruth, who won 94 games in the majors, was one of Boston's top throwers.

Ruth was winning Red Sox officialdom over to his point and had just about everybody convinced he should be a full-time position player after setting a new major league record with 29 homers in 1919. Then Boston owner Harry Frazee sold him to the Yankees.

The New York Yankees had been an American League bottom-feeder, a perpetual second-division club. The arrival of Ruth, his lean and hungry frame growing into his 6'2", 215-pound size in his prime,

Babe Ruth warms up before a pitching appearance for Boston in 1918. Before moving to the outfield, Ruth won 89 games as a Red Sox pitcher. *(Mark Rucker/Transcendental Graphics/ Getty Images)*

changed all of that. It was impressive enough to slug 29 homers in a season, but given that Ned Williamson mashed 27 in 1884 and Buck Freeman had stroked 25, it was not an outrageous total.

What no one realized was that the 1919 campaign was Ruth's opening act. In his first full season with the Yankees in 1920, Ruth astonished the nation by connecting for 54 home runs. That made Ruth the first player to ever hit 30, 40, and 50 home runs in a season. It nearly

doubled the previous record, which belonged to him already, and did double the highest total of another player. This was like a running back in the National Football League upping his seasonal yardage total from 1,000 to 2,000 with no intermediate steps, or a professional basketball player averaging 20 points per game when the best anyone else had ever done was average 10.

Americans—and sports fans everywhere, really—have always been fascinated by feats of speed and strength. Smacking home runs beyond the walls of ballparks with startling regularity counts as a feat of strength. Wielding a bat that weighed about 44 ounces, Ruth took big cuts. When he connected, the ball soared out of sight. When he missed he generated big breezes and elicited moans from the crowds.

As soon as Ruth began his assault on the home run record book, he created excitement. More and more fans wanted to see this phenomenon up close. The Yankees' ballpark was inadequate, and the team set out to build a huge baseball palace, seating more than 50,000 people. Yankee Stadium opened in 1923 and became known as "The House That Ruth Built." The cause-and-effect line was clear. Ruth hit home runs. Ruth's home runs created demand for tickets. The Yankees built a park with more seats to accommodate fans who demanded those tickets.

After leading the American League in home runs twice with the Red Sox, Ruth's domination ratcheted up after his trade to the Yankees when he became a full-time right-fielder and gave up pitching.

UNPRECEDENTED POWER

Ruth's 54 home runs in a single season so astounded fans that they clamored to see him play. It was an unprecedented, stunning total of home runs for one man in one season. That brought Ruth his third home run title. The next year, 1921, with expectations so sky-high airplanes hadn't flown there yet, Ruth did it again. He eclipsed his year-old record by hitting 59 home runs.

Ruth was such an amazing hitter compared to all those who had come before

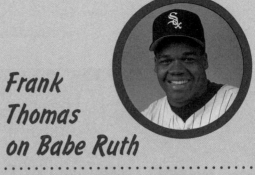

Frank Thomas on Babe Ruth

"Babe was Babe. That's why he was one of the greatest legends to ever play the game. He could throw a no-hitter, or he could hit three or four home runs a day. He was a special talent, and no one back then compared. They might have one or two guys who were close, but really no one compared to Babe Ruth. Today you don't have that one athlete who is 10 times better than anybody else because there's so much training you can do to close the gap. Back then no one had the training to close the gap."

him that one day in 1921 famed sportswriter Hugh Fullerton, whose persistence uncovered most of the details of the Black Sox Scandal, dragged him to Columbia University for scientific testing. In summary, Fullerton wrote, Ruth was 90 percent efficient compared to the average person's 60 percent; Ruth's eyes were 12 percent faster than the average person's; his hearing functioned 10 percent faster than ordinary people; his nerves were steadier than 499 out of 500 people; and his intelligence and understanding were 10 percent above normal.

"The secret of Babe Ruth's ability to hit," wrote Fullerton, "is clearly revealed in these tests."

Now a full-fledged celebrity, within a short span of time Ruth had become

> "I guess a lot of people think I was half-stiff all the time I was playing. But that's not true. I never took a drink during a game. Sure, afterward. And sometimes I would play with a bad hangover."
>
> *—1930s Cubs slugger Hack Wilson*

one of the most famous Americans. He was the most prominent person in the nation's most prominent sport. Once scratching-for-milk-money poor, Ruth began commanding a salary that put him in the top one percent of wage-earners in the United States.

Ruth hit the longest home run of his career outside of the spotlight of the majors. In 1926, immediately after the World Series, Ruth hooked up with a traveling team for some exhibitions and played a game at Artillery Park in Wilkes-Barre, Pennsylvania. Ruth locked onto a pitch and sent it zooming beyond the fences. Accounts from that day, including the Associated Press, reported breathlessly that Ruth had hit the ball 700'! Another estimate put the shot at 650'. Later research by people determined to pin down the accuracy of the distance could do no better than to round off the hit at a remarkable 625'. Ruth always said the longest homer he ever hit in his life was on this day in Pennsylvania.

A spectator sitting in the bleachers as a youth was tracked down at age 87 and with clear memory he recounted the scene: "They used to have a little zoo outside the stadium," the fan said. "There were about eight to 10 cages with animals lined up along one fence way past right field, and I remember the ball Ruth hit took one big bounce before hitting the bear cage."

In addition to his fast start with the Yankees, Ruth also led the American League in homers in 1923, 1924, 1926, 1927, 1928, 1929, 1930, and 1931. It was in 1927, anchoring the batting lineup for the famed "Murderers Row" Yankees team, which some have called the greatest of all time, when Ruth hit his fabled 60 homers. That set a single-season mark that lasted for 34 years.

RUTH PLAYED HARD—ON AND OFF THE FIELD

Identified with college football star Red Grange, heavyweight boxing champion Jack Dempsey, golfer Bobby Jones, and tennis player Bill Tilden, as emblematic of "The Golden Age of Sport," Ruth

In September 1921, Babe Ruth underwent scientific tests at Columbia University to prove his superiority in speed of eye, brain, and muscle. *(Mark Rucker/Transcendental Graphics/Getty Images)*

turned New York City into his personal playground. He was a night owl who seemed to never sleep, who rolled into the Yankee clubhouse late, nursing a hangover. He wore trendy raccoon coats and was known to dine, date, and drink to excess yet always produced when it was his turn to hit.

Ruth knew every other famous figure in American society, made numerous appearances for charity, visited children in hospitals, and made promises to hit home runs for sick kids and—almost mysteriously and phenomenally—kept them.

A confluence of circumstances, including the Black Sox Scandal, the introduction of the lively ball, and a unique talent made Babe Ruth into an enduring symbol of the home run and baseball itself.

Ruth operated at full throttle off the field as a party boy who lived secure in the knowledge that newspapermen of the day would not report his worst mistakes and flaws. There is a famous story that Ruth ate a large number of hot dogs and made himself sick enough to be taken to the hospital. This was termed "the stomach ache heard 'round the world." But in later years some speculated that such an incident never took place at all and he was hospitalized because he overdid it with booze.

A COMPLETE PLAYER

With Ruth's human errors restricted to a need-to-know crowd, he remained a beloved figure. He was a mythic figure, belting the ball harder and farther than anyone who had ever played, turning the home run into a weapon employed on an unprecedented scale. In later years baseball would see players come along who could do nothing but hit home runs. They were specialists who were not particularly adept fielders, who swung wildly and never worked pitchers for walks, and who did not help their teams offensively in other ways. They were one-dimensional bombers.

Not so in Ruth's case. Although he was by far most closely identified with cracking homers, Ruth was an all-around top-level ballplayer. The quality of his pitching set him apart from the beginning, and he was a capable outfielder. But Ruth also hit for average. His lifetime average was .342, among the best ever, and he won the 1924 batting title with a .378 average. That was just a year after Ruth hit .393. Imagine the accolades if Ruth was the all-time home run leader and hit over .400. He also knocked in 2,213 runs, scored 2,174, and collected 2,062 walks. Ruth set dozens of records, and it took decades for some of the big ones to be broken.

The 60 homers in 1927 was Ruth's signature record. The Washington Senators' Tom Zachary was the man who threw the pitch that led to Ruth breaking his own single-season record, and Zachary always insisted the ball was foul. "The ump signaled homer," Zachary said, "and I leaped on the grass and yelled 'Foul!' But I guess I was the only one who saw it that way." Newspaper accounts called the swat barely fair, perhaps by inches, so Zachary was not hallucinating. One of the most famous homers of all time went into the record books. Zachary, who later became a teammate, and Ruth, kidded one another about the blast for 20 years. Only when Zachary saw Ruth two months before his death did he agree with Ruth that it was fair. He later said he was glad he did so to make Ruth feel better at the time.

AN AMERICAN ORIGINAL

Ruth was thinner when he broke into baseball, but the image of him that lingers from his later playing days is of a top-heavy man taking short, mincing steps when he ran on skinny legs. Yet not having a more sculpted, athletic body never seemed to hurt Ruth at the plate. His talent with a bat overrode every obstacle from every pitcher and every obstacle he put in his own way. Ruth's face decorated newspapers, ads, and newsreels.

In 1935, in an article for *American Magazine*, Ruth authored a first-person story about what it was like to be so famous. For a ballplayer who seemed to lap up attention, indeed suck all of the light in a room to him, Ruth seems surprisingly philosophical.

"Fame is a spotlight one minute and a bull's-eye the next," he wrote. "The people who cheer loudest when you succeed are those who throw pop bottles when you fall. The crowd begins by overrating you. When you don't

Babe Ruth watches one of his 59 home runs in 1921 leave the yard. *(Mark Rucker/ Transcendental Graphics/Getty Images)*

live up to its exaggerated opinion of you, it underrates you. Nobody would be famous if people didn't go to such extremes. Loud cheers make heroes. Pop bottles make martyrs.

"It's all very well to be known all over the world. It pays big dividends. But dividends alone won't make a man happy. I know because I've spent them. I think it is better to be known well by a few good

1920–1939 Home Run Champions

AMERICAN LEAGUE			NATIONAL LEAGUE		
1920	Babe Ruth	54	1920	Cy Williams	15
1921	Babe Ruth	59	1921	George Kelly	23
1922	Ken Williams	39	1922	Rogers Hornsby	42
1923	Babe Ruth	41	1923	Cy Williams	41
1924	Babe Ruth	46	1924	Jack Fournier	27
1925	Bob Meusel	33	1925	Rogers Hornsby	39
1926	Babe Ruth	47	1926	Hack Wilson	21
1927	Babe Ruth	60	1927	Cy Williams and	
1928	Babe Ruth	54		Hack Wilson	30
1929	Babe Ruth	46	1928	Hack Wilson and	
1930	Babe Ruth	49		Jim Bottomley	31
1931	Babe Ruth and		1929	Chuck Klein	43
	Lou Gehrig	46	1930	Hack Wilson	56
1932	Jimmie Foxx	58	1931	Chuck Klein	31
1933	Jimmie Foxx	48	1932	Chuck Klein and	
1934	Lou Gehrig	49		Mel Ott	38
1935	Jimmie Foxx and		1933	Chuck Klein	28
	Hank Greenberg	36	1934	Mel Ott and	
1936	Lou Gehrig	49		Ripper Collins	35
1937	Joe DiMaggio	46	1935	Wally Berger	34
1938	Hank Greenberg	58	1936	Mel Ott	33
1939	Jimmie Foxx	35	1937	Mel Ott and	
				Joe Medwick	31
			1938	Mel Ott	36
			1939	Johnny Mize	28

friends—trusted and liked and respected by them in spite of all of one's weaknesses and shortcomings—than to be cheered on every continent by people who think you're great. A famous man always feels as if he were living under false pretenses, that sooner or later he will be found out and showered with pop bottles."

This type of introspection seemed rare for Ruth. But there is no doubt about it, his gargantuan home runs were real, and if he sounded insecure it likely did not stem from any lacking on the diamond.

By all accounts, Ruth was a fun-loving man. His pleasures were adult, even if he excelled at a little boy's game. When his annual salary for the Yankees reached $80,000 and it was noted that he was making more than the president, he famously commented, "Why not? I had a better year than he did."

Ruth had a better year than almost everyone every year. One former Yankee backup gained fame for rooming with Ruth in hotels on the road. He set inquirers straight by tidying up their assumptions of what this meant. Technically, he did room with Ruth, but in actuality, he said, he roomed with Ruth's suitcase. The Babe kept his own hours in his own special places.

Ruth winked and said hello to everyone with a broad smile, calling young men "Kid" and older men "Doc." That's because he could never remember names, no matter how many times he met you. That included teammates who had been with the Yankees for months.

Occasionally teammates, and frequently manager Miller Huggins, sought to reform Ruth, to calm him down, urge him to watch his bad habits and his weight, but when he left the orphanage he was a

kid turned loose in a new wide world. He never could get enough of it, and he never changed.

Certainly, Ruth's personality contributed to the fresh love affair with the home run, and his name is forever inseparable from the image of man and bat swinging and connecting, with the marvelous wood on ball sound. Home runs had always been part of the game, but Ruth elevated their importance, gave them cachet, and provided a role model for up-and-coming sluggers.

Players who had never before thought about hitting home runs liked the idea of blasting the ball out of sight. Managers had never considered home runs part of game strategy before, but when they saw Ruth ruining their pitchers, they had to pause.

CONTAGIOUS POWER

Ruth ushered in a whole new era, a whole new way of looking at baseball. Followers were not far behind. By the mid-1920s, a new face in the Yankee lineup provided protection for Ruth in the batting order and offered up another home run hitter. As soon as Lou Gehrig ensconced himself in the lineup, he and Ruth became the most formidable one-two punch in baseball history.

Gehrig hit behind Ruth in the order, but in 1927, the same year Ruth hit 60 homers, Gehrig smacked 47, the first of five times he topped the 40 barrier. Despite his career being cut short by the illness that would kill him at age 37, Gehrig hit 493 home runs and was a three-time American League home run champ.

Just a few days after sweeping the Pittsburgh Pirates to win the 1927 World Series, Babe Ruth, left, and Lou Gehrig pose at an exhibition game during a postseason barnstorming tour. The "Bustin' Babes" and the "Larrupin' Lou's" were the names of their respective barnstorming teams. *(AP Images)*

Gehrig should have had at least one more homer on his résumé. During a 1931 game at Griffith Stadium in Washington, D.C., Gehrig powdered the ball over the right-field wall. Teammate Lyn Lary was on base and apparently thought the ball had been caught since it bounced back onto the field and was picked up by a Washington outfielder and thrown back into the infield. Lary ran into the dugout. The umpires ruled Lary out and Gehrig's shot invalid. That year Gehrig and Ruth tied for the American League home run lead, but Gehrig lost the one that would have given him the title outright.

Ruth created an epidemic. In 1922, Ruth did not lead the American League

in homers. Ken Williams of the St. Louis Browns hit 39. The same year in the National League, Rogers Hornsby slugged 42 homers for the Cardinals. Hornsby, the greatest hitting second baseman of all-time with a .358 average, twice led the senior circuit in homers. A hitting fanatic, Hornsby would not attend movies because he thought they would weaken his batting eye.

Home run lore began taking shape, too. In 1921, Max Flack, a Cubs hitter, gave a souvenir to himself. Flack lived across the street from Wrigley Field in one of the apartment buildings that loom over the right-field wall. Flack got hold of one pitch and sent it flying out of the park. It crashed through a window of the apartments across the street, and when Flack got home he found his home run ball in his own living room.

Decades later, Kansas City Royals outfielder Hal McRae, who hit 191 homers in a 19-year career, made one of the most apt descriptions of the lure of the home run to the sports fan. "It's like a heavyweight fight," McRae said. "Everybody enjoys that one swing, the knockout punch."

Ruth and Gehrig begat Jimmie Foxx, a four-time American League home run leader who came close to erasing Ruth's name as the single-season homer record-holder. Foxx starred for both the Philadelphia A's and the Boston Red Sox. His arms were more muscular than Popeye, and he hit home runs that stayed aloft longer than the Wright brothers.

It is little-remembered that if not for inconvenient weather, Roger Maris might have been chasing Foxx along with Ruth. In 1932, Foxx led the American League with 58 homers, just two behind The

Babe Ruth congratulates Jimmie Foxx before a September 21, 1932, game in Philadelphia. Foxx led the American League with 58 home runs in 1932, ending a run of six seasons in which Ruth either led or tied for the league lead in homers. *(AP Images)*

Babe. But two home runs Foxx bashed during the season were washed out by rained-out games.

Foxx so terrorized Yankees Hall of Fame pitcher Lefty Gomez that Gomez routinely made jokes about Foxx's long shots off him. For decades, Gomez, a prominent after-dinner speaker at sports banquets, told stories about facing Foxx. Once, with Foxx at the plate, Gomez shook off all of catcher Bill Dickey's signs. When Dickey trotted out to the mound for clarification, Gomez said something on the order of, "Maybe he'll get bored and go away." During the heyday of America's space program, Gomez referred to another time Foxx took him deep. A mysterious object found on the surface of the moon was a home run Foxx hit off him in the 1930s, Gomez said.

Foxx, who sometimes trimmed the sleeves of his uniform shirts so as not to constrict his fabulous muscles, hit 414 home runs in the decade of 1931 to 1940 following Ruth's 462 between 1921 and 1930.

33

Most Home Runs (Team) in One Season

AMERICAN LEAGUE

Seattle Mariners	264	1997

NATIONAL LEAGUE

Houston Astros	249	2000

Fewest Home Runs (Team) in One Season

AMERICAN LEAGUE

Chicago White Sox	3	1908

NATIONAL LEAGUE

Pittsburgh Pirates	9	1917

NATIONAL LEAGUE BOPPERS

Although the American League and the National League have not always been on the same page with trends, from dominating pitchers to dominating hitters, from designated hitters to pitchers hitting, the American League's power seemed daunting to the National Leaguers.

Yet stubby, barrel-chested outfielder Hack Wilson of the Chicago Cubs, who stood just 5'6" and had a child's shoe size of 5½, performed feats that rivaled Ruth's. The four-time National League homer champ smashed 56 home runs in 1930, and the league mark lasted much longer than Ruth's. Wilson held the record from 1930 to 1998, when Mark McGwire slammed 70. Wilson's 191 runs batted in during the same 1930 season is a record that may never be topped.

Wilson's longevity in the sport was affected by alcoholism, and he died young as well. "I guess a lot of people think I was half-stiff all the time I was playing," Wilson said. "But that's not true. I never took a drink during a game. Sure, afterward. And sometimes I would play with a bad hangover."

The next most prominent National League basher of the period was Chuck Klein, who smote 43 homers in 1929 and also won home run crowns in 1931, 1932, and 1933. Klein is one of the Philadelphia Phillies' all-time greats, who batted .320 and hit 300 home runs in 17 seasons in the big leagues.

Signed for $400 at age 16 at a tryout session in 1925, Mel Ott was 17 years old when he made his debut for the New York Giants in 1926. When he retired 21 years later, Ott was the National League's all-time leader in home runs with 511. The shortest member of the 500-home run club at 5'9", Ott also had perhaps the quirkiest batting stance. A left-handed hitter, when a pitch to his liking approached, Ott raised his right foot in the air about to the height of his left knee. He was seemingly off-balance, but his Hall of Fame hitting credentials proved he was not.

At his height and weighing about 170 pounds, Ott was not to be confused with the more rotund Ruth or the beefier Foxx. He did not slam homers with the frequency of those men in any season, but he produced solid home run numbers every year. Ott led the National League in homers six times with between 30 and 38

Giants slugger Mel Ott raises his foot before hitting a fly ball during Game 5 of the 1936 World Series. Ott retired as the National League record holder in career home runs with 511. *(AP Images)*

homers each time. The only time he hit more than 40 he was beaten out for the title by Klein.

Ott's stance and swing were tailor-made for his home ballpark, the Polo Grounds, and its short right-field fence just 257' from home plate. When Ott clouted his 500th homer, it was pointed out that 313 of them were hit at home.

Ott called his manager John McGraw, "Mr. McGraw," and many around the Giants called Ott "Master Melvin" in his early years with the club. McGraw kept Ott around to learn the game, but he hit 18 home runs at age 19. In 1929, when he was 20, Ott showed his greatness. He hit 42 homers and drove in 151 runs.

McGraw was wise enough to recognize talent in Ott from the beginning, and he chose to tutor the young player himself rather than send him to the minor leagues. One thing McGraw sought to protect was Ott's peculiar batting stance, just right for only him. Game after game, McGraw ordered Ott to sit next to him on the dugout bench and learn the sport by watching. McGraw was prone to blowing up over scenes he did not like to witness on the field, like his team making errors, and the boy from Gretna, Louisiana, certainly had his vocabulary enhanced by McGraw's outbursts.

Sometimes the displeased McGraw yelled at Ott because he was a handy

Leading Lifetime Home Run Hitters Ranked Behind the 25 Members of the 500 Club

26.	Lou Gehrig	493
	Fred McGriff	493
28.	Stan Musial	475
	Willie Stargell	475
30.	Carlos Delgado	473
31.	Dave Winfield	465
32.	Jose Canseco	462
33.	Carl Yastrzemski	452
34.	Jeff Bagwell	449
35.	Dave Kingman	442
36.	Andre Dawson	438
37.	Vladimir Guerrero	
	Chipper Jones	436
39.	Juan Gonzalez	434
40.	Cal Ripken Jr.	431
41.	Mike Piazza	427
42.	Billy Williams	426
43.	Jason Giambi	415
44.	Darrell Evans	414
45.	Albert Pujols	408
46.	Andruw Jones	
	Duke Snider	407

customer, not a wrong-doer. Ott replied, "But Mr. McGraw, I'm not even playing."

Brought back to earth, McGraw said, "I know, Ott. But I just don't want you to make the same stupid mistakes as those dumb such-and-such, so-and-sos out there now."

Ott became a 12-time National League All-Star and ultimately became the Giants' player-manager, and then manager. Giants owner Horace Stoneham liked to hire and promote from within, but he let himself in for problems when he made Ott manager only because managers always get fired. "If I fired Mel, my mother and sister wouldn't speak to me." But the Giants didn't win under Ott the way they had under McGraw and his successor Bill Terry, and Ott was eventually fired.

The Giants retired Ott's No. 4 uniform jersey, and in 1951 Ott was elected to the Baseball Hall of Fame. In 1958, when he was just 49, Ott died from injuries suffered in an automobile accident. In 2009, in observance of the 100th anniversary of Ott's birth, the community of Gretna built a life-sized bronze statue of Ott.

A CALLED SHOT?

Ruth's charisma translated to all ages. Kids wanted to see him play and adults wanted to witness blasts that soared into the sky. When Ruth retired, one sportswriter pulled out a pencil and his elementary school arithmetic background and calculated that in ticket sales alone Ruth contributed $20 million to baseball. And that was in the 1920s and 1930s.

It is fitting that Ruth not only set the bar for single-season and career home run totals but that he also belted one of the most talked-about and famous homers of all time. The play occurred in the fifth inning of the third game of the 1932 World Series between the Yankees and the Chicago Cubs and it is referred to as "Ruth's called shot." Did or did not Babe Ruth point to the outfield and predict that he was going to hit a home run in his at-bat against pitcher Charlie Root? Maybe, maybe not.

Most sportswriters on the scene covering the October 1 game made no mention of anything special happening. A few did. Root always denied that Ruth had called his shot. If he had, the hurler said, he would have knocked Ruth into

the dirt of the batter's box with his next pitch.

There is definitely vagueness about what occurred. There was a particular animosity between the Cubs and Yankees that postseason. Mark Koeing, a one-time Yankee mainstay, was picked up by the National League club during the season. Word filtered back to his old friends in New York that Koeing was being short-shrifted on the percentage of his World Series share, and they called the Cubs cheap.

Ruth was vocal about this. But he always attracted fan buzz, good and bad, wherever he traveled, so his being razzed

Babe Ruth hits a home run in Game 3 of the 1932 World Series against the Chicago Cubs. It was during this game that Ruth allegedly gestured with his hand before hitting a home run giving birth to the legend of the "Called Shot." *(B. Bennett/Getty Images)*

37

"He got a hold of that ball and hit it over the triple deck clear out of the ballpark in right-center. I'm telling you, it was the longest cockeyed ball I ever saw in my life. I tipped my hat just to say, 'I've seen everything now.'"

—Guy Bush, pitcher who gave up Babe Ruth's final two major league home runs

when he stepped up to the plate was not that unusual. Also, as usual, he played to the crowd. This is the sequence that supposedly unfolded with the score 4–4: As Ruth was being booed, he gazed out at Root. Root breezed a strike past the Bambino and Ruth held up one finger. Root breezed a second strike past Ruth and he held up two fingers. Then Ruth either waved his hand or pointed his finger to a spot in the outfield where he intended to deposit the next throw, which he promptly did with a mighty swing of the bat. Ruth also supposedly laughed as he ran around the bases and talking to himself said, "You lucky so-and-so."

There is some film footage of Ruth's at-bat. One suggests Ruth engaged in several hand gestures between pitches. The other suggests that Ruth was pointing at the Cubs dugout as part of the yelling contest between the two sides. In postgame interviews, Ruth did not make a big deal of the

hit. But as days passed, he was quizzed about the play more, and Ruth's natural showmanship kicked in. He teased the sportswriters about the event, gradually claiming more ownership of his actions being premeditated.

Still, over the years, a variety of people present on the day of the homer stood up to claim that they knew what they had seen and Ruth had indeed pointed to the distant seats. One home-made 16 millimeter film became public in 1994 showing Ruth making four gestures while he was at the plate. Some take that as conclusive evidence that Ruth called his shot. At the Baseball Hall of Fame in Cooperstown, New York, there is tape in Ruth's voice reviewing what he says happened. By then Ruth is fully engaged in preserving the image of him calling the homer. Nearly 80 years have passed, but the play is still the object of debate. It has only added to the Ruth legend, and the slugger wouldn't have wanted it any differently.

FINISH FITTING FOR A (HOME RUN) KING

Ruth hit his milestone 700th home run on July 13, 1934, during a Yankees game against the Tigers in Detroit. The ball sailed over the wall of Navin Field and was chased down by a 16-year-old boy named Lennie Bielski after it rolled under a car. Police officers then captured Bielski and paraded him into the park and to the Yankees' dugout. After the game, Ruth gave him $20 and autographed a ball "To the boy who got my 700th home run. Best Wishes, Babe Ruth."

Dreaming of becoming a major league manager without any apprenticeship in the minors, Ruth turned down the chance to run New York's Newark farm club. In 1935 he signed with the Boston Braves under the mistaken belief that he would end up running the team. A part-time player, Ruth, then 40, was disappointed when he was relegated to coaching duties.

As a slugger, however, he had one last hurrah left in his war club of a bat. On May 25, 1935, the Braves played the Pirates in Pittsburgh, and Ruth, summoning the Ruth of old, whacked three home runs, the last ones of his career. Guy Bush surrendered the final two, giving Ruth 714.

Bush recalls Ruth's first home run off of him as just a puny fly ball taken by the wind and landing in the front rows of the stands. He was determined to use his best stuff to get Ruth out his next at-bat. The plan was to fire fastballs only. That didn't work. "He got a hold of that ball and hit it over the triple deck clear out of the ballpark in right-center," Bush said. "I'm telling you, it was the longest cockeyed ball

I ever saw in my life. I tipped my hat just to say, 'I've seen everything now.'"

Maybe, maybe not. In 2006 the ball that Ruth hit an exhibition homer with off Walter Johnson in Yankee Stadium in 1942 and was billed as Ruth's "last home run ball," was auctioned off for $86,250. The ball was autographed by Ruth and Johnson after it was caught by a 15-year-old boy from Georgia. Then 78, the man sold the ball to pay off his grandson's college loans. In 2008, a baseball memorabilia collector paid $328,000 for a game-used, sweat-stained Babe Ruth Yankees cap. It was not known if he hit a home run while wearing it.

When Ruth died in August 1948, his body lay in state at St. Patrick's Cathedral in New York and 75,000 fans filed past. More than 6,000 people attended the funeral service. Among the pall bearers at Ruth's funeral were former teammates Joe Dugan and Waite Hoyt. It was a stifling hot day in New York and in a story long recounted, Dugan whispered to Hoyt, "Lord, I'd give my right arm for an ice-cold beer." Hoyt responded, "So would the Babe."

Years later, the prominent baseball writer Roger Kahn reflected on Ruth for *Esquire* magazine. Kahn called Ruth, "a holy sinner. He was a man of measureless lust, selfishness, and appetites, but he was also a man undyingly faithful in a manner to both his public and to his game."

Whether fans believe that Babe Ruth was the greatest baseball player of all because of his combined hitting, pitching, and fielding talents, there is little doubt he is the most famous baseball player. And no one is more closely identified with the home run.

(Mark Rucker/Transcendental Graphics/Getty Images)

CHAPTER 3

AFTER RUTH

450

440

430

420

410

400

390

380

370

360

350

340

330

320

310

300

290

280

270

260

> "Maybe one of us will hit that 61 mark to beat his best record, but that won't give us the right even to carry Ruth's bat. Ruth was more than just a ballplayer, more than just a game hitter. Ruth was baseball."
>
> —*Hank Greenberg*

Hank Greenberg faced prejudice nearly 20 years before Jackie Robinson. His skin color was white, but because his religion was Jewish, Greenberg took fan and player verbal abuse. He was called names, and his beliefs were insulted.

At 6'4" and 220 pounds, Greenberg was big and strong and nobody put shackles on him about retaliating to uphold his honor the way Robinson was asked to refrain from responding to troublemakers the first two years of his major league career. Greenberg had one additional answer for tormentors. He could hit the ball from England to France, and he hit home runs nearly as frequently as Babe Ruth for a little while.

One of the greatest players in Detroit Tigers history, Greenberg, born in New York City on New Year's Day, 1911, was a member of the generation of young power hitters spawned by Babe Ruth's success. Ruth made it not only socially acceptable to hit home runs but also made it publicly desirable. Greenberg won the first of four home run titles in 1935, and in 1938, when Ruth's 60 taters were still fresh in the record book, he tied Jimmie Foxx for next-best on the list when he slammed 58.

If Ruth was indeed "The Sultan of Swat," both Foxx and Greenberg proved that Ruth's 60 homers in a single season was a record that could go at the right time. Players began to think that way, and fans swooned whenever a slugger emerged who looked as if he might hit a bunch of homers.

SLUGGING AWAY PREJUDICE

As a pure slugger, first baseman Greenberg rated highly. He once knocked in 183 runs in a season and was named American League Most Valuable Player in 1935 and 1940. Like many of his contemporaries, however, Greenberg missed several of his prime playing seasons while serving in the U.S. Army Air Corps, four and a half years in all. However, when he came out of the service in 1945 in time to play 78 games, Greenberg hit a pennant-clinching grand slam for the Tigers.

As a minority, Greenberg's religion was in the news when he played. In 1934, the Jewish high holy days of

Hank Greenberg takes batting practice before a 1946 game against the White Sox at Chicago's Comiskey Park. In 1938, Greenberg chased Babe Ruth's single-season home run record of 60, finishing with 58. *(Mark Rucker/Transcendental Graphics/Getty Images)*

Rosh Hashanah were in conflict with key Tigers games. Greenberg consulted a rabbi about whether he should play or spend the holiday in prayer. He was cleared to play. However, 10 days later for Yom Kippur, the holiest day on the Jewish calendar, Greenberg spent the day in a synagogue. At that time the notorious Father Charles Coughlin was publicly disparaging Jews and blaming them for the country's Depression-era economic woes. Greenberg's attendance in temple for the Day of Atonement made national news.

As a large athlete, Greenberg was quite conscious of presenting the image of a formidable Jew in the face of anti-Semitism and Germany's menacing Nazi policies. He said that when he batted he felt "added pressure of being Jewish. How the hell could you get up to home plate every day and have some son-of-a-bitch call you a Jew bastard and kike and sheenie?" Ultimately, Greenberg, "came to feel, that if I, as a Jew, hit a home run, I was hitting one against Hitler."

When Greenberg failed to increase his total of 58 in the Tigers' last five games, rumors spread that anti-Semitic pitchers conspired to give him nothing to hit so he wouldn't break the record. However, Greenberg always denied any belief in those theories. "I ran out of gas," he said of his finish.

Lou Gehrig and Hank Greenberg chat before a 1935 Yankees-Tigers game at Yankee Stadium. *(FPG/Archive Photos/Getty Images)*

After Greenberg posted his 58 homers in the 1938 season, reporters wanted to know if he could top Ruth. In *Collier's* magazine in the spring of 1939 as the next season was starting, Greenberg wrote about the likelihood of hitting 60. He didn't seem intimidated.

"There was only one Babe Ruth and there will never be another," Greenberg said. "Maybe Jimmie Foxx will break that record of 60 home runs. Maybe Joe DiMaggio, Rudy York, or Hal Trosky, or Bill Dickey. Maybe I will. That won't make any of us a second Babe Ruth. Maybe one of us will hit that 61 mark to beat his best record, but that won't give us the right even to carry Ruth's bat. Ruth was more than just a ballplayer, more than just a game hitter. Ruth was baseball."

Growing up in New York, Greenberg visited Yankee Stadium to watch Ruth play. As a curly-haired kid he hung around the player's entrance waiting for him to emerge after games.

"When I say that I worshipped Babe Ruth I'm putting into words what every New York kid felt in those days," Greenberg said.

Greenberg had interesting takes on several home run related subjects, not the least was the headline on his first-person article reading, "How to Hit a Home Run." He pretty much debunks the notion that anyone can hit home runs at any time.

"It's a funny thing about home runs," Greenberg said. "You can't learn how to do it from someone else. If I ever tried to bat as the Babe used to bat, I wouldn't hit three home runs a year."

Greenberg said whoever broke Ruth's single-season home run record would have to be relaxed at the plate and swing straight without upper-cutting or down-swinging on the ball. Greenberg had 58 homers in the books with a week to play in 1938, and everyone was telling him he would catch Ruth easily. He did not.

"I didn't feel tired during that final week, and I did not feel tense," Greenberg said. "But the pressure was on me. I realized that when it was all over. I'm going

after it [60] this coming season, all right. Do I think I'll do it? I wouldn't bet on it."

Greenberg was right. He had another good year and made the All-Star team but hit just 33 homers.

RIGHT-HANDED ROCKET LAUNCHER

Jimmie Foxx was both the contemporary of Babe Ruth and Hank Greenberg and someone who nearly out-lasted both while winning three Most Valuable Player awards. Foxx, nicknamed "Double X," had huge home run hitting seasons for two teams, a rarity. Foxx had his 58-homer

Jimmie Foxx hit at least 30 home runs for 12 straight seasons and knocked in at least 100 runs for 13 consecutive seasons. *(Rogers Photo Archive/Getty Images)*

season for the Philadelphia Athletics in 1932 but also hit 50 for the Boston Red Sox, then a team record, in 1938. That year Foxx also accumulated 175 RBIs. For his career, Foxx drove in 1,922 runs. Regarded as one of the physically strongest of hitters, Foxx developed his upper body strength working on the family farm in Maryland when he was growing up. Not only did Foxx hit at least 30 home runs for 12 straight seasons, he also knocked in at least 100 runs for 13 consecutive seasons.

Foxx was recommended to Connie Mack and the A's by Frank "Home Run" Baker and was only 17 when he attended his first spring training camp in Florida. He was not shy and talked of hitting the ball a long ways back in Maryland. Talking with Al Simmons, another future Hall of Famer, Foxx pointed out a distant palm tree more than 400' away and bragged that he used to hit the ball farther than that.

Simmons didn't believe Foxx and said, "Oh yeah? We play with baseballs, not golf balls, in this league."

In his next at-bat, Foxx hit the ball over the palm tree.

Many a time Yankee great Lefty Gomez spoke of Foxx as his particular nemesis. "He could hit me at midnight with the lights out," Gomez said.

Foxx retired with 534 career homers, well behind Babe Ruth, but behind no one else, and he held second place on the all-time career list for more than 20 years. A right-handed batter, Foxx said he would have feasted on a diet of Gomez pitches and others who threw from the southpaw side.

"If I could have hit only against lefthanders I would have batted .500," Foxx said.

Foxx, who retired in 1945, was only 59 when he died in 1967. He choked to death on a piece of meat stuck in his throat while eating at his brother's home.

THE "BIG CAT"

He did not have the enduring or transcending-the-game fame of many of the other best hitters of his time, but first baseman Johnny Mize was an extraordinary slugger. He led the National League in homers four times and smacked 359 four-baggers in his 15-year career with the St. Louis Cardinals, New York Giants, and New York Yankees. He was also a solid fielder who at 6'2" and 215 pounds earned the nickname "Big Cat" for his graceful play.

Mize maintained a philosophy that indicated patience at the plate. "The pitcher has to throw a strike sooner or later, so why not hit the pitch you want to hit and not the one he wants you to hit?" Mize said.

Mize was a good all-around hitter with a lifetime .312 average, and he was elected to the Hall of Fame.

GREENBERG'S PROTÉGÉ

In 1947, although he was at the tail end of his career, Greenberg signed with the Pittsburgh Pirates and became baseball's first $100,000-per-year player. The affiliation with the Pirates also gave Greenberg the chance to befriend and mentor the next great slugger, Ralph Kiner.

A year later, after Kiner had put his first season of 50-plus home runs in the books, Greenberg predicted that the

young slugger would break Ruth's record of 60. "I'm convinced that Ralph Kiner, Pittsburgh Pirates left fielder, will break Babe Ruth's record of 60 home runs in one season," Greenberg said in a first-person article in *Look* magazine. "He may do it this year. If not this year, then some year soon."

Kiner said he did not receive much batting instruction in the minors and tried to learn from old photos of Babe Ruth. He wanted to copy the swing of the Bambino. "I figured he was the greatest hitter who ever lived so I better figure out what he was doing," Kiner said.

After his debut in the minors, Kiner went into the service during World War II. He bulked up from 165 to 195 pounds and became more of a long-ball hitter then.

Kiner struck out 109 times as a rookie, but with Greenberg's tutoring he never came close to that figure again. He and Greenberg became so close that Greenberg was Kiner's best man at his wedding. Kiner called Greenberg, "the biggest influence in my life."

From Greenberg's vantage point, the prognostication seemed sound. After all, both he and Jimmie Foxx had slugged 58 in a year, and Hack Wilson had collected 56. That 60 did not seem out of reach. It was a reasonable thought, but Ruth's 60 endured as a record far longer than Greenberg and others felt likely.

"To beat the 60 mark, a fellow must be a good natural hitter with power and a home run swing," Greenberg said. "Kiner is that. Kiner has youth in his favor. He's

> "Home run hitters drive Cadillacs; singles hitters drive Fords."
>
> —*Ralph Kiner*

only 25. He has five to seven years of improvement to look forward to."

Kiner emerged as the preeminent National League slugger of the post–World War II era. He won his first of seven straight home run crowns (albeit two shared with Johnny Mize and one with Hank Sauer) in 1946 and kept on rolling. Twice Kiner topped 50 homers in a season. When he and Mize each smashed 51 homers in 1947, no one had done it in the NL since Hack Wilson's record of 56 in 1930. Then, in 1949, Kiner increased his personal best to 54.

A right-handed hitter of powerful dimensions, Kiner was 6'2" and 195 pounds in his playing days, and he helped return the home run to glamour status after a lull of sorts as the pioneer generation of clouters retired and World War II, with its diminished baseball rosters, intervened.

KINER'S HOME RUN LIFESTYLE

Kiner, who later became a longtime broadcaster for the New York Mets and was known for his Yogi Berra–type malapropisms, lived a Hollywood lifestyle, too. His first marriage was to another celebrity, tennis star Nancy Chaffee, and he loved the orange groves, warm weather, and movie culture of Southern California.

Kiner was like a flash of light streaking across the night sky with his long bombs and his frequently quoted attitude about hitting them. Kiner was prone to make pronouncements to sportswriters that not only displayed his confident attitude but burnished the entire reputation of home run hitters.

"Homers win more games than hits," Kiner said. Although there was some doubt that Kiner actually uttered the phrase most frequently attributed to him, the sentence "Home run hitters drive Cadillacs; singles hitters drive Fords," did sum up both his approach and his results.

Kiner hit so many home runs—and stood out for doing it—that some managers created game plans to cope with his at-bats as if they were football coaches plotting new defenses. When managing the Cleveland Indians, Hall of Fame shortstop Lou Boudreau devised the famous Ted Williams shift. The left-handed hitting Williams came to bat one day during the long American League season and found a fielding alignment heavily stacked to the right of second base and in right field.

Soon after Kiner clubbed two home runs against the Indians in a spring training game, Boudreau introduced the reverse shift. It was like the Williams shift, only tilted toward left field, with the third

Pittsburgh Pirates slugger Ralph Kiner led or tied for the National League lead in home runs for seven straight seasons in the 1940s and '50s. *(Rogers Photo Archive/Getty Images)*

baseman standing on the foul line and three infielders positioned to the left of second base. Boudreau dared Kiner to try to beat his team by hitting to right instead of his preferred left-field destination for sharply hit balls.

National League teams picked up on Boudreau's innovation, and for a while it bothered Kiner. He was hard-pressed to get any hits through the infield, and although suggestions rolled in that he should bunt to the right side or change his stance to

hit more to right, in the end Kiner beat back defensive challenges by doing what he did best—hitting home runs over all of the fielders' heads. Kiner lamented that the shifts probably cost him enough hits that he could not hope to hit .300, but he danced with the date he brought, remaining true to the home run.

Kiner, who played just 10 seasons in the majors, made his debut with 23 homers in 1946, and that serves as an illustration about how the homer had

Home Run Leaders 1940-49

AMERICAN LEAGUE

1940	Hank Greenberg	41
1941	Ted Williams	37
1942	Ted Williams	36
1943	Rudy York	34
1944	Nick Etten	22
1945	Vern Stephens	24
1946	Hank Greenberg	44
1947	Ted Williams	32
1948	Joe DiMaggio	39
1949	Ted Williams	43

NATIONAL LEAGUE

1940	Johnny Mize	43
1941	Dolph Camilli	34
1942	Mel Ott	30
1943	Bill Nicholson	29
1944	Bill Nicholson	33
1945	Tommy Holmes	28
1946	Ralph Kiner	23
1947	Ralph Kiner and Johnny Mize	51
1948	Ralph Kiner and Johnny Mize	40
1949	Ralph Kiner	54

1926. Kiner busted out the next year with 51. Boudreau created the shift in 1948, but Kiner hit 40 home runs that year and resumed his torrid pace with 54, 47, 42, and 37, all league-leading totals, over the next several years.

CHASING RUTH

Kiner's high production, and his two seasons topping 50, thrust him into the discussion as a candidate to break Babe Ruth's single-season 60–home run mark. One of the chief challenges for sluggers that homered early and often during the season was trying to stay equal with Ruth through the month of September. The year he swatted his 60 Ruth finished like a marathon champ, setting a single-month record with 17 blows that lasted for years. That late surge generally finished off pretenders for the crown.

"Almost every threat to Ruth's record has kept pace with the Babe's mark through the first half or two-thirds of the race," Kiner said. "Some of them have been ahead of the Babe going down the stretch. I was in 1948. But nobody has been able to match Babe in [the last part of the] season. I think his late-season home runs were the most remarkable part of his record. The home run gets tougher to hit as the baseball season wears on."

Kiner never did truly challenge the Ruth record, but he did hit one home run that traveled just about as far as any credibly researched distance applied to a homer. In an April 22, 1950, game at Forbes Field, Kiner blasted a ball off of Cincinnati Reds pitcher Kent Peterson that cleared the left-field wall and scoreboard by an estimated 50' and landed approximately 570' from

temporarily dropped off as a weapon. The league-leading 23 was the lowest total by a National League home run leader since

home plate. That's what's called putting good wood on a ball!

Although Kiner never hit four home runs in a single game, he four times hit three. He was also always a grand-slam threat. One day he came to the ballpark weakened by a high fever and was held out of the starting lineup. The game see-sawed, and the Chicago Cubs held a 10–8 lead when Kiner was told he might be needed for pinch-hitting duty. He responded, "I have one good swing in me." When the Pirates loaded the bases in the eighth inning, Kiner was inserted in the game. He got his one good swing. It went for a game-winning grand slam.

Between his three marriages, Kiner took advantage of his friendship with singer Bing Crosby, who was part-owner of the Pirates, and invited Kiner to exclusive parties. When dating Elizabeth Taylor or Janet Leigh, Kiner's flirtations made it into the gossip pages of newspapers as regularly as his sports accomplishments did.

Kiner was a member of the Pirates during some of their darkest seasons. The team was so bad during the early 1950s that a young catcher named Joe Garagiola gathered enough humorous stories to last a lifetime on the banquet and broadcasting circuit.

"Although I was playing for a bad ballclub, at least I had these individual goals to go after," Kiner said, "and that kept me going. What happens when you're with most bad clubs is that most players just go through the motions and end up quitting. But I always had these personal goals to motivate me."

Kiner was the one reliable All-Star on the team, but not even his prodigious home run hitting could keep the Pirates

Ralph Kiner dated multiple Hollywood starlets during his major league career. Here he arrives at a Hollywood movie premiere in 1949 with date Elizabeth Taylor. *(AP Images)*

out of the cellar. When general manager Branch Rickey tried cutting Kiner's salary of $100,000 by 25 percent, Rickey said, "We finished last with you, and we can finish last without you." Rickey traded a shaken Kiner, who was very fond of Pittsburgh, to the Chicago Cubs. Rickey was right, too. The Pirates could finish last without Kiner.

Others thought more highly of Kiner and his achievements. He was voted into the Hall of Fame in 1975 and had a long, successful career as a baseball broadcaster. Although he shared three of those crowns, it is unlikely that Kiner's mark of leading his league in homers for seven straight

> "All I want out of life is that when I walk down the street folks will say, 'There goes the greatest hitter who ever lived.'"
> —*Ted Williams at 20 years old*

years will ever be broken. Kiner's career lasted just a decade (back problems contributed to his retirement), but he hit 369 home runs during that span, averaging just about 37 a season. That pays well enough to drive Cadillacs in any era.

THE SPLENDID SPLINTER

Ted Williams was hardly just a slugger. He wanted to be known as the greatest hitter who ever lived, and he may just have accomplished that goal. Williams is a member of the 500-home run club, retiring with 521, the same figure as Willie McCovey and Frank Thomas. But he also walked nearly as often as Babe Ruth and hit .344 lifetime. Williams is also remembered as the last man to hit .400 for his stupendous 1941 season when he hit .406.

When he was 20 years old, fresh from San Diego, Williams said, "All I want out of life is that when I walk down the street folks will say, 'There goes the greatest hitter who ever lived.'" If one takes into account the most home runs hit coupled with the highest average, it might well be said that Williams' dream came true. The comment, to describe a magnificent hitter, was so poetic that it was borrowed for the

movie *The Natural* and uttered by Robert Redford's lead character.

Williams had the eyesight of Superman, the reflexes of a karate instructor, and the sweet swing of a lumberjack. He showed up in Boston in 1939, took root in left field at Fenway Park, and didn't exit until 1960, except for two lengthy military commitments during World War II and the Korean War as a pilot that probably cost him 130 or so homers off of his lifetime total.

"The Splendid Splinter" as Williams was called because he was tall at 6'3" and lanky at 205 pounds, was a supremely discerning hitter. He refused to be panicked into changing his style or approach by any pitcher. If a pitch was not in the strike zone, he would not swing, and his eyesight and judgment were said to be so sharp that umpires chose not to disagree with him.

A true all-around hitter, Williams was always considered a long-ball walloper who could disrupt a game but was not seen primarily as a home run hitter. Still, the homers added up, and Williams led the American League in home runs four times. He won the home run title in 1941, 1942, 1947, and 1949. The last year he stroked 43, his career high.

Two of the best sluggers of their era, Pittsburgh's Ralph Kiner and Boston's Ted Williams chat before the start of the 1950 All-Star Game at Chicago's Comiskey Park. *(AP Images)*

TEDDY BALLGAME'S LONGEST LONG BALL

One of Williams' most famous home runs was struck in 1946 at Fenway Park. It was not a particularly busy day despite a doubleheader. In the first inning of the second game, Williams' sweeping, picturesque turn of the bat mashed a ball thrown by Detroit Tigers hurler Fred Hutchinson. On that day the ball was estimated to fly 450' deep into the bleachers. Alas, with the sun in his eyes, a patron named Joseph Boucher, a devoted Red Sox fan who split

his time between Albany, New York, and Boston, failed to duck, and the ball hit him right on top of his straw hat. The ball ripped the straw hat and conked its wearer solidly on the noggin.

"How far away must one sit to be safe in this park?" Boucher asked rhetorically. "I didn't even get the ball."

That's because the ball bounced off his head and continued another 12 rows higher. Boucher was taken into custody for a cursory look by medical people on hand at Fenway, before being quickly released

Ted Williams is greeted at home plate by teammate Joe DiMaggio (5) and coach Marv Shea after hitting a ninth-inning home run to give the American League a 7–5 victory over the National League in the 1941 All-Star Game at Briggs Stadium in Detroit. *(AP Photo)*

back to his seat, but the ball was long gone. It was unclear if the hat would be wearable again. At least it made for a good souvenir.

Given that the home run was Williams' longest ever in his home park and the stature of his Hall of Fame career, Red Sox officials later determined more precisely the flight and landing spot of the ball. It was determined that the seat Mr. Boucher was lounging in was Seat 21 in Row 37 of Section 42 in the right-field bleachers. The seats at Fenway Park are green, but this seat has been painted red to commemorate the special moment.

A half century after the swat, *Boston Globe* sports columnist Dan Shaughnessy called Williams at his Florida home to see how much he remembered about the play. Williams' remarkable memory, as crisp as his youthful eyesight, kicked in immediately upon mention of the hit.

"I could pick up his arm," Williams recalled of Hutchinson's style. "He threw me a change-up and I saw it coming. I picked it up fast and I just whaled into it. I got just the right trajectory. Jeez, it just kept going. In distance, it was as long as I ever hit one."

The Red Sox pretty much proved that with their measurement of 502' from home plate to the seat.

ALL-STAR SHOWMAN

For a guy who never had that one monstrous home run season, Williams did manage to pick his spots judiciously and often at impressive times, especially in All-Star play.

In 1941, the American League trailed 5–4 in the bottom of the ninth when Williams came to the plate with two men on base against the Cubs' Claude Passeau. With the count 2–1, Williams launched a deep shot to the right-field stands for the game-winning home run. Film clips of Williams running the bases show a young man of 22 with a long stride and a busting-out-all-over grin.

Williams' first All-Star Game after his World War II service was in 1946. Pitcher Rip Sewell of the Pittsburgh Pirates had invented a weapon he called "the eephus pitch." The ball was thrown with a high arc, little movement, and at a slow speed. Except for its trajectory, it resembled the baffling knuckleball. Being out of the game for a few years and being in the other league, Williams had never faced the eephus pitch. Williams said he could hit it. Sewell said he couldn't.

By the time Sewell got into the game and Williams came to bat, the American League led 8–0. Sewell claimed he told Williams the pitch was coming. He lofted it into the air, Williams stepped into the ball and unleashed a mighty cut. The ball soared out of play for a home run, the only one surrendered by Sewell during a career that included 390 regular-season games.

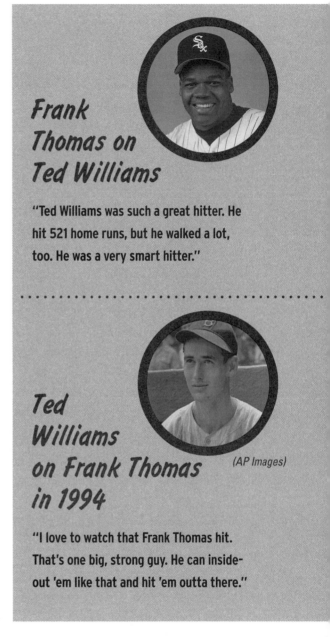

Frank Thomas on Ted Williams

"Ted Williams was such a great hitter. He hit 521 home runs, but he walked a lot, too. He was a very smart hitter."

Ted Williams on Frank Thomas in 1994

(AP Images)

"I love to watch that Frank Thomas hit. That's one big, strong guy. He can inside-out 'em like that and hit 'em outta there."

Both men laughed when Williams tagged the ball, but Williams later admitted that he had started running toward the mound to seal off the angle of the pitch, movement that carried him out of the batter's box and would have been declared illegal if noted by the umpires.

Most Home Runs in One Day of Major League Play

On July 2, 2002, there were 62 home runs hit in the National League and American League combined.

GODS DON'T ANSWER LETTERS

Williams was always credited for having an eagle eye at the plate, but he never liked being intentionally walked. At one point in the 1940s when there was discussion about doing away with the play, he came out loudly in favor of change. And that was after leading the American League in intentional passes for five straight years. Managers have long employed the strategy in key moments of issuing bases on balls to players with big bats who were inclined to hurt them with one swing. It should have been no surprise to anyone who knew him that Williams would rather take his chances hitting away.

"I understand, naturally, that a lot of people are going to say I'm being selfish about this," he said, "and I admit the charge might have some merit. Because there are few things in life I like doing better than belting a baseball, as far and as often as possible. But I also think the feelings of the vast majority of fans should be considered by the men who make the game's rules. A chorus of boos always greets an intentional pass.

"This fact and the observation that, even in a one-sided game, a majority of customers always sticks around to see one more long clout convinces me that most fans want to see the big thump above everything else."

"The Big Thump" was just another clever way to say home run. Williams pulled out a story he had heard about Ken Williams, the American League leader in 1922. Ken Williams once took advantage of a loosely thrown, poorly aimed intentional ball pitch by reaching across the plate and smacking it out of the stadium. "I'd like a chance to do that myself someday," Ted Williams said.

As the 1960 season began, Williams was mum about his future. In June he stroked his career 500th home run. At that point in baseball history, only Babe Ruth, Jimmie Foxx, and Mel Ott had 500 home runs. Ruth had his 714, Foxx had 534, and Ott, the National League record holder, 511. Williams' milestone crush job took place on June 17 against the Cleveland Indians, and he said, "My goal now is 512 homers."

His manager, Mike Higgins, said his goal for Williams was 550. That would have been some year. As it was, Williams entered the final home game of the Red Sox's season on September 28 with 520 homers, just three days after announcing this indeed would be his final season of play. The Red Sox faced the Baltimore Orioles on a day they announced that Williams' No. 9 would be retired and he would be honored with the presentation of many gifts. It was a cool, gray day in Boston, and that seemed to hold back the ball from traveling on its usual trajectories. Williams noted that when he flied

"This fact [intentional walks being booed] and the observation that, even in a one-sided game, a majority of customers always sticks around to see one more long clout convinces me that most fans want to see the big thump above everything else."

—*Ted Williams*

Ted Williams takes a swing before a 1941 home game at Fenway Park. *(Mark Rucker/ Transcendental Graphics/ Getty Images)*

Ted Williams talks with fellow Hall of Famers Cal Ripken, left, Juan Marichal, second left, and Frank Robinson at Boston's Fenway Park prior to the start of the 1999 All-Star Game. The players took part in the announcement of baseball's All-Century Team. *(AP Images)*

out deep to right field earlier in the fifth inning.

Williams came to bat in the bottom of the eighth inning against relief pitcher Jack Fisher. On a 1–1 pitch, Williams saw a delivery he liked and creamed the ball. It headed into the thick air and found a safe landing in the right-field bullpen area. As Williams circled the bases for the last time, author of a special moment in his own career, in Red Sox and baseball history, he barely looked up at the fans at Fenway giving him a standing ovation.

He sped past home plate, briefly accepting the hand-touch congratulations of Sox catcher Jim Pagliaroni, and dashed into the dugout. The ovation continued for four minutes, accompanied by a "We want Ted" chant, but not even Williams' teammates could convince him to take a bow or tip his cap. "I was gunning for the big one," Williams admitted about the home run. "I really wanted that one."

On a magazine assignment, author John Updike watched the denouement of a famous baseball career and how Williams, ever obstinate, refused to acknowledge his fans. Updike then penned one of the most famous lines in baseball reporting. Williams' failure to respond to the cheers was not terribly surprising, he wrote, for "Gods don't answer letters."

Williams ran off into the sunset. But before he was through with the stage he graced and the game that gave him fame, he became a manager, an elder statesman of the sport, and in 1999, indeed a god. He returned to Fenway Park for the All-Star Game and the introduction of the Major League Baseball All-Century Team, riding in a golf cart because of the infirmities of age. The current-day All-Stars flocked to him as if he was a major-leaguer and they were little boys bearing pens and programs for autographs. It was considered the greatest gathering of living baseball talent ever assembled, and Williams was at center stage.

On this nationally televised warm night in July, he even tipped his cap.

(Joseph Scherschel//Time Life Pictures/Getty Images)

CHAPTER 4

MINOR LEAGUE WHAMMERS

450
440
430
420
410
400
390
380
370
360
350
340
330
320
310
300
290
280
270
260

> "It seemed like that ball looked like the size of a cantaloupe the whole summer. That year it all came together for me. It was quite a season."
>
> —Joe Bauman on his 72-home run season in 1954

We have had Hack Wilson, Jimmie Foxx, Hank Greenberg, Mickey Mantle, and Roger Maris in hot pursuit of Babe Ruth's single-season home run record of 60 just as if they were trying to reel in the leader in the Olympic marathon. But in reality there have been several less-publicized seasons where sluggers came after the Babe. The big difference is that those hitters were playing in the minors.

This is baseball trivia at its most obscure—and finest. In most cases, the names have been dusted over by the passage of time, yet the accomplishments of these sluggers will always elicit a "Wow" reaction when pointed out.

The cast of characters that makes up the list of all-time home run kings in the minors is fascinating. Some like Crash Davis in *Bull Durham*, piled up the homers year after year. Some were one-year wonders. Most remain little-known, but a few enjoyed some measure of fame on the big-league stage.

THE ROSWELL ROCKET

Joe Bauman was Barry Bonds before Barry Bonds was born. Playing in the now-defunct Class C Longhorn League for the Roswell, New Mexico, Rockets, Bauman clubbed 72 home runs in 1954. Bauman put together one of the greatest all-around hitting seasons of all time at any level of professional baseball. That season Bauman, a 6'5", left-handed–hitting first baseman not only swatted the 72 homers, but he also batted .400, drove in 224 runs, scored 188 runs, and walked 150 times. His slugging percentage was a phenomenally ridiculous .916. Ruth's best was .847.

"It seemed like that ball looked like the size of a cantaloupe the whole summer," Bauman said of his dream season. "That year it all came together for me. It was quite a season."

While Bauman garnered his share of attention at the time, if he had posted those numbers in present-day baseball, a few things would have gone differently. Bauman, who was followed by a group of photographers, would be besieged by ESPN, Fox, and every newspaper from the *Albuquerque Antelope* to the *New York Times* and he would be pushed through some major league team's farm system at a swifter rate than a race car running laps at the Indy 500. He never would have

Joe Bauman jogs home after hitting his 69th home run for the Roswell Rockets on September 3, 1954. *(AP Images)*

languished at a lower level minor league club long enough to hit his 72 bombs.

Even more amazing, Bauman had already spent two years in the Longhorn League, having seasons that featured 50 and 53 home runs. Yet no scout whispered sweet nothings into his ear.

Bauman grew up in Oklahoma City, and in his last year of American Legion ball he batted .846, an eye-popping figure that earned him a chance to sign with Little Rock in 1941. His brief baseball career was interrupted by military service.

Bauman spent four years in the navy during World War II. After the war, Bauman played three seasons of minor league ball and then retired to run a gas station in Elk City, Oklahoma. As property of the Boston Braves, Bauman was never run through the farm system, and he got just one at-bat at Triple A. After his hiatus, Bauman was talked into joining a team in Artesia in the Longhorn League and had his contract negotiated away from the Braves. Bauman jokingly speculated that his new team boss might have invested "a dollar bill or

Joe Bauman, who hit 72 home runs for the minor league Roswell Rockets in 1954, is shown at his home in Roswell on Oct. 9, 1995. *(AP Images)*

a jockstrap" to steal him away from the Braves. Either way it became a good deal for the Longhorn League.

Roswell is best known for its quirky, hazy, somewhat bizarre connection to UFOs. Bauman's season of 72 thumpers is the next-most famous occurrence related to the small town and occasionally it is mentioned that he sent 72 UFOs into orbit. The alleged landing of aliens in 1947 put Roswell on the map. Bauman was a local hero who put a human face on the community.

At the time, the minor league single-season home run record was 69, held by Joe Hauser of the Minneapolis Millers in 1933 and Bob Crues of the Amarillo

Gold Sox in 1948. It came down to the last day of the season and a Roswell doubleheader against Bauman's old Artesia team for him to establish the new record. On September 5, 1954, Bauman hit one home run in the opener and two home runs in the nightcap.

In time-honored minor league tradition, after his blasts, a hat was passed among fans to make donations as a reward for Bauman putting on a good show. With each homer, the hat got passed again, and so many people were pushing dollar bills through the backstop that teammates had to help Bauman gather the money. He made $800 that night, a very good tip for top-notch service. This was a bigger reward than Bauman was used to; players normally received hams when they hit homers. "We were the best-fed ballclub in the country," Bauman said.

Unlike some other hitters fortuitously matched with tailor-made ballparks for their batting strengths, Bauman was slamming homers to Park Field's right field, fronted by a fence 330' from home plate. Deep center was 385', a little short but not outrageously so. What he did have in his favor was playing in a desert locale at high altitude that had thin air. It was like having Coors Field in Denver as a home ballpark.

Bauman was 32 years old during his spectacular season, age working against his promotion to the majors. Even so, the Braves did no more for him than send him back to Roswell in 1955. By Bauman's standards, that was a pedestrian year—he hit "only" 46 homers. In 1956 the Braves wanted to transfer Bauman to Atlanta of the Southern Association, a higher league, but they also wanted him to take a pay cut.

"I told them that I could make more money selling 24-inch shoestrings on any corner in Oklahoma City," Bauman said.

Instead of accepting the assignment, Bauman bought his own release from the team and moved to Roswell permanently, where he opened Joe Bauman's Texaco Service. He retired to the site of his greatest fame. For years, Bauman operated a gas station and later a beer distributorship. Bauman donated the bat he used to smack his 70th home run to Louisville Slugger. The bat manufacturers gave Bauman a black bat with gold engraving to commemorate his season. At the start of the new millennium, *Baseball America* asked readers to vote for their top choice of minor league legend in the 20th century. Bauman topped the vote list. A panel of experts representing the publication also rated Bauman's 72 homers second only to Jackie Robinson signing a contract with the Brooklyn Dodgers' organization as the biggest story of 1945.

Bauman could never quite respond to why major league teams did not express more interest in him.

"I don't really know," Bauman said. "I was no speed merchant. But I didn't strike out more than most other people, and I think I was an adequate fielder at first base."

After retiring from baseball in 1956, Bauman mostly stayed out of the limelight. However, whenever a younger slugger came along with the potential to hit 60 or 70 home runs in a season, sportswriters called to ask Joe Bauman what he thought about the young whippersnapper.

One of those later-generation hitters was Barry Bonds, who in 2001 clouted 73 home runs for the San Francisco Giants.

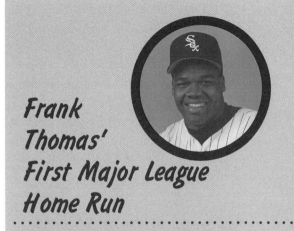

Frank Thomas' First Major League Home Run

DATE: August 28, 1990
OPPOSING PITCHER: Gary Wayne of the Minnesota Twins
DESCRIPTION: Fly ball to deep left field

"Gary Wayne. He was a left-hander, good curveball. He just found a sweet spot for me. I think everybody remembers their first home run. You have to. I didn't get the ball back. You can't always get them back."

Bonds' major league record eclipsed Bauman's mark, too. After 47 years of holding professional baseball's single-season homer record, Bauman saw it evaporate. He was home in New Mexico watching on television when Bonds collected his record swat.

"It didn't bother me or anything," said Bauman, who expected his total to be topped years earlier. "I just thought, 'There goes my record.'"

Bauman was the answer to a trivia question, but also believed he had done something pretty special when he slugged 72 home runs in a season.

"I'm proud of it," Bauman said, "even if it's just minor league trivia."

On August 11, 2005, Bauman was invited to his old ballpark for a special ceremony. Roswell renamed Park Field Joe Bauman Stadium. However, he took a fall at the ballpark and broke his pelvis. While hospitalized and recovering, Bauman contracted pneumonia and died on September 20 at age 83.

THE BABE RUTH OF MEXICO

Hector Espino is a sports hero in Mexico but almost completely unknown in the United States, especially as his feats recede with the passage of time. Espino, who was nicknamed "The Babe Ruth of Mexico," is considered the all-time career minor league home run hitter. The greatest player in the history of the Mexican League, Espino spent 24 years in uniform from 1960–84 and stroked 484 homers.

Espino was born in 1939 and died in 1997. At first he was an outfielder but later shifted to first base. In 1964, his first season at the new position, Espino hit .371 to win the first of his five batting crowns. He also won four home run titles. Also in 1964, Espino's skills earned him

the attention of the St. Louis Cardinals. He signed and was sent to Triple A Jacksonville for 32 games. However, after that short stint, Espino chose to return to Mexico for the rest of his career. At various times he gave various reasons, but allegiance to his home country was certainly one of them and homesickness and experiencing racism in the United States were also mentioned.

For many years, Espino was pretty much a year-round player. He was the king of the Mexican Winter League, which routinely attracted big-leaguers, and in 24 years of off-season play, Espino added eight batting titles, six home run titles, and six Most Valuable Player awards to his résumé.

Espino's continued prowess with the bat kept major league teams calling, with the New York Mets, San Diego Padres, and California Angels being the most serious suitors. Always Espino turned them down to stay in Mexico. He is a member of the Mexican Baseball Hall of Fame, and his No. 21 uniform jersey has been retired by all Mexican summer and winter teams in the professional leagues.

Espino was only 58 when he died of a heart attack.

THE ALL-TIME GREATEST MINOR LEAGUER

For those who have difficulty categorizing Espino's dual winter-summer play or counting the Mexican League as a full-service minor league year-round, Buzz Arlett is sometimes considered the biggest bomber in minor-league history.

Arlett, who was born Russell Loris Arlett in 1899, stood 6'4" and weighed 230 pounds at a time when most ballplayers

Babe Ruth's First Major League Home Run

MAY 6, 1915

For Boston Red Sox

Off New York Yankees pitcher Jack Warhop

were shorter and lighter. He also played when there were only eight teams in each major league and it was challenging to break in regardless of how well a hitter did in the minors.

Arlett's brother Pop was a pitcher for the Pacific Coast League's Oakland Oaks in 1918 when Buzz made his play-for-pay debut as a hurler. Buzz Arlett won 99 games as a pitcher through 1922 but became a full-time outfielder in 1923. Arlett was 32 when the Philadelphia Phillies took a chance on him in 1931, and he hit well, compiling a .313 average with 18 home runs during the year. However, Arlett was a weak fielder, and long before there was a designated hitter, that flaw forced him to the bench in a part-time role. Although Artlett's heft might have contributed to him bashing the ball long distances, his lack of fitness slowed him in the field.

The Phillies did not consider Arlett a keeper and sold him to the Baltimore Orioles. Alas for Arlett, the Orioles were a minor-league team at the time in the International League. Once again Arlett showed he was a multitalented guy, most impressively leading the league in homers with 54. Wherever he went, Arlett hit with power.

Of all the sluggers in the majors or minors, Arlett most resembles Babe Ruth. They both began as pitchers. Arlett won 108 games in all. They were both heavy-set. They both routinely powdered the ball out of sight. Arlett retired in 1937 with 432 minor league homers. His 1,786 minor league RBIs was also a record. In 1984 the Society for American Baseball Research chose Arlett as the best minor-league player of all time.

Mickey Mantle's First Major League Home Run

MAY 1, 1951

For New York Yankees

Off Chicago White Sox pitcher Randy Gumpert

After retirement, when he ran a bar in Minneapolis, Arlett was chosen for the Pacific Coast League Hall of Fame. With its West Coast monopoly of the nation's largest cities, the PCL provided a high-caliber haven for ballplayers who did not want to play in the East, to those on the way up, and to some players who squeezed out a few more years of play after the majors rejected them.

STRONG AS A MOOSE

The Pacific Coast League bordered on a third major league. Joe DiMaggio started out with the San Francisco Seals before moving on to the Yankees. Tony Lazzeri, another Hall of Famer, was a 60-homer man in the minors with the Salt Lake City Bees in 1925 and became the second baseman for the Murderers' Row New York Yankees of 1927. Lazzeri and DiMaggio were two of the Bay Area's famous Italian-American players.

One PCL franchise, the Sacramento Solons, contributed to home run lore because of the dimensions of their stadium in 1975. The left-field wall was just 233' from home plate. As a direct result, what would be routine fly balls or pop ups in other

Hall of Famer Tony Lazzeri slugged 60 home runs for the Salt Lake City Bees of the Pacific Coast League in 1925. *(AP Images)*

parks sailed over the wall for home runs. Many league records were set in the park that season, including most round-trippers by a home team, 305, most homers by two teams, 491, and most home runs by two teams in one game, 14.

Fans must have bought football helmets for protection instead of baseball caps. It was raining baseballs in California's state capital that summer.

The year after Lazzeri mashed his 60 homers in an extended PCL season, a slugger named John "Moose" Clabaugh distinguished himself by smacking 62 home runs for Tyler in the Class D East Texas League. One would think such a performance would put Clabaugh on a

fast track to the majors even without an Amtrak train. And it did—at first. Taking a chance Clabaugh could take the giant steps between Class D and the majors, the Brooklyn Dodgers sent for him at the end of the 1926 season, and he got into 11 games. Clabaugh's only hit was a pinch-hit double, but he thought he was on his way and would be invited to spring training with the big club for 1927. It didn't happen.

"After the season was over, I never heard from the Dodgers again," Clabaugh said.

Despite Clabaugh's wicked power and ability to hit for average, he never was called by any other major league team again. Clabaugh played 16 frustrating years in the minors with 17 teams waiting to be summoned, hitting .339 with 346 homers. He was 6' tall, weighed 185 pounds, and stole as many as 40 bases in a season. He admitted having poor vision, but it never interfered with his hitting. However, his depth perception was affected in the outfield when he tried to flag down fly balls. Yet one of Clabaugh's other rare achievements was pulling an unassisted triple play in an exhibition game, also in 1926.

"I talked to the major league scouts," Clabaugh said. "They all told me the same thing. They said my fielding was holding me back. I'd make easy plays look hard. I could do everything else."

The fans in Texas loved Clabaugh in 1926.

"I hit No. 62 on the last day of the season," he said. "They took up a collection for me."

The most home runs Clabaugh hit in a season the rest of his career was 32, one of three other seasons he topped 30. In

> "When you're in a groove and you're hitting good, everything is like in slow motion. A guy could be throwing 90 mph, but when you're in that groove, it just seems to come slow."
>
> —Bob Lennon

1984, Clabaugh died at age 82 in Arizona, where he had become an avid golfer and earned his nickname, "Moose." It was a reference to Clabaugh being able to swing a mean club—as anyone who saw him swing a baseball bat could attest.

NASHVILLE'S GREATEST SLUGGER

Although Bob Lennon was a minor league slugger, too, he was fortunate enough to have a few cups of coffee in the majors. Lennon was from Brooklyn, and the Dodgers signed him, deploying him to Thomasville, Georgia, in 1945 after Lennon spent 16 months in the Army during World War II. He started slowly but stamped his name in the minor league record book in 1954, hitting 64 homers for Nashville, a Southern Association mark.

Not only did Lennon smoke so many home runs, he also hit .345, drove in 161 runs, and scored 139, contributing to his selection as MVP of the Southern Association. He hit about 10 home runs in one week when his parents were visiting, and he got a special kick out of that.

"I led the league in stolen jockstraps," joked Lennon about his single-season domination of the league. He said he hit 38 or 39 of his home runs with one bat, singular longevity for a single war club. He described it as, "The best bat I ever had. It was just as hard as a rock." The movie *The Natural* lay quite a bit in the future, but Lennon's favorite bat could have been called "Wonder Boy," too. "When you're in a groove and you're hitting good, everything is like in slow motion. A guy could be throwing 90 mph, but when you're in that groove, it just seems to come slow."

Lennon was swiped from the Dodgers by their rivals, the New York Giants following the 1947 season, and Lennon got into three games with them in 1954, although he did not hit safely. Lennon killed minor league pitching the next year with Minneapolis, and after belting 31 homers there, the Giants brought him back to the big city. Lennon appeared in 26 games but hit only .182.

Hitting coach Johnny Mize, the big slugger by then retired, tutored Lennon one on one in 1957.

Roger Maris' First Major League Home Run

APRIL 18, 1957

For Cleveland Indians

Off Detroit Tigers pitcher Jack Crimian

"Nobody tried to tell me anything last year," Lennon said. "Sure, I read in the papers that I was getting instruction, but [manager Leo] Durocher never said one word to me. I'll listen to Mize. He's a great hitter. I wish he was here last year and I would have listened to him last year."

Mize said Lennon's stance prevented him from reaching low pitches on the outside corner and that he may never have needed to adjust in the minors because hurlers he faced couldn't throw them. But not even Mize's wisdom paid off for Lennon.

Losing faith in Lennon, the Giants started him in Minneapolis again in 1957 but then let him go to the Chicago Cubs. Lennon appeared in nine games there and bottomed out with a .143 average.

Hank Aaron's First Major League Home Run

APRIL 23, 1954

For Milwaukee Braves

Off St. Louis Cardinals pitcher Vic Raschi

A series of injuries to his shoulder, ankle, and arm all contributed to his lack of big-league hitting, said Lennon, who batted just .165 in 38 major league games. The ankle injury occurred when he was playing winter ball in the Dominican Republic during that country's 1956–57 season. Lennon said the team owner paid bonus money for hits, $10 for a single, $20 for a double, and $30 for a triple.

"So I hit one off the center-field wall [an easy double] and I went for the triple, for the extra $10," Lennon said. "That's when I tore the ankle up. He [the outfielder] had it, and I tried to give him a decoy. I went one way and my ankle went the other, and I ripped all the ligaments and everything. The next day they sent me with an interpreter to a voodoo doctor. I was on crutches. He was about four feet tall and 80 years old and he gave me a lot of mumbo jumbo, but the ankle didn't get any better. The interpreter said, 'Hey, Bob, he wants you to stamp your foot.' I said, 'Jeez, I can't do that.' He told me everything would be okay, but I always thought he put the whammy on me."

Overall, Lennon's winter ball experience was exceptional, playing on four pennant-winners, winning a home run title in Venezuela, and playing in Puerto Rico with guys like Roberto Clemente and Orlando Cepeda.

One player Lennon admired, even if he was a Brooklyn fan, was Mel Ott. In some ways Lennon mimicked Ott's stance, lifting his leg off the ground as he gauged the approach of a pitch.

Like so many young players of his era, Lennon loved Babe Ruth, and in the 1930s when Ruth was briefly a coach for the Dodgers, Lennon saw him close up. "He

The Brooklyn Dodgers pose for a team photo in 1947. Joe Hauser (standing, far right) was a minor league manager in the Dodgers system. Playing in the minor leagues in the 1930s, Hauser twice topped 60 home runs in a season. *(AP Images)*

was a great ballplayer, a home run hitter and a pitcher, and I wanted to be just like him." Lennon actually hit more homers in a season than Ruth did, albeit in the minors, of course. Lennon also met Ruth briefly at Florida spring training in 1947 and shook his hand. The young hitter could see Ruth was already sick with the throat cancer that would kill him the next year.

Lennon said he was playing for a Sioux City, Iowa, minor-league team in Denver in 1948 when it was announced that Ruth had died from the illness that had been afflicting him for the previous two years.

"I said, "Dear Lord, please let his power come into me,'" Lennon recalled. "And the next time up I hit a home run."

After his brief appearances in the majors, Lennon played four more seasons in the minors after 1958. He died in Dix

Hills, New York, in July 2005 at age 76, remembered in the sport he loved mostly for his 64 long balls in one year.

"THE BABE RUTH OF THE MINORS"

One of the kings of swat who predated Lennon was Joe Hauser. Hauser did something few hitters at any level of baseball ever did. He hit more than 60 homers in a season twice. Hauser slammed 63 homers for the Baltimore Orioles in the International League in 1930 and 69 homers for the Minneapolis Millers of the American Association in 1933. It was his record of 69 homers that Joe Bauman broke with his season of 72.

Hauser's career followed a very different trajectory than those of the other 60-homer men. Born in 1899 in

71

> "When you hit a home run there are so many feelings inside you. You see the ball headed out for the fence and you say to yourself, 'There's another one. It's gonna make it.' Me, I liked the inside pitch. When I got my pitch, I went for the big job. That was my pay dirt."
>
> —*Joe Hauser*

Milwaukee, Hauser broke into the majors in 1922 with the Philadelphia Athletics and appeared in 111 games as a rookie at first base. He produced a top-flight average of .323 even though he hit just nine homers.

His second year, Hauser hit 17 home runs, drove in 94 runs, and batted .307. As a third-year man for Connie Mack, Hauser smacked 27 homers (second to Ruth in the American League that year) and drove in 115. Clearly, he was on his way to a first-class career. However, in spring training of 1925, Hauser broke a knee cap. He missed the entire season and was never the same major league player, appearing in only parts of three seasons between 1926 and 1929.

In Hauser's six big-league seasons he hit 80 home runs and batted .284. But so much more was promised.

The 5'10", 185-pound Hauser was 19 when he joined Providence of the Eastern League in 1918 for his first minor league stint. His brother, a police officer in Milwaukee, rewarded him with $1 for every home run he hit. That didn't exactly break big bro's bank account that year, because Hauser hit just one four-bagger. The pace began increasing the next year during his return engagement in Providence when Hauser hit six home runs. He got to play in Milwaukee of the American Association in 1920 and 1921, by the second year punching out 20 homers and affecting his brother's take-home pay.

Actually, in his early days in the minors, Hauser legged out more triples than homers, with 21 for Providence in 1919. But his nickname of "Zip" was applied not for his running ability but when he was a fastball pitcher growing up. When Hauser was called to the A's, his brother was probably as relieved as he was. Playing at home in Milwaukee for the old Brewers was a big deal for Hauser. The heavily German fan base called him "Unser Choe," or "Our Joe."

A light-hearted man who was a noted raconteur, Hauser had very large hands, enabling him to swing a large bat with ease. Hauser almost made it into the

500-home run club by combining his 80 major league homers with his 399 minor league dingers.

Hauser's injured knee was not back to full strength when he showed up for the 1926 season and he was gradually phased out of full-time duty at first base by an up-and-coming star—Jimmie Foxx. The two roomed together, and there was no resentment when one took the playing time from the other.

"Nice guy, Double X," Hauser said. "He was a good guy."

And such a great player that Hauser was no longer needed. He was waived from the A's and claimed by the Cleveland Indians.

After recovering from his severe knee injury, Hauser never again played 100 games in the majors, though one might think clubs would have seen him as a potential asset following a 1930 season in which he slugged the 63 homers for Baltimore.

"There's nothing in baseball to compare with the feeling you get hitting a home run," Hauser said. "When you hit a home run there are so many feelings inside you. You see the ball headed out for the fence and you say to yourself, 'There's another one. It's gonna make it.' Me, I liked the inside pitch. When I got my pitch, I went for the big job. That was my pay dirt."

Hauser was given a new Studebaker as a reward for the 63 homers.

No big-league team came calling after the season of 63, and Hauser ended up in Minneapolis for 1933. He could hardly make a decent payday during the Depression, gathering just $400 a month in Minnesota. Still, as the season wound

Barry Bonds' First Major League Home Run

JUNE 4, 1986
For Pittsburgh Pirates
Off Atlanta Braves pitcher Craig McMurty

down, Hauser was closing in on his old best of 63 homers.

The Millers were playing a double-header against St. Paul on Labor Day with the first game starting at 10 AM.

"I didn't even have my eyes open yet," Hauser said.

He was sitting on 62 homers when a rain delay of an hour kicked in, creating a sea of mud in the batter's box upon resumption of the game in the fifth inning.

"I get into the box, the pitcher throws the ball, and bang!" Hauser said. "The ball goes out of the park and I tie my old record in Baltimore. That ball was really hit, 375' right down the chalk line. In the eighth, I come up again. I hit another one over the fence and that's the 64th, breaking my Baltimore record. It made me feel terrific."

When he hit 69, Hauser was given some bonus compensation, $500, and some gifts from the fans.

Hauser became known as "The Babe Ruth of the Minors," and he knew the real Babe Ruth, whom he called the real home run king.

"A great man," Hauser said. "We talked many times when I was playing for

73

Philadelphia but never about home runs. We talked other things."

Too bad. That might have been an entertaining confab.

Before Hauser's epic Orioles season began, the Yankees played an exhibition game in Baltimore as they headed north. Hauser said Ruth asked him how many home runs he was going to hit that year. If they only knew. But Hauser said, "I don't know, Babe. We haven't played any games yet."

Although Hauser was unhappy that he wasn't even offered a raise from Minneapolis after banging 69 home runs, he returned to the Millers because he had nowhere else to go. He began the 1934 season hitting at the same remarkable pace. At one point he hit five home runs in two games on a road trip to Kansas City and after 82 games he had 33 homers, 88 RBIs, and a .348 average.

"I thought I was gonna hit 100," Hauser said. "Then I broke my leg."

End of season.

Hauser was out of baseball between 1937 and 1939. Then he returned for three more seasons playing for Sheboygan in the Wisconsin State League. That's where he retired and opened a sporting goods store. Hauser also stuck close to the game, managing Sheboygan's minor league outfit for eleven seasons between 1940–53 with time out for World War II. He won six pennants.

Hauser proved he could play again in the 1930s, but no one in the big leagues gave him a chance. He attributed the lack of interest to lingering concern over his leg injuries.

"I had those broken legs," Hauser said, "and they were scared to take me. That's what I think, yeah."

For many years later in life Hauser maintained an apartment in Sheboygan, and he kept his sporting goods store open until 1984. He smoked five cigars a day and had a drink or two a night. He also answered a steady stream of fan mail asking for his autograph from baseball aficionados thrilled by his two 60-homer seasons. In his nineties, Hauser moved into a nursing home and had to give up the cigars in a

"Sure I strike out a lot. I struck out on the last time at bat on the last day of the season to lead the league by one. I kind of hate to see Pancho Herrera out of the league. He was my main competition. But [Mickey] Mantle strikes out over a hundred times a year and nobody says anything."

—*Dick Stuart*

Playing for the Lincoln Chiefs of the Class A Western League, Dick Stuart connects for one of his 66 home runs in 1956. *(Joseph Scherschel/Time Life Pictures/Getty Images)*

no-smoking environment. He was 98 years old when he passed away in 1997.

DR. STRANGEGLOVE

Probably the most colorful minor league 60-homer man who did fairly well in the majors was Dick Stuart. The Pittsburgh Pirates and Boston Red Sox first baseman wielded a big bat but was such an atrocious fielder that he was nicknamed "Dr. Strangeglove" as a play on words with the 1960s movie *Dr. Strangelove.*

Not that Stuart minded. He mostly cared about hitting the ball a long way. Stuart became enamored with the home run and thought others should be enamored with him—from waitresses in coffee shops to managers and owners of big-league teams—because he belted 66 home runs for Lincoln, Nebraska, in the Class A Western League in 1956. He also struck out a league-record 171 times. Stuart thought he was great and thought he was Hollywood handsome, spending long moments carefully combing his thick, wavy dark hair while looking in the mirror before emerging from the locker room in public. For a long time Stuart went around signing his autograph, "Dick Stuart 66."

It was hard to be considered exaggerating by terming Stuart a one-dimensional player when he did the self-identifying for you.

75

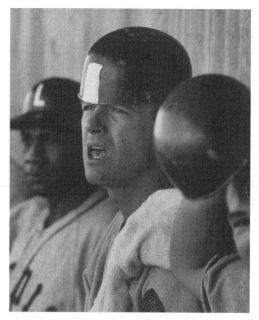

Despite hitting 66 home runs in a single minor league season and 228 homers in the majors, Dick Stuart was best known for his strikeouts and struggles in the field that earned him the nickname "Dr. Strangeglove." *(Joseph Scherschel//Time Life Pictures/Getty Images)*

Stuart, born in San Francisco, was 18 years old when he signed with the Pirates for $10,000, a pretty good price in 1951, even if he did not think so. Already Stuart was thinking big, as in thinking about hitting a lot of home runs wherever he went, which he was sure was to the majors on a high-speed train.

"The guy who breaks Babe Ruth's record will be worth a fortune," Stuart said at the time, clearly not considering $10,000 a fortune. "They better save up. I'm going to want it all in cash."

Stuart's timing was off, is all. He broke Babe Ruth's record of 60 home runs, except he did so in the minors, not the majors, and he didn't surpass Joe

Hauser or Joe Bauman, neither of whom derived riches from their feats. Whether it was inner insecurity or something else, Stuart tended to brag about his hitting even though he was far from a polished ballplayer. Fielding aside, Stuart also struck out too much. It was all or nothing for him. He got his share of home runs when he reached the majors, for sure, but he also led the National League in strikeouts.

"Sure I strike out a lot," Stuart said before the 1962 season. "I struck out on the last time at bat on the last day of the season to lead the league by one. I kind of hate to see Pancho Herrera out of the league. He was my main competition. But [Mickey] Mantle strikes out over a hundred times a year and nobody says anything."

After pounding the 66 dingers, Stuart figured his reputation had preceded him every step of the way through the minors and to the Pirates. He expected the mere mention of his name would bring out ticket-buyers. Instead, in Pittsburgh, he was sort of the tolerated wayward son on a team with a hard-nosed manager, Danny Murtaugh, and a mix of Latinos and black players who were a tight-knit group with excellent fielding skills. Stuart brought the long ball to the mix, but he couldn't understand why all everyone wanted to do was talk about his strikeouts. It was a big fuss over something inconsequential, he felt.

Stuart hit 228 homers in the majors, as many as 35 in a season with the Pirates and as many as 42 with the Red Sox. He struck out 957 times in his 10-year career, and his fielding average was a mere .982. Sometimes Stuart was referred to as "The Man in the Iron

Glove," as opposed to the famous novel, *The Man in the Iron Mask*.

Red Sox reliever Dick Radatz, a teammate of Stuart's for two years in the 1960s, suggested that Stuart buy a Massachusetts vanity license plate with "E-3" on it, the symbol for error, first baseman.

Stuart was good-natured and did tell jokes that helped put tense teammates at ease. He could even make fun of his fielding. Once watching a player accidentally step on his glove, Stuart said, "Well, here goes the pennant."

Red Sox manager Johnny Pesky was frustrated trying to get the message across to Stuart that missing balls he should have caught was not much better than making errors and that striking out could cost the ballclub in key situations. Yet Pesky also confessed, "Don't ask me why, but I like the guy. There isn't a mean bone in his body."

Stuart was really just born too early. He was a natural designated hitter, a guy who could sit on the bench for a couple of innings at a time focused on nothing but his next at-bat instead of worrying about someone having the impertinence to hit a line drive at him when he was in the field. Eventually, Stuart's atrocious fielding and too-free swinging got him drummed out of the majors after he made short stops with the Phillies, Mets, and Dodgers.

So Stuart fled to Japan in 1967, where he signed on with a Tokyo team as a home run hitter and conversation piece. It worked out pretty well for him. Stuart hit 10 home runs and drove in 27 runs in his first 34 games before pulling a leg muscle, and he enjoyed mingling with the people and seeing the sights.

Minor League Single-Season Home Run Leaders

1. **Joe Bauman, Roswell Rockets, Longhorn League, 1954** — 72
2. **Joe Hauser, Minneapolis Millers, American Association, 1933** — 69
   Bob Crues, Amarillo Gold Sox, West Texas–New Mexico League, 1948 — 69
4. **Dick Stuart, Lincoln Chiefs, Western League, 1956** — 66
5. **Bob Lennon, Nashville Volunteers, Southern Association, 1934** — 64
6. **Joe Hauser, Baltimore Orioles, International League, 1930** — 63
7. **Moose Clabaugh, Tyler Trojans, East Texas League, 1926** — 62
   Ken Guettler, Shreveport Sports, Texas League, 1956 — 62
9. **Tony Lazzeri, Salt Lake City Bees, Pacific Coast League, 1925** — 60
   Frosty Kennedy, Plainview Ponies, Southwestern League, 1956 — 60

"This is a new experience for me," he reported, "and I love it."

Presumably, he learned how to say "66" in Japanese.

Sadaharu Oh and Henry Aaron show their batting forms at a November 1, 1974, news conference in Tokyo. Aaron was in Japan for a home run hitting contest against Oh, who totaled 868 home runs during his career in the Japanese leagues. *(AP Images)*

THE WORLD RECORD HOLDER

Japan has had a long love affair with baseball, predating World War II. Babe Ruth and his family traveled to Tokyo in 1934 as part of an exhibition tour, and the fans knew who he was. Years later, his daughter Julia told the story about how as soon as Ruth checked into the Imperial Hotel a man wearing a kimono knocked on the door and said, "Sign baseball?" Ruth obliged, but the man kept reaching into the pockets of his garment and pulled out baseball after baseball to be signed. Julia Ruth Stevens guessed the man brought two dozen balls with him.

He left Ruth laughing, but he signed them all.

"They loved Daddy over there," Stevens said in 2000. She said when Ruth and the other star players rode in open cars to the hotel fans that lined the road and shouted, "I love Bay-bee!"

The Japan League was considered minor league in quality after World War II and well into the 1960s when American ballplayers like Stuart who were past their prime sought to tack on a few more years in the game.

It was only in the 1990s and early 2000s that home-grown Japanese players began to make an impact in the majors and lead fans to believe that the caliber of play was higher than previously thought. This raised the question of the comparative value of the 868 home runs hit by Japanese icon Sadaharu Oh, who hit more than Barry Bonds, Hank Aaron, and Ruth but also played in smaller parks.

Oh had seasons of 55, 51, and 50 homers and in all hit 40 home runs or more 13 times, with six more seasons over 30. He was the 15-time single-season Japan League home run champ.

Oh had a batting stance that was in some ways reminiscent of Mel Ott's. Oh swung left-handed, and like Ott, he raised his right leg when he was poised to swing at a pitch. He was also more popular than Lady Gaga, Tom Cruise, or any other singing or acting figure who is cover material for magazines in the United States.

Former major league pitcher C.J. Nitkowski, who also pitched in Japan, summarized Oh's popularity as being Babe Ruth, Joe DiMaggio, Mickey Mantle, and Ted Williams "all rolled into one." And that was 27 years after Oh's retirement as an active player.

More remarkable in a country that cherishes its homogeneity, that popularity honors Oh as a deity when he is not 100 percent Japanese. He is half-Chinese.

"Mr. Oh is like a god here," a *Chicago Tribune* reporter quoted a Japan League team marketing executive as saying.

What numbers would the Japanese slugger have produced if he played in the United States? Nobody can know, but the increasing reputations of foreign players coming to the United States and starring in recent decades has only added luster and respect to Oh's accomplishments.

A Home Run Cycle

Tyrone Horne did not hit 60 homers in a single season, but he recorded a home-run achievement that was one of the most unusual of all time.

On July 27, 1988, Horne was playing left field for the Arkansas Travelers against the San Antonio Mission before 5,010 fans in Texas. On that day, Horne hit four home runs and drove in 10 runs, a pretty special performance. But what made Horne's display stand out even more is that his four home runs were a solo, a two-run job, a three-run shot, and a grand slam.

One proponent of Oh's skills compared to major leaguers has always been Davey Johnson. Johnson, the former Atlanta second baseman who had a solid career in the United States before he moved to Japan where he teamed with Oh for two seasons, might as well have been Oh's publicity agent.

"I believe Oh would hit 700 home runs over here [in the United States]," Johnson said. "He would be a good hitter anywhere in the world. Quality is still quality."

Johnson was also Hank Aaron's teammate with the Braves and was on the team the year Aaron broke Babe Ruth's record.

"Aaron had a short, powerful swing, while Oh's is more classic," Johnson said.

Japanese home run king Sadaharu Oh smashes a grand slam to lift the Yomiuri Giants over the New York Mets in the first game of an 18-game exhibition series in October 1974. *(AP Images)*

"They're both fastball hitters but intelligent hitters. Both are good breaking ball hitters as well.

In a tantalizing bit of theatre, in November 1974 Aaron journeyed to Tokyo for a home run hitting contest against Oh. It was Home Run Derby come alive for 50,000 fans at Korakuen Stadium. The competition lasted just 20 minutes, but Aaron hit 10 out of 18 fair balls at least 300' into the stands. Oh hit nine home runs out of 20 fair balls.

Televised by CBS, Aaron was paid $50,000 and Oh $20,000. As far as proving home run hitting superiority, Aaron said the one-on-one contest proved nothing. Oh said when he started off hot with three quick homers he thought he might win.

"How many homers he would hit here, I don't know," Aaron said later, "but he's a very good hitter."

In the decades since Oh's prime, Japanese ballplayers have become major leaguers in great numbers. Some fizzle

> "I believe Oh would hit 700 home runs over here [in the United States]. He would be a good hitter anywhere in the world. Quality is still quality."
>
> *—Davey Johnson, Sadaharu Oh's teammate in Japan*

and go home. Some, like Ichiro Suzuki, become international superstars.

Oh removes himself from any controversy about whether he is the true home run champion or discussions about the sizes of ballparks and lengths of seasons.

"The number of home runs I hit were in Japan," Oh said in 1997. "People want to say that I'm the world champion, but that doesn't concern me. If you don't play on the same field, it's impossible to make a comparison."

Oh played his entire 22-year career for the Yomiuri Giants and then managed until 2008. Despite the rise of other stars playing in the United States, Oh remains the gold standard in Japan, the greatest baseball celebrity in his country.

When he retired, Oh gave the simplest of reasons.

"Mentally, I have not been able to inspire myself to maintain my true stature," he said. "All this season I tried to regain it, but I never could."

For most of his career, Oh said his biggest home run thrill was hitting his first as a 19-year-old rookie. As a 40-year-old, Oh said his biggest home run thrill was hitting his career 756th in 1977, one more home run than Hank Aaron.

What did it all mean? Well, the major league record still stands because Sadaharu Oh played in the Japan League. But if Oh and baseball fans grope for an easy phrase to describe his feat, it would be safe to say that Oh has the world record for home runs.

CHAPTER 5

WILLIE MAYS AND FRIENDS

450

440

430

420

410

400

390

380

370

360

350

340

330

320

310

300

290

280

270

260

> "Man, after you get two in a game, you don't start looking for a third one. Sure, this was my best game and my biggest thrill in baseball, too."
> —*Willie Mays after hitting four home runs in one game*

Some people receive a gift at birth, but they do not arrive fully formed. Willie Mays was such a star who was bestowed with speed, strength, and aptitude, but who also was fortunate enough to nurture his talent under the proper tutors.

By the time his father, Cat; his Birmingham Black Barons manager/guide Piper Davis; and his New York Giants manager, Leo Durocher, stopped treating Mays like a son and stepped back far enough to watch the fruits of their teaching bloom, he was perhaps the greatest baseball player of all time.

If there is a photo of the candidates for greatest-ever players, Mays is in the picture. Some say he would be there alone, but even so no one suggests he would be crowded out by anyone other than Babe Ruth or Hank Aaron.

THE "SAY HEY" KID

Years into his career, Mays was asked who was the best baseball player he ever saw. He stated rather matter-of-factly that he was. The comment did not smack of hubris as much as flat truth.

When Mays retired from baseball in 1973 after 22 years in the sport, mostly with the Giants and a few minutes with the New York Mets, he had 660 home runs to his credit. He was second only to Ruth on the all-time list, though he could see Aaron approaching the rearview mirror.

The thing about Mays and home runs is that they did not define his game the way they did for so many other sluggers, including many of his contemporaries. The 1950s was a golden age for members of the 500–home run club with overlapping careers, including Ted Williams, Aaron, Mays, Mickey Mantle, Willie McCovey, Harmon Killebrew, Eddie Mathews, Frank Robinson, and Ernie Banks.

Home runs just seemed to pop off Mays' bat at the right time, in between all of the other excitement he created with his feet and glove. One example being that Mays' first big-league hit was a homer on May 28, 1951, at the Polo Grounds against the Boston Braves.

There was so much more to Mays' game than home runs. It has often been said that the baseball scout's dream when gazing upon raw talent is finding the five-tool player, a young guy who can hit, hit with power, run, throw, and field. Mays was the poster example of that player.

Willie Mays goes airborne to snag a drive off the bat of the Dodgers' Duke Snider during a 1954 game at Ebbets Field in Brooklyn. *(Charles Hoff/NY Daily News Archive via Getty Images)*

Mays was born in 1931 and grew up in Westfield, Alabama, near Birmingham. It was not a warm time for race relations in the Deep South, but in Mays' little corner of the continent, the local kids, white and black, got along well, one main reason being their shared enthusiasm for sports.

Although he showed talent as a budding star running back in high school, a broken leg convinced Mays that his future lay in the safer game of baseball rather than football. He was also so good, so young that he was offered the chance to play for the Black Barons of the Negro Leagues when he was just 17. Mays was literally a boy among men as he rode the countryside from game to game on buses, doing homework some of the time in hotel rooms while his older teammates caroused in bars.

Piper Davis looked out for Mays like a close uncle, as he had promised Mays' father, and shaved some of the rough edges off his game. Davis toughened Mays up at the plate, telling him what to do when pitchers threw at him, how to run the bases to get back at them, and also how to play with freedom. That was already in Mays' soul, along with the keenest instincts seen in a player, but it was important that Davis did not try to curtail any of them.

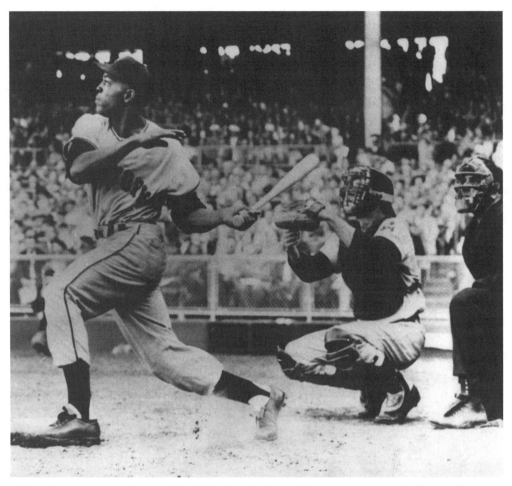

Willie Mays watches the ball fly off his bat during a 1954 game against the Boston Braves. Mays hit 41 home runs in 1954. *(Mark Rucker/Transcendental Graphics/Getty Images)*

Soon enough, Mays was hitting .477 for Minneapolis in the New York Giants' system and breaking into the Giants' lineup in center field in 1951. Despite a slow start that left him distraught, Leo Durocher, who believed in Mays' greatness from the first minute he saw him play, displayed blind faith in him.

Durocher's confidence in Mays was an elixir for the young player. He won the National League Rookie of the Year award and despite a stint in the Army, continued to mature as an all-around hitter and brilliant fielder. Called "The 'Say Hey' Kid" for his exuberance, the singular, signature play of Mays' career is a fielding play. His run-to-the-wall, turn-his-back, hat-flying-off-his-head stab of a ball in deep center, turn, and throw at the Polo Grounds in the 1954 World Series against the Cleveland Indians is probably the most famous catch of all time.

Mays could do anything on the field, and that included hitting home runs. He bashed 51 in 1955, 49 in 1962, 47 in 1964, and 52 in 1965 and led the National League all four of those seasons.

Mays also became one of the many players who shared the record for most home runs in a game when he crushed four against the Milwaukee Braves on April 30, 1961, after spending most of the night sick to his stomach, likely from food poisoning. In addition to feeling weak from vomiting, Mays was in a slump, using a bat borrowed from light-hitting infielder Joey Amalfitano against Braves All-Star Lew Burdette.

It was not a bad showing by a player who felt so lousy that he was going to ask his manager for the day off. Who knew?

Mays hit his first homer in the first inning, a solo swat traveling 420' off Burdette that exited County Stadium in Milwaukee in center field. In the third inning, Mays hit a two-run shot off of Burdette to left-center. In the sixth inning, with reliever Seth Morehead on the mound, Mays crunched a pitch that soared over the left-field fence and landed in a picnic area 480' from home plate. In the eighth, Mays was facing reliever Don McMahon.

Braves first baseman Joe Adcock called time out, strolled to the mound, and offered a simple solution to the Mays problem. "Don't let this guy hit the ball this time," Adcock said. McMahon replied, "Don't worry. I got him." The next pitch traveled 430' into the bleachers for Mays' fourth homer of the day.

Mays ended up with eight RBIs that day, and given the obstacles facing him that morning, he was pretty happy about his achievement.

"Man, after you get two in a game, you don't start looking for a third one," he said. "Sure, this was my best game and my biggest thrill in baseball, too."

The Giants stroked eight home runs that day in a 14–4 victory and some guy

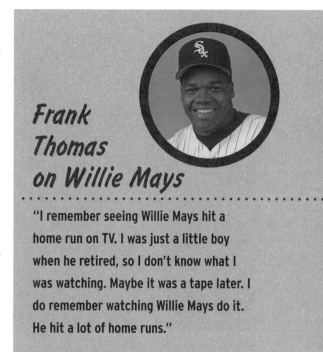

Frank Thomas on Willie Mays

"I remember seeing Willie Mays hit a home run on TV. I was just a little boy when he retired, so I don't know what I was watching. Maybe it was a tape later. I do remember watching Willie Mays do it. He hit a lot of home runs."

named Hank Aaron hit two for the host Braves, but Milwaukee sports writer Bob Wolf summed up the occasion of the damage done by Mays and his teammates with this lead on his story: "The best thing that could be said about the Braves Sunday was that none of them got hurt."

THE MICK

Willie Mays and Mickey Mantle were compared to one another throughout their careers because they both played center field for New York teams, both broke into the majors in 1951, and both were sublime talents. Like Mays, Mantle was a five-tool player, although Mantle's wheels were damaged early with knee injuries. Gradually they took a toll and turned Mantle into a sympathetic figure that stoically bore pain as he swathed the weak knees in enough tape

The three greatest sluggers of their era, from left, Willie Mays, Mickey Mantle, and Henry Aaron pose before a June 1969, game between the Atlanta Braves and San Francisco Giants. *(Diamond Images/Getty Images)*

to conceal a mummy. One difference between Mantle and almost all other sluggers in the 500–home run club was his ability as a switch-hitter. Only Eddie Murray in that club also hit from the left and right sides.

Mantle was the fair-haired boy from Oklahoma, like Mays somewhat naïve upon his elevation to a storied position in the nation's news media capital. He was replacing Joe DiMaggio in the field, to boot.

Mantle played hard. On the field he could smash breathtaking home runs. Off the field he stayed up late, sometimes all night, carousing with his closest friends, Billy Martin and Whitey Ford. He had a shy grin and supreme belief in his own talent, and he was driven by a belief that, like his father, he would die young.

THE LONGEST HOME RUN EVER

Early in his career, Mantle hit a drive right-handed out of Washington's Griffith Stadium that may not have landed yet. The 565' blast in April 1953 against the Washington Senators made the *Sporting News* salivate. The multilayered headline read, "Mantle Makes Home Run History at 21; Power Kings of the Past Move Over for Oklahoma Kid"; "The Shot That Shook the Records"; and "Mickey's 565-Foot Drive Recalls Ruth, Foxx Feats."

Later, upon selectively reviewing Mantle's home runs, *Sport* magazine referred to the Washington homer as, "reputed to be the longest home run in baseball history." The ball is in the Baseball Hall of Fame in Cooperstown.

Only by some good fortune did the ball that Mantle powdered off a Chuck Stobbs pitch end up anywhere other than in private hands. Immediately recognizing the significance of the smash, Yankees public relations man Red Patterson sped from the press box to the outside of the stadium and tracked down a 10-year-old boy named Don Dunaway. The ball came to rest in his backyard. A neighbor woman corroborated the place where the ball landed, and it was jokingly suggested some thought it was a flying saucer as the ball dropped from the sky.

In an age well before much financial worth was attached to sports memorabilia, Dunaway sought to charge just 75¢ to turn the ball over to Patterson. Patterson gave him a dollar that day after pinpointing the landing spot of the ball but later mailed Dunaway $5 plus two autographed baseballs.

MICKEY HITS 500

Mantle's early evidence of prodigious power made a believer out of Yankees coach Bill Dickey, the Hall of Fame catcher who was once a teammate of Babe Ruth and Lou Gehrig and saw the other 1920s, 1930s, and 1940s power hitters up close. "For sheer power," Dickey said, "Mickey ranks with the best of them."

Despite his bum legs, Mantle survived 18 years in the majors and hit 536 home runs. He won four home run titles, leading the American League with 52 homers in 1956 and posting his best total of 54 for a season in 1961 when he and teammate Roger Maris engaged in their legendary race to top Babe Ruth's 60.

Frank Thomas on his own 200th career home run on June 9, 1996, and his 300th home run on August 7, 1999

"My 200th home run came off of Jimmy Haynes with the Orioles. My 300th, I hit in Oakland. That came off of Kevin Appier, a very good pitcher. Both of those were hit to deep left field, pretty much down the left-field line. I definitely don't remember all of my home runs, but I remember a lot of the big ones."

Mantle hit his 500th career home run on May 14, 1967, against the Baltimore Orioles. At the time, that made him the sixth player to reach the 500 mark. Mantle slugged a Stu Miller change-up in the seventh inning at Yankee Stadium. Mantle had gone 28 at-bats without a homer when he cracked the big one and was getting itchy about it.

"I'm glad it's over," Mantle said. "It's a relief. It's like winning the last game of a

89

This photo shows the path of Mickey Mantle's 565' home run, hit off of the Washington Senators' Chuck Stobbs at Griffith Stadium on April 17, 1953. *(AP Images)*

World Series. It's always been one of my ambitions to hit 500."

Third-base coach Frank Crosetti, who must have been hard to impress, shook Mantle's hand as he ran past the bag, and Mantle took note, saying it was the only time in his 500 blasts that Crosetti did so. Miller, irritable after losing a 6–5 game, did not seem likely to shake Mantle's hand that day.

"I don't care if it was his first or his 800th," the reliever said. "That means nothing to me. All I know is I was doing my damnedest to get him out, as I always try to do."

After going through a home run slump that delayed him reaching 500, the night before this game Mantle told his wife he planned to hit it on Mother's Day. Mantle's former teammate Hank Bauer, then managing the Orioles, witnessed many a Mantle homer but was gracious about being on the losing end of the game.

"It was Mickey's hour," Bauer said.

Mantle's next target was Mel Ott and his 511 homers, though he said he was hoping to avoid a countdown in the newspapers the way his chase to 500 had been approached. Mantle said he hoped to play a few more years and pass Jimmie Foxx's total of 534. But Mantle's legs wouldn't support him very much longer. He finished out the 1967 season and retired after 1968. However, he did catch Foxx and completed his career with 536 homers, about as many as he could squeeze out of his ailing body.

> "Mickey Mantle was the best player I ever saw. He was magnificent. He was head and shoulders above everybody else."
>
> —*Phil Linz, Mantle's Yankees teammate*

Mickey Mantle holds the ball he hit for a home run that traveled 565'. The Yankees slugger points to the dent in the ball, where it hit a house after clearing center field.
(AP Images)

Mantle's final season was The Year of the Pitcher. Bob Gibson was pitching shutout after shutout for the St. Louis Cardinals in the National League, and Denny McLain of the Tigers was on his way to 31 victories,

the only 30-game–winning season by a pitcher since 1934 when Dizzy Dean did it.

In late September 1968, with the season and Mantle's career winding down, as well as McLain's 31st win with the Tigers leading 6–1, Mantle was presented with a gift. McLain subtly let Mantle know he was going to throw him a gimme pitch. Call it a career tribute or an outrageous act by a perpetual prankster, McLain grooved a fastball, and Mantle smashed it for his 535th home run.

As it slowly dawned on Mantle that McLain was going to serve up a batting practice-type pitch, he actually signaled for a chest-high fastball. He fouled it off, signaled again, and darned if McLain didn't throw the next pitch, in the same place, too. Mantle teed off on this one.

In the locker room after the game Mantle was asked if McLain let him hit the pitch. "I have no doubt about it," he said. McLain, however, denied any complicity in such an action. "You don't think I'd deliberately throw him a home run ball, do you?" McLain said. "There would be a scandal and an immediate investigation." The Tigers, who had already clinched the American League pennant, won 6–2. Mantle hit one more homer and retired.

> "My winning was winning the respect of the fans, the people in the community, my children, the media. I feel that most everything I've been involved in, I won in my own way of thinking. It's not a ring, not a trophy, not a plaque, but in my own mind I felt that I won."
>
> *—Ernie Banks*

Contrary to his long-held belief that he would die before he was 40, Mantle lived until 1997, passing away at 63, but only after his body gave out from a life of hard living and drinking. Liver cancer was the cause of death shortly after he had a liver transplant. The cancer spread to several other organs, making the transplant useless.

Mantle's was a poignant passing. In the months leading up to his death, he reflected publicly about how he had abused his body with alcohol and how he might have accomplished much more on the baseball diamond.

"God gave me the ability to play baseball," Mantle said. "God gave me everything. For the kids out there…don't be like me."

Despite Mantle's harsh late-in-life assessment, there were many who preferred to remember him more for his grace on the baseball field than his foibles off of it.

"He was the best player I ever saw," one-time Yankees teammate Phil Linz said. "He was magnificent. He was head and shoulders above everybody else."

"LET'S PLAY TWO"

Like some of the best black ballplayers of the post–World War II generation who marched through the gate opened by Jackie Robinson, Ernie Banks spent some of his formative years in the Negro Leagues.

Growing up in Dallas, Texas, Banks was a latecomer to organized baseball. His father Eddie gave him instruction, and Banks was known for breaking windows with his clouts. He learned the rudiments of the sport by playing serious softball because there was no baseball team for him to play on in his home area. Banks was only a teenager, though, when his talents shone brightly enough to catch the attention of the Kansas City Monarchs, one of the powerhouses of the Negro Leagues.

Banks fell under the spell of his wise manager, Buck O'Neil. O'Neil later not only became the first African-American coach in the majors for the Chicago Cubs but also became the driving force behind the establishment of the Negro Leagues Museum in Kansas City and the most eloquent spokesman for his fellow players

Ernie Banks takes a cut during a 1955 game. The shortstop hit 44 home runs that season, just his second full year in the big leagues. *(John Dominis//Time Life Pictures/Getty Images)*

that had labored in the shadows, ignored by mainstream media. O'Neil, who is now honored with a statue in the Baseball Hall of Fame, steered Banks to the Cubs.

It was a fortuitous match. Banks swiftly rose to the majors, the first black player to compete for the Cubs when he broke into the lineup in 1953, but he also emerged as the most popular Cub in history. The combination of Banks' always sunny, optimistic, and upbeat attitude was exemplified by his "Let's play two," outlook when he came to the ballpark each day. Banks would declare, "What a beautiful day for baseball!" even if it was raining, and although he played before free agency and the focus on players garnering millions of dollars, he summed up the opportunity through grateful eyes. "The riches of the game are in the thrills," Banks said, "not the money." Baseball seriously disappointed Banks in only one way, the inability of his Cubs to win a pennant and reach the World Series during his playing days.

"My winning was winning the respect of the fans, the people in the community, my children, the media," Banks said. "I feel that most everything I've been involved in, I won in my own way of thinking. It's not a ring, not a trophy, not a plaque, but in my own mind I felt that I won."

While playing, and still today, Banks is known as "Mr. Cub" for his allegiance to the organization and for his friendly demeanor.

That is an appellation Banks enjoys.

"That's kind of what my life has always been about," he said. "I wanted to

Ernie Banks hit 512 home runs in 19 seasons with the Chicago Cubs. Known as "Mr. Cub", Banks won the 1958 and 1959 National League MVP awards. *(Diamond Images/Getty Images)*

finish my career with one team, in one city, one mayor, one park, one owner. I did that."

Banks was 6'1" and weighed 180 pounds, a rangy shortstop with unprecedented power for the position, a power that resided in quick wrists. Although he later shifted to first base, Banks hit home runs at a surprising rate for a middle infielder and won two Most Valuable Player awards for a bad team. On his way to a lifetime total of 512 homers, one more than Mel Ott, Banks five times hit more than 40 homers in a season, twice leading the National League.

Years before Banks was watched for moving up on the home run list he exhibited hints of what he might accomplish. In 1955, Banks hit a record five grand slams in a season. The single-season record had been shared by 10 other players, including Babe Ruth.

"It's the greatest thrill of my life," Banks said. "I still can't believe it's true."

Banks not only chatted away with reporters, he kept on talking to his fellow infielders while the game was in progress or to opposing base runners when they came to first base after a hit or a walk. No telling what topic might come up.

Years after retirement, Banks told a questioner that his ambition in life had not been to become a Hall of Fame baseball player but to attend Harvard and become an international lawyer. Still later, Banks, then in his seventies, said his biggest remaining goal in life rather than perhaps becoming president of the Cubs, was to win the Nobel Peace Prize. His goal was to get rich athletes to essentially tithe from their earnings and use the money to help end world poverty.

"OLD MAN BANKS" HITS 500

Banks attained his 500th homer on May 12, 1970, at Wrigley Field, his favorite ballpark, in a game against the Atlanta Braves. On a soggy field after night-long rains that held attendance down to 5,264 fans, Banks clouted his milestone homer to left field off Pat Jarvis. Those fans gave Banks a standing ovation that he twice came out of the dugout to acknowledge. At that point he was the ninth man to hit 500 homers.

"The pitch was a fastball inside and up," Banks said. "They've been pitching me inside lately because I haven't been getting around on the ball."

He got around on that pitch fine, and as he was getting around the bases Banks had several thoughts in his mind.

"I was thinking about my mother and dad, about all the people in the Cubs' organization that helped me and about the wonderful Chicago fans who have come out all these years to cheer me on," Banks said.

At the time, the Cubs held a weekly promotion for discount tickets on Senior Citizens Day, and Banks burst out laughing

American League Home Run Champions (1950–59)

Year	Player	HR
1950	Al Rosen	37
1951	Gus Zernial	33
1952	Larry Doby	32
1953	Al Rosen	43
1954	Larry Doby	32
1955	Mickey Mantle	37
1956	Mickey Mantle	52
1957	Roy Sievers	42
1958	Mickey Mantle	42
1959	Harmon Killebrew and Rocky Colavito	42

National League Home Run Champions (1950–59)

Year	Player	HR
1950	Ralph Kiner	47
1951	Ralph Kiner	42
1952	Ralph Kiner and Hank Sauer	37
1953	Eddie Mathews	47
1954	Ted Kluzewski	49
1955	Willie Mays	51
1956	Duke Snider	43
1957	Hank Aaron	44
1958	Ernie Banks	41
1959	Eddie Mathews	46

Eddie Mathews selects a bat with Boston Braves manager Tommy Holmes looking on in spring training, 1952. Mathews hit 25 home runs as a rookie for the Braves that season. *(AP Images)*

at the symmetry of an "old" player getting the big hit on such a day. "Old Man Banks hit No. 500 on Senior Citizens Day," he said as if writing a newspaper headline. Banks was 39 that season, and the end of his career was on the horizon. He appeared in 72 games in 1970 and just 39 the next year when he wrapped it up.

However, on the day Banks slammed his 500th, he thought more about the past and his present than what the future would be. In typically light-hearted fashion, Banks jumped in the air and clicked his heels together the way third baseman Ron Santo did during the 1969 pennant chase. "I'm 12 years old again," Banks pronounced.

For Cubs fans, Ernie Banks will be forever young.

HANK'S HAMMERIN' PARTNER

One of Banks' 1950s and 1960s slugging contemporaries who actually beat him to 500 was Eddie Mathews. Mathews and Hank Aaron formed the most fearsome power-hitting tandem of the second half of the 20th century, and when it comes to sheer numbers they eclipse the combination of Babe Ruth and Lou Gehrig. Aaron, of course, broke Ruth's career record with 755 homers. Mathews concluded his long third-base career with 512. Ruth's total was 714 and Gehrig, his career cut short by the illness that led to his early death, hit 493 homers.

Mathews, then wearing the uniform of the Houston Astros, hit his 500th home run off Hall of Fame San Francisco Giants pitcher Juan Marichal on July 14, 1967. As he approached the 500 mark, Mathews said it was difficult to keep the situation in the back of his mind, even though he wanted to.

"I didn't want to think about it," Mathews said, "but there is no way you can forget it because people keep reminding you of it."

Mathews was a left-handed hitter who broke into the majors in 1952 when the Braves were still in Boston. He had a 17-year career, mostly with the Braves but also with Houston and the Tigers at the end. Mathews led the National League in homers twice in 1953 and 1959 and four times hit at least 40 homers in a season. He also had the distinction of appearing on the cover of the first issue of *Sports Illustrated*—without apparently being jinxed. Mathews was a nine-time All-Star.

One of Mathews' teammates along the way was catcher Bob Uecker, who gained more distinction as a radio broadcaster, television actor, and witty speaker than he did as a backup major leaguer. Uecker used to go around telling audiences that he and Mathews had 400 home runs between them. At the time Mathews had 399 and Uecker one.

Mathews, also a big-league manager after he retired, said when he broke into the majors he never dreamed he would hit so many home runs, but once he reached 500, "I realized it was quite a milestone. There was no 500–home run club then. But once they started that, it became a lot of fun and important to me that I was a member of that."

Although the end of his career was fast approaching when Mathews knocked his 500th home run, he said he still harbored the goal of catching Ott. He did and totaled exactly one more home run than Ott's 511.

TWO-LEAGUE MVP

Frank Robinson was always a fiery player, and later, after he became the first African-American manager, he was a feisty field leader. Robinson was a cornerstone of the Cincinnati Reds' offense after he reached the majors in 1956 and a cornerstone of the Baltimore Orioles' attack after he was surprisingly traded before the 1966 season.

Robinson, a 6'1", 195-pound rock-hard (in physique and attitude) outfielder, accumulated 586 home runs in his 21-year career. He almost surely would have surpassed 600 if he had chosen to remain a full-time player a little bit longer instead of becoming a pioneer player/manager with the Cleveland Indians.

Robinson's biggest home run year was 1966 when he hit 49 and led the American League. Robinson, who hit 30 or more homers 11 times, played angry that season after his trade from the Reds. Forty-five years later, it is not clear whether Robinson has forgiven the Reds or not. He completed a rare sweep of the Triple Crown hitting categories with his 49 homers, 122 RBIs, and .316 average. That was a Most Valuable Player season, and Robinson is the only player to win the MVP award in both leagues.

During Robinson's early season hot streak that introduced him to the American League, he hit a home run out of Baltimore's Memorial Stadium, the predecessor of Camden Yards. The ball sailed beyond the wall and landed in a parking lot 540' from home plate, the first ball hit cleanly out of the yard.

Cincinnati Reds manager Birdie Tebbetts, center, poses with muscular sluggers Frank Robinson (left) and Ted Kluszewski before a June 1956 game. Robinson hit 38 home runs as a rookie in 1956. *(Mark Rucker/Transcendental Graphics, Getty Images)*

"I lost sight of the ball as I ran the bases," Robinson said. "When I reached the dugout, they told me I had just hit the first ball ever knocked out of the ballpark. 'You've got to be kidding,' I said."

If Robinson played mad after being disposed of by Cincinnati, a trade accompanied by some insulting comments, he had always played hard and was standoffish to other players. He was not on the field to make friends but to make war and win games. Longtime manager Bobby Bragan said, "He was almost defiant at the plate." It was as if Robinson stood at the plate to inform pitchers they had no right to think they could get him out.

Robinson's final approach landing on 500 was different from other 500-homer bashers. The homer was recorded during the latter part of the 1971 season. The Orioles were engaged in a day-night doubleheader that was awkward in construction. Robinson hit his 499th home run in the first inning of the first game against the Detroit Tigers. Then, hours later, at nearly midnight, in the ninth inning of the second game, Robinson unleashed his 500th.

Peculiar, but that's the way the cards were dealt. Robinson said it was distracting to hear fans shout, "Hit it! Hit it now!" each time he went up to the plate during the doubleheader. When he did get a pitch to hit and the ball left Robinson's bat, he did not think it was gone. He was a bit surprised when it traveled into the stands.

Frank Robinson swings for the fences in May 1966. In his first year with the Baltimore Orioles, Robinson won the Triple Crown, leading the American League in home runs, RBIs, and batting average. *(AP Images)*

"It was not one of my best," Robinson said, "but I file no complaint. It was 500."

MINNESOTA MASHER

Harmon Killebrew came up to the majors with the Washington Senators for a cameo appearance in 1954 and moved with them to Minnesota in 1961 when they became the Twins. During his residence in the nation's capital, Killebrew was called the most exciting Senators player since Walter Johnson. Killebrew was pure muscleman slugger, not fleet afoot and not born to roam the outfield. He was a little bit like Ralph Kiner, a home run hitter who could carry a team on his back when he was hot and a player

that experts targeted as the one from the 1950s most likely to break Ruth's record of 714.

"A Modern Ruth?" the *Sporting News* asked in April 1965. It was the type of question many publications posed when big sluggers came along. Sports outlets searched as intently for "nexts" as entertainment publications did for future leading men or ladies in the movies.

At least Killebrew was no one-year bust. He was the real deal, a slugger with longevity. Killebrew collected 573 career homers, hit 40 or more eight times, and led the American League in home runs six times. An 11-time All-Star in his 22 years of play, Killebrew stood 5'11" but weighed 215 pounds. In stature he probably most resembled Jimmie Foxx among the big bashers

> "Harmon [Killebrew] hit home runs like Babe Ruth. They hit fly balls so high they didn't look like they'd go out of the park, but the ball just carried and carried."
>
> —*Longtime manager Chuck Dressen*

Harmon Killebrew visits with young fan Johnny Guiney, 9, at Yankee Stadium on September 12, 1964. Killebrew had visited the lad in May after he was hospitalized with critical burns suffered when his altar boy robes caught fire. Johnny asked his idol to hit a homer. Killebrew responded with two-run blast in the first inning, and added another home run in the eighth. *(AP Images)*

Killebrew was a third baseman, outfielder, and first baseman at various times. He was no Ozzie Smith with the leather, but he was no Iron Glove Dick Stuart either. Still, at a later time he might well have been a full-time designated hitter. No debate was involved in assessing the genial, popular Killebrew's power with the bat. He definitely carried a big stick but also did not wish to boast about it.

"I don't like to set goals for myself or worry about records," Killebrew said repeatedly as questions buzzed at him from different angles at different times.

Killebrew was compared to Babe Ruth in one way beyond just sheer home run titles. Ruth was known for visiting children in hospitals and he promised one young man who was not supposed to survive his illness that he would hit a home run for him that day. Ruth did so, and, as it so happened, the youth recovered.

Less publicized, or at least less enduring as a story, Killebrew was summoned through the intervention of the *New York Post* to the bedside of an eight-year-old fan who had been burned over 50 percent of his body in a fire. Killebrew autographed a ball to "My pal John" and signed the boy's baseball glove. He also promised that if he

of the past. In 1962, 1963, and 1964 he was the first American League player to lead the circuit in homers three years in a row since Ruth.

Harmon Killebrew shows off his two home run balls after the Minnesota Twins' home game at Metropolitan Stadium on August 10, 1971. Killebrew became just the 10th player in major league history to reach 500 career home runs. *(Bruce Bennett Studios, Getty Images)*

got well by the next time Killebrew was in town to play the Yankees, he would bring him to the park to meet the players. "Maybe I'll hit you a couple," Killebrew said of bashing home runs in that night's game.

Later that day Killebrew hit a home run in the first inning and another in the eighth. For his pal.

In April 1969, 15 years after making his debut, Killebrew tagged his 400th career homer. At that time he ranked 14th all-time in homers, and he revealed that his wife, Elaine, had set a lifetime goal for him. "Harmon's going to hit 600," she said. "I won't let him quit until he does."

Killebrew added another 100 homers to his total in less than two and a half years, though he didn't inch up from 498 to 499 for nearly a month. He cracked his

500th shot off Baltimore's Mike Cuellar in August 1971. The blast zoomed 385' to the left-field bleachers at Metropolitan Stadium.

"I'm glad that's over with," said Killebrew, who hit a second homer in the game in the sixth inning. "When people keep asking you when you're going to hit it, you try a bit harder. The only time I thought about it was when people kept asking me about it. The Hall of Fame in Cooperstown has asked for the bat," Killebrew said. "I'll keep the ball [which was returned by a fan]."

Killebrew was 35 when he hit his 500th homer but slowed considerably over the next few years and fell a little bit shy of that 600 goal. He was inducted into the Hall of Fame in 1984, and Chuck Dressen, the longtime manager who saw Ruth play, compared the two sluggers' home run styles.

"Harmon hit home runs like Babe Ruth," Dressen said in the 1950s. "They hit fly balls so high they didn't look like they'd go out of the park, but the ball just carried and carried."

Killebrew had those bulging muscles that could psych out pitchers when he moseyed into the batter's box and made those baseballs fly when he connected. Growing up, Killebrew built muscle by toting 10-gallon cans while doing his summer job on a milk delivery route. But he also thought some of his power was hereditary.

"I always had good strength, even though they never worked with weights in those days," Killebrew said. "I think I got natural strength from my father, who was a former college football player."

When Killebrew meshed his natural strength with timing and experience, for pitchers it was time to watch out.

MAYS CHASES 600

Everyone in sports likes to make big deals about round numbers, from newspaper reporters and television sportscasters to team officials and fans. But Willie Mays was just not a numbers guy and it was hard to get him excited when he hit his 400th career home run in August 1963.

"My first homer was just as important," Mays said after the game against the St. Louis Cardinals that he helped his Giants team win with the blow. "If I hadn't ever hit that one, I probably wouldn't have been here for this one."

Logically, that is true, but a whole bunch of players hit one home run. Not so many hit 400, 500, or Mays' 660, so

whether he got giddy about the achievements or not, others would on his behalf. Warren Spahn, the winningest left-handed pitcher of all time with 363 victories, was in the ballpark when Mays knocked the 500th in Houston in late September 1965.

"I saw your first one, Willie, and now I saw your 500th," Spahn said. "You're a wonder."

Mays said of his 500th homer, "I just want to keep winning, to win the pennant. If the home runs come along the way, fine, but I don't count them."

Others needed an adding machine to count them. Early the next season Mays passed Ott's 511 to set a new National League home run record. The clout took place in his home park in San Francisco, and the accomplishment merited a five-minute standing ovation. Dodgers pitcher Claude Osteen was not as appreciative of the swat. "It was a milestone in Willie's career, but it's just another lousy home run to me," he said.

It was September 1969, with Mays showing wear and tear on his body and slumping because of the growing pressure on him to hit the 600th, when he stepped to the plate in San Diego on a night when just 4,779 paid their way in. Mays was supposed to rest, and Giants team officials wanted to see him smack the landmark homer in San Francisco. But Mays got his chance on a pitch from Mike Corkins, and his 391' swat won the game.

"I wondered if I was ever going to get a hit," Mays said. "I knew I was going to get 600, but I was beginning to wonder when."

He wasn't the only one. Frank Torre, the former Braves first baseman and brother of Joe Torre, had retired from baseball but was working for the

Adirondack Bat Company. As a gimmick the company offered Mays company stock, valued at $9 a share, for each foot the 600th home run traveled. Mays was in such a slump, however, that Torre followed him around the country for six weeks. Torre estimated that he traveled 12,000 miles and spent $4,200 (more than Mays got in stock) following Mays' quest.

Maybe Mays was waiting for the stock price to increase in value, but he ended up with a $3,519 payout on distance from Adirondack, a sports car, and other goodies as a reward for the historic hit that left him the only other player besides Ruth to hit at least 600 homers.

Mays said the 600th was his most satisfying home run because of the way his teammates reacted. They poured out of the dugout and mobbed him at the plate. Afterward, Mays said, "I'm just glad Torre can go back to his family."

Mays retired in 1973, spending his last few years as a bench player with the Giants and then the Mets when he was traded back to New York during the 1972 season. His final homer, the 660th of his career, came in a Mets uniform.

Frank Robinson, Harmon Killebrew, and Reggie Jackson, from left, celebrate in the clubhouse after the American League defeated the National league 6–4 in the 1971 All-Star game. Each player—members of baseball's 500–home run club—homered in the victory. *(AP Images)*

CHAPTER 6

HOME RUN DERBY AND HOME RUN POTPOURRI

450

440

430

420

410

400

390

380

370

360

350

340

330

320

310

300

290

280

270

260

Pittsburgh Pirates first baseman Dick Stuart smiled as he gazed at the man in the batter's box.

"I've seen this fella hit 'em a mile," Stuart said as Cincinnati Reds outfielder Frank Robinson swung his bat.

The black and white images flickered across the television screen showing baseball sluggers in a way they had never been portrayed. They were still in their home uniforms, but Stuart, Robinson, Willie Mays, Mickey Mantle, Harmon Killebrew, Hank Aaron, and others were up close and personal in ways they had almost never interacted with the public. They were casual, easygoing, and chatty.

And their acting roles were simple. All they had to do was play themselves and do what they did best as the cameras rolled.

Home Run Derby made its television debut in January 1960. Each episode featured two of the majors' top sluggers going one on one per 30-minute show. The series ran for 26 episodes.

The creation of this television show illustrated once again that the home run was a special play in baseball. There was no suggestion of creating a sequel called *Singles Derby*. In the show, as host Mark Scott put it, it was "a home run or nothing."

The show's signature scene on the screen was flashing to a special *Home Run Derby* scoreboard, with the lettering in an arch above a genuine scoreboard with innings marked out 1 through 10. On the left were two crossed bats and on the right was a baseball.

Filmed at Wrigley Field in Los Angeles—not the iconic Wrigley Field of Chicago—Scott announced at least once per show that the unnamed park was chosen because it offered no advantage to either a left-handed or right-handed batter. The frequently shown dimensions were 340' down the left-field line and 339' down the right-field line.

The format was basic. There was a batting practice pitcher hired to serve up meatballs from the mound, a catcher, an umpire, and a couple of guys spread around the outfield to catch line drives and the like that fell short of the fences. Pitcher Tom Saffell, a former major leaguer, was not identified, although Scott pointed out to the players and the audience that he got paid a bonus for throwing home run balls. The catcher was John Van Ornum, a minor leaguer. The umpire was Art Passarella, and he was named in each episode.

Babe Ruth is greeted at home plate by Yankees teammate Lou Gehrig and the White Sox batboy after Ruth homered in the first All-Star game at Chicago's Comiskey Park on July 6, 1933. Ruth's two-run shot gave the American League a 3–0 lead. *(Mark Rucker/Transcendental Graphics/Getty Images)*

Players came to bat nine times, each time representing an inning. They were given three outs per inning, as in any game, but their three outs could be a foul ball, a swing and a miss, or even a long bomb off the top of the wall. Anything that was not a home run was an out, so the game moved along quickly and fit into the half-hour structure.

One player represented the visiting team in the top half of the inning and the other player represented the home team. The player who hit the most home runs was the winner. The winner's share was $2,000, the loser's share $1,000. Bonuses

were paid to anyone hitting three or more homers in a row.

Jackie Jensen, of the Red Sox at the time and certainly of lesser stature than several of the Hall of Famers who participated, was the only one to earn such a bonus. He hit five in a row. Even with $500 at stake for those streaks, it proved impossible for some of the greatest home run hitters of all time to hit three in a row. That development supported the notion of just how difficult it is to hit a home run even with gift pitches and illustrated how not even the best sluggers could hit home runs whenever they wanted to.

Boston Red Sox slugger Jackie Jensen crosses the plate after hitting a grand slam on July 10, 1958, at Fenway Park. Jensen participated in four episodes of the television show *Home Run Derby*, **winning twice.** *(AP Images)*

When one player was at bat, the other joined Scott at a table, where the announcer wrote down the score and they chit-chatted briefly about the player's hitting style or the opponent. They occasionally pointed out the difference between the *Derby* and a real game. When Frank Robinson smashed a ball off of the left-field wall, Scott called it this way: "It's off the wall for an out." Stuart said, "There's that double again."

Robinson recalled seeing Stuart put a ball into orbit during a regular-season game. "He hit one out at Crosley Field; I think it went downtown," Robinson said.

The first show pitted Mantle against Mays, and Mantle won 9–8. Mantle then beat Ernie Banks and Jackie Jensen before Killebrew beat Mantle. Aaron won six times in a row, besting Ken Boyer, Jim Lemon, his Braves teammate Eddie Mathews, Al Kaline, Duke Snider, and Bob Allison. Stuart won twice before running up against Robinson and falling 6–3.

Although the appearance of such home run celebrities as Aaron, Mays, and Mantle give *Home Run Derby* an enduring quality, some of the players were home run hitters of the moment, such as Lemon, Allison, and Bob Cerv. Cerv bested Robinson 8–7.

"Good-bye," Scott commented about one of Cerv's shots leaving the park.

In one match-up, Mays polished off the Washington Senators' Allison with a destructive run that ended in an 11–3 win.

"It's getting to be real embarrassing now, Mark," Allison said to Scott as Mays powdered balls deep and deeper.

While the show is a cherished memory for some, like *Maverick, Wagon Train*, or other television programs of the era, *Home Run Derby* ran just a single season. It was popular and was likely to be renewed, but Scott, who was also the producer, died of a heart attack in July 1960, less than two weeks after the final episode aired. His premature death at 45 years of age shelved the show.

Home Run Derby was gone but not forgotten. It had made fans for life among baseball spectators, and in 1985 a slightly modified version of the show was introduced as a live competition at the annual All-Star Game. ESPN obtained the rights to rerun the original 1960 *Home Run Derby* matches in 1988 and 1989, and it has been said that the viewing popularity helped convince the sports network to start its ESPN Classic station.

ALL-STAR BREAK DERBY

The current major league home run derby between present-day sluggers takes place the night before the All-Star Game and is reminiscent of the NBA's three-point shooting contest. The event pits eight hitters against one another over a series of rounds

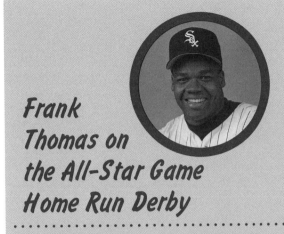

Frank Thomas on the All-Star Game Home Run Derby

"I think it's the greatest thing. I just think that it's gotten to the point where it's too long with 10 outs instead of six outs. I think the rounds should be shortened to make it more competitive. The urgency is there.

"Winning the home run derby in 1995 was probably one of my proudest moments ever. It was so hot out in Arlington, Texas. I saw guys that were in the competition that just felt like giving up because it was so hot. I had a good battle with Albert Belle, and I beat Albert in the final. Belle, Mo Vaughn, Manny Ramirez, Ron Gant, Sammy Sosa, Reggie Sanders, and Raul Mondesi were in it. There were probably the best four young hitters in the league. It was a great competition. To win that thing I had to work to prepare mentally, how I was going to win it all through the rounds. And it worked out. Albert had one more home run than I did, 16-15, but I beat him in the finals."

that provide 10 outs each, with swing-offs in the case of ties. There have been minor adjustments to the format over the years, changing the number of players competing for each league and whether or not homers hit in early rounds should carry over to later rounds.

Regardless, the basic premise remains the same from the original television show and the first live showdown: who can hit the most home runs when only home runs count?

The first All-Star home run derby lined up Jim Rice, Eddie Murray, Carlton Fisk, Tom Brunansky, and Cal Ripken Jr. for the American League and Dave Parker, Dale Murphy, Steve Garvey, Ryne Sandberg, and Jack Clark for the National League. The format consisted of two innings with five outs in each inning. The AL won 17–16, and Parker's six home runs were tops.

A year later, in 1986, only six hitters swung. Wally Joyner of the Angels and Darryl Strawberry of the Mets each hit four homers.

Not every slugger wanted to play every year, but sooner or later just about every slugger appeared at least once. Ken Griffey Jr. did not want to participate in 1998, was talked into it, and won. He had already won in 1994 and won again in 1999.

One of the most electrifying moments in home run derby history was supplied by the Texas Rangers' Josh Hamilton in 2008. Hamilton astounded himself, the crowd, the other players, and television announcers when he clubbed 28 home runs in the first round. The balls flew out of Yankee Stadium in every direction. Fans were disbelieving, roaring, on their feet. Hamilton was the man of the hour, turning in a performance no would one forget.

Under the rules in effect at the time, however, Hamilton did not win the title that year. His 28 smashes did not carry over out of the first round, and the championship went to Minnesota's Justin Morneau, who beat Hamilton 5–3 in the finals. Still, Hamilton's longest blast measured 518' and Morneau's farthest homer traveled 512'.

Not all homers have been measured, but there have been some doozies. In 2005, winner Bobby Abreu tagged one and sent it 517'. In 2002, Sammy Sosa knocked a ball 524'.

None of the home runs hit in the home run derby count on players' records, of course, although an impressive performance in the competition can enhance a reputation or at least provide bragging rights. Not that most of the players chosen for the starring roles need either form of adulation.

OUT-OF-THE-PARK DEBUTS

Even in real games, not all home runs are equal. Some are more important than others because they provide the margin of victory. Some are more memorable than others because they represent a milestone of one kind or another. Just about every player remembers the first home run of his major league career, but some are even more memorable because the player creamed the ball in his first at-bat.

Consistent with baseball's unpredictability, there is no correlation between a rookie hitting a home run in his first at-bat and superstardom. That rookie may never blossom into a solid player, or he might become one of the greatest players of all time. There is a randomness to the completion of the act that is one of baseball's unique traits. If a player hits a home run in his first at-bat it is the result of circumstance, who is pitching, and hitter readiness. If star sluggers can't even be counted on to hit home runs regularly in a home run derby when the pitch is being grooved, then no matter how great the player, there is no telling when he will be able to hit a home run.

FIRST-TIME-UP FOUR-BAGGERS

Among those players who managed to send the ball out of the park in their first at-bat are: Whitey Lockman, Hall of Fame relief pitcher Hoyt Wilhelm (who never hit another homer in 21 years), Chuck Tanner, Bill White, Will Clark, Jose Offerman, Jermaine Dye, Adam Wainwright (another pitcher), Jason Heyward, and Starlin Castro. Heyward and Castro hit their memorable home runs in 2010 as they broke in with the Braves and Cubs, respectively.

As only baseball would know with its fastidious record-keeping, the first player to homer in his first at-bat was Joe Harrington of the Boston Braves on September 10, 1895. In his two-season career Harrington hit three home runs.

The ultimate first at-bat debut was recorded by Kevin Kouzmanoff of the Cleveland Indians on September 2, 2006. Kouzmanoff became the first player to hit a grand slam off of the first pitch thrown to him during his major league career. It took 130 years of major league ball for it to happen but less than four years for it to happen again.

Boston Red Sox rookie Daniel Nava stepped to the plate on June 12, 2010, during a game that turned into a 10–2 win over the Philadelphia Phillies. During a

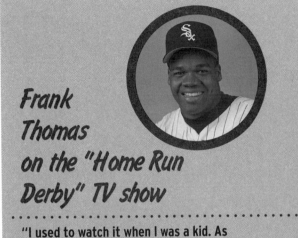

Frank Thomas on the "Home Run Derby" TV show

"I used to watch it when I was a kid. As far as I remember they used to sit up there [at a table] and just casually talk about home runs. It was a fun show."

pregame radio show, Nava, called up that day from Triple A Pawtucket after spending 2009 with the Portland Sea Dogs, was told by Sox broadcaster Joe Castiglione, "Hit that first pitch out." The throwaway comment was like telling an actor about to make his Broadway debut, "Break a leg."

Nava had been cut from his college team; cut from an independent league team, the Chico Outlaws; and really had no reason to believe just a few years earlier that he would earn the chance to walk into the batter's box at Fenway Park with the bases loaded in the second inning. Pitcher Joe Blanton threw the ball and Nava swung. It landed in the Red Sox bullpen beyond right field, and the fans, including Nava's parents, were going crazy.

Nava had progressed from student manager to all-conference player at Santa Clara. Yet the Red Sox were still able to purchase his rights from an independent

Carlos Lee of the Chicago White Sox is congratulated by third-base coach Wallace Johnson after homering in his first major league at-bat on May 7, 1999. *(John Zich/AFP/ Getty Images)*

team for $1—with the proviso that if he made the majors they would fork over $1,500. They got a good deal.

"I guess it's pretty ridiculous," Nava said of his story after the remarkable clout. "As I was rounding the bases, I think that's when I kind of said, 'Oh, man, I just hit a grand slam.'"

The homer was caught by Sox reliever Manny Delcarmen, rescuing the ball as a souvenir for Nava. Nava, 27 at the time, sprinted around the bases with his head down and ran right back into the dugout.

The fans made so much noise that David Ortiz pushed Nava out for a curtain call. It was definitely a moment to savor.

ALL-STAR GAME HOME RUNS

If virtual unknowns can push themselves into the baseball world's consciousness with home runs like Nava did, then hitting a home run in an All-Star Game is something else entirely. That's because a player has to be good enough to be selected to

"Everybody's always talking about my strikeouts. If I played every day I could strike out maybe 400 times. I have no idea how many home runs I could hit if I played every day."
—*Dave Kingman*

Atlanta Braves outfielder Jason Heyward blasts a three-run homer in his first major league at-bat on Opening Day, 2010. *(Scott Cunningham/Getty Images)*

play in an All-Star Game before he can hit a home run in one.

Some lesser known players have hit home runs during All-Star Games, but it is for the most part the stage of stars.

The first home run hit in All-Star Game history was by Babe Ruth. The first game was played in 1933, and the American League won. Ruth's two-run shot was the key blow. Among other greats who hit home runs in the All-Star Game during its first two decades of operation were Frankie Frisch (two), Joe Medwick, Jimmie Foxx, Lou Gehrig (two), Joe DiMaggio, Lou Boudreau, Johnny Mize, Ralph Kiner (three), Ted Williams, and Stan Musial. Williams and Musial were unusual cases. They both played so long (more than 20 years) and appeared in so many All-Star Games, that their homers were sprinkled over decades.

Williams homered in 1941, 1946 (twice), and 1956, and Musial homered in 1948, 1949, 1951, 1955, 1956, and 1960.

Those who smacked All-Star Game homers who were not nearly as famous include Augie Galan, Max West, Vince DiMaggio, Hoot Evers, Bob Elliott, Frank Malzone, Dick McAuliffe, Dick Dietz, Jimmy Wynn, Lee Mazzilli, Frank White, Terry Steinbach, Jeff Conine, and Hank Blalock. These are not obscure players, but their lifetime credentials wilt compared with the records of the longtime stars.

> "There'll be a man on the moon before Gaylord Perry hits a home run."
>
> —*Former Giants manager Alvin Dark, seven years before Perry hit his first major league home run on the same day as the Apollo 11 moon landing*

HOME RUN HAT TRICKS

Any fan who attends a major league game and witnesses one player hitting three home runs is going to go home talking about it. It is a rare and special feat and spectacular enough to warrant admiration. However, it has occurred around 500 times in major league play dating back to Ned Williamson's documented three-homer game for the Chicago White Stockings in May 1884.

Some of the biggest sluggers of the dead-ball era also came through on this front, posting single-game homer binges worth remembering. Some of the finest players of their age and most powerful swingers of the period before Babe Ruth and the lively ball hit three home runs in a game.

Among the really old-timers, Cap Anson, Dan Brouthers, and Roger Connor did it. Ruth's first three-homer game took place in the 1926 World Series against the Cardinals. He also hit three in another World Series game in 1928 and finally did it during the regular season in 1930. Ruth's famous denouement in uniform for the Boston Braves on May 25, 1935, represented his last three-homer show. Those were the final three home runs of his career.

The three-homer list is dotted with intriguing stats. One might have thought Ruth would have done it more often and that some players on the list might never have come close. Among those who have smacked three home runs in a game is Ty Cobb, who never quite believed in the long ball. And he did it when he was older, in 1925. Joe Hauser, the minor-league home run king, had a three-homer moment of glory for the Philadelphia A's in 1924.

Fairly obscure players, such as Carl Reynolds, Hal Lee, Ed Coleman, George Watkins, Moose Solters, Johnny Moore, Alex Kampouris, Merv Connors, Jim Tabor, Hank Leiber, Jim Tobin, Clyde McCullough, Gene Hermanski, and Pat Mullin have all hit three home runs in a game.

Lou Gehrig hit three homers in a game four times, and Johnny Mize did it six times.

Throughout the 1950s, a decade that produced several of the most prolific home run hitters of all time, players kept battering

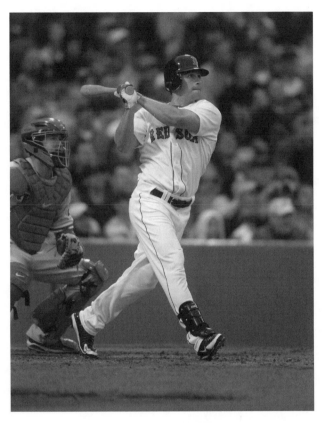

Red Sox rookie Daniel Nava watches the first pitch he saw as a major leaguer leave Fenway Park for a grand slam on June 12, 2010. *(Michael Ivins/ Boston Red Sox/Getty Images)*

the ball over the fence, and many of those big names hit three homers in a game. Guys such as Duke Snider, Larry Doby, Roy Campanella, Gil Hodges, Joe DiMaggio, Eddie Mathews, Stan Musial, Al Kaline, Mickey Mantle, Ernie Banks, Ted Williams, Rocky Colavito, Hank Aaron, and Frank Robinson all hit at least three homers in a game during that time period.

Later, famed players such as Willie Mays, Harmon Killebrew, Willie McCovey, Willie Stargell, Roberto Clemente, Billy Williams, Reggie Jackson, Johnny Bench, Orlando Cepeda, Carl Yastrzemski, Gary Carter, Jim Rice, Pete Rose, Dave Kingman, Mike Schmidt, George Brett, Eddie Murray, Andre Dawson, Mark McGwire (five times), Dave Winfield, Jim Thome, Barry Bonds, Ken Griffey Jr., Cal Ripken

Jr., Sammy Sosa, Edgar Martinez, Ivan Rodriguez, Carlos Delgado (five times), Manny Ramirez, Alex Rodriguez (four times), Albert Pujols (four times), Chipper Jones, and Ryan Howard all hit three homers in one game. Frank Thomas did it twice. Sammy Sosa, who bashed 609 career homers, did it six times. Mize and Sosa share that record.

Although an amazing achievement, hitting three home runs in a game has been accomplished on an average of three to four times a year since the inception of the National League. It goes in cycles, but the pace picked up after World War II. The three-homer game was recorded 23 times in the 1940s and 55 times in the 1950s.

During the late 1990s and the mid-2000s, when baseball was infected with

Home Run Derby TV Series

EPISODE NO.	RESULTS
1.	Mickey Mantle defeated Willie Mays.
2.	Mickey Mantle defeated Ernie Banks.
3.	Mickey Mantle defeated Jackie Jensen.
4.	Harmon Killebrew defeated Mickey Mantle.
5.	Harmon Killebrew defeated Rocky Colavito.
6.	Ken Boyer defeated Harmon Killebrew.
7.	Hank Aaron defeated Ken Boyer.
8.	Hank Aaron defeated Jim Lemon.
9.	Hank Aaron defeated Eddie Mathews.
10.	Hank Aaron defeated Al Kaline.
11.	Hank Aaron defeated Duke Snider.
12.	Hank Aaron defeated Bob Allison.
13.	Wally Post defeated Hank Aaron.
14.	Dick Stuart defeated Wally Post.
15.	Dick Stuart defeated Gus Triandos.
16.	Frank Robinson defeated Dick Stuart.
17.	Bob Cerv defeated Frank Robinson.
18.	Bob Allison defeated Bob Cerv.
19.	Willie Mays defeated Bob Allison.
20.	Willie Mays defeated Harmon Killebrew.
21.	Willie Mays defeated Jim Lemon.
22.	Gil Hodges defeated Willie Mays.
23.	Ernie Banks defeated Gil Hodges.
24.	Jackie Jensen defeated Ernie Banks.
25.	Jackie Jensen defeated Rocky Colavito.
26.	Mickey Mantle defeated Jackie Jensen.

steroids use, there was a spike in home runs and concurrently a jump in three-homer games. There were 27 three-homer games in 1998 and 1999, in those two years eclipsing the decade of the 1940s. In 2001 alone, there were 22.

One player who hit three home runs in a game during the 2010 season was Cincinnati Reds outfielder Drew Stubbs. Stubbs wrecked the Chicago Cubs on the Fourth of July with his three-homer performance at Wrigley Field. The only ones setting off fireworks for the holiday at the venerable old park were the Reds, who won 14–3.

Stubbs, age 25 during the 2010 season, had played in just 42 games before the campaign began and was not about to go around making predictions about hitting home runs, but he felt pretty good during batting practice that day.

"I could tell during batting practice that the wind was blowing out," Stubbs said.

Students of the Chicago Cubs know that when the wind blows out, things can get funky and home runs can pile up. Stubbs took advantage of the atmospheric conditions. Ted Lilly was the Cubs' starter, and Stubbs greeted him rudely with his first home run of the day soaring out of the park in left-center.

"It was a good way to start the day," Stubbs said.

Stubbs' second homer of the afternoon was clubbed off of reliever Jeff Stevens, this one exiting in right-center field.

"I was not sure I got it all," Stubbs said.

Stubbs' third homer of the occasion came off of a pitch thrown by Andrew Cashner, another reliever.

Major League Home Run Derby Champions

YEAR	WINNER(S)	HOME RUNS
1985	Dave Parker	6
1986	Wally Joyner and	
	Darryl Strawberry	4
1987	Andre Dawson	4
1988	Rained out.	
1989	Eric Davis	3
1990	Ryne Sandberg	3
1991	Cal Ripken Jr.	12
1992	Mark McGwire	12
1993	Juan Gonzalez	7
1994	Ken Griffey Jr.	7
1995	Frank Thomas	15
1996	Barry Bonds	17
1997	Tino Martinez	16
1998	Ken Griffey Jr.	19
1999	Ken Griffey Jr.	16
2000	Sammy Sosa	26
2001	Luis Gonzalez	16
2002	Jason Giambi	24
2003	Garret Anderson	22
2004	Miguel Tejada	27
2005	Bobby Abreu	41
2006	Ryan Howard	23
2007	Vladimir Guerrero	17
2008	Justin Morneau	22
2009	Prince Fielder	23
2010	David Ortiz	11

Cincinnati Reds outfielder Drew Stubbs, right, celebrates with teammate Jonny Gomes after hitting his third home run of the day against the Chicago Cubs on July 4, 2010. *(AP Images)*

"I just got a slider," Stubbs said. "I liked the way it looked when it left the bat. Sure enough, there goes another one."

Stubbs became the Reds' regular center fielder and leadoff man as they won the National League Central Division title, hit 22 homers on the year.

"That's the first time at any level I had a three-home run game," he said.

"BASEBALL'S GREATEST SINGLE-GAME ACCOMPLISHMENT"

Rarer is a four-home run game. Four home runs in a major league game is the record, and it has been the record since our grandparents were children. This is a record frequently tied but never broken, and a record that is more than 115 years old. There aren't even Frank Sinatra records dating back that far.

The first incidence of four homers being hit in a single ballgame was recorded by Bobby Lowe of the Boston Beaneaters on May 30, 1894, in a 20–11 mashing of the Cincinnati Reds. Lowe supposedly impressed the fans so much that they spontaneously threw silver coins on the field after his fourth blow as a way to reward the extraordinary showing. The total from Lowe's metal detecting was $160.

Lowe did not make a habit out of hitting four home runs in a game. He hit just 71 homers total in his career. In fact, no player has ever hit four home runs in a game more than once. The wait for five in a game continues.

In the meantime, sharing the record with Lowe are Ed Delahanty, 1896; Lou Gehrig, 1932; Chuck Klein, 1936; Pat Seerey, 1948; Gil Hodges, 1950; Joe Adcock, 1954; Rocky Colavito, 1959; Willie Mays, 1961; Mike Schmidt, 1976; Bob Horner, 1986; Mark Whiten, 1993; Mike Cameron, 2002; Shawn Green, 2002; Carlos Delgado, 2003.

This was one achievement for Gehrig in the home run realm that Ruth did not match. Seerey played seven seasons in the outfield for the Cleveland Indians and Chicago White Sox and totaled 86 home runs. He had good pop in his bat but batted just .224 because he was busy striking out. He led the American League in strikeouts four times.

Adcock, the Braves' first baseman in the 1950s when he teamed with Hank Aaron and Eddie Mathews to give Milwaukee a Murderers' Home Run Row, also stroked a single in his four-homer game for 17 total bases. Horner was a young, strutting power hitter who could hit them a long way but could not sustain a high average.

Whiten was as unlikely as anyone to hit four homers in a game, despite the nickname "Hard-Hittin' Mark Whiten." The St. Louis Cardinals' outfielder had a day for the ages but was not really a home run man. He hit a career high of 25 in 1993 but only 105 in an 11-year career. Most notably, in Whiten's four-homer game versus the Cincinnati Reds, he drove in 12 runs. That also tied the existing and still-standing major league record set by "Sunny" Jim Bottomley in 1924.

No one would have bet a farthing that Mike Cameron, most respected for his fielding and his steady ability to get on base,

would ever hit four home runs in a game, either, although he has accumulated a respectable number—269—in a 16-year-long career that continues into 2011.

The *Sporting News* once called hitting four home runs in a game "baseball's greatest single-game accomplishment," and although fans of the perfect game might argue, there have been fewer four–home run games than perfect games in baseball history.

GRAND SLAMS

The single hit that can most shake up a game and change its complexion is the grand-slam home run. Hitting home runs with the bases loaded is the result of good timing, opportunity, and ability. Few players hit very many in their careers. They are not as rare as comets, but they are hardly common for a team or especially for an individual. They do not constitute bonus points for clutch hitting, but grand slams represent the ultimate clutch hit.

Lou Gehrig's career total of 23 grand slams has been the major league record for decades, but a couple of active players are closing in. Outfielder Manny Ramirez, nearing the end of his potential Hall of Fame career, has 21 as does Alex Rodriguez. Rodriguez is both young enough and active enough to keep adding to his total and even surpass Gehrig. Others who have accumulated a large number of grand salamis are Eddie Murray with 19 and Robin Ventura and Willie McCovey with 18.

KING KONG

Following on the career grand slam list are Ted Williams, Jimmie Foxx, Babe

Mark Whiten watches his major league record–tying fourth home run sail over the fence at Cincinnati's Riverfront Stadium on September 7, 1993. *(AP Images)*

Ruth, Henry Aaron, and Dave Kingman. Kingman had perhaps the weirdest career of any prolific home run hitter.

Kingman was quite deserving of the description of slugger. He hit 442 career home runs between 1971 and 1986 and drove in 1,210 runs. He was a feared hitter during his era, but he was also a vulnerable one. The 6'6" Kingman, nicknamed "King Kong" batted just .236 and struck out 1,816 times. That included striking out more than 100 times in a season 14 times. With Kingman, it was all or nothing as he swung for the fences, with hurricane force winds following if he missed.

In 1975, four years into his career, Kingman was still growing into a full-time player.

"Everybody's always talking about my strikeouts," Kingman said. "If I played every day I could strike out maybe 400 times. I have no idea how many home runs I could hit if I played every day."

Kingman could make outrageous comments and sometimes quite humorous ones. He took two of the best relief pitchers in the game, Rollie Fingers and Tug McGraw, out on a deep-sea fishing trip and said, "If I pushed these guys overboard, my batting average would improve by 50 points."

The former University of Southern California All-American was a three-time major league All-Star and led the National League in home runs twice, with a high of 48 in 1979 while he was with the Cubs.

Most aspects of Kingman's game were magnified: his personal size, his outsized swing, the prodigious distances on his home runs, his very sketchy fielding, and a penchant for alienating people, especially sportswriters, with sarcastic remarks. He was not known for cooperating with the writers, and in big markets such as Chicago and New York, that would haunt him.

Pulitzer Prize–winning news-side columnist Mike Royko was a lifelong Cubs fan supremely annoyed by Kingman's habits. At the time the White Sox were undergoing a revival during the second ownership of Bill Veeck, the colorful entrepreneur who had an ashtray installed in his wooden leg.

"I'd prefer an owner with a wooden leg to a left fielder with a wooden head," Royko said.

Kingman's foibles contributed to his bouncing from team to team. Counting the Mets twice, he made eight big-league stops. Teams always seemed ready to take a chance on Kingman because of his home run reputation, but they tired of the baggage that came with the homers.

Kingman's biggest faux pas occurred with the Oakland A's in 1986 when he put a live rat in a pink box and had it delivered to a female sportswriter during the first inning of a game. It was not a present that was appreciated. Kingman was fined $3,500 by the A's. When asked if he would apologize, Kingman dismissed the incident as a practical joke. "I've pulled practical jokes on other people and I didn't apologize to them," he said. The A's apologized to the writer, and that was Kingman's final season in the majors.

Year-by-Year Home Run Leaders (1960-69)

AMERICAN LEAGUE

Year	Player	HR
1960	Mickey Mantle	40
1961	Roger Maris	61
1962	Harmon Killebrew	48
1963	Harmon Killebrew	45
1964	Harmon Killebrew	49
1965	Tony Conigliaro	32
1966	Frank Robinson	49
1967	Harmon Killebrew and Carl Yastrzemski	44
1968	Frank Howard	44
1969	Harmon Killebrew	49

NATIONAL LEAGUE

Year	Player	HR
1960	Ernie Banks	41
1961	Orlando Cepeda	46
1962	Willie Mays	49
1963	Hank Aaron and Willie McCovey	44
1964	Willie Mays	47
1965	Willie Mays	52
1966	Hank Aaron	44
1967	Hank Aaron	39
1968	Willie McCovey	36
1969	Willie McCovey	45

The Chicago Cubs' Dave Kingman watches the flight of the ball off of his bat during a 1980 game. Kingman hit 442 home runs for seven major league teams over 16 seasons, but his career average was just .236. He topped 100 strikeouts in a season 13 times. *(Jonathan Daniel/ Getty Images)*

HOME RUN LINGUISTS

Kingman was a perfect example of how home run hitters can seem bigger than life. That accounts for the many variations and the compelling need of hitters to describe home runs as something perhaps more than home runs. The official name for the play removing a fair ball from the action with a swing of the bat is home run.

However, "home run" just seemed too tame for some over the years, hence, the application of words like taters, dingers, bombs, four-baggers, round-trippers, and other affectionate terms for home run invading the lexicon.

No one has ever applied such vivid imagery to other forms of hitting rather than home runs than the comment uttered by Reggie Jackson in 1978. "Hitting," he said, "is better than sex." Frank Thomas was one of the power hitters from a generation later who wasn't so sure about Jackson's hitting-sex correlation. "I don't know about that," Thomas said. "Better than sex?" said non–home run hitter Roberto Alomar. "He's a power hitter. I think maybe Reggie is lying a little bit."

> *"A no-hitter would mean more for me because I am a pitcher. I wasn't trying to hit a home run either time. "*
> *—Tony Cloninger on his two grand-slam day*

Although showboating is officially frowned upon as batters run around the bases, bashing a serious clout almost demands some sort of response from someone somewhere. Given that if the hitter is too demonstrative he is likely to be knocked on his butt his next time up by a resentful pitcher, the most colorful part of a home run may never be seen by the players or fans in the ballpark. The guys who have the most fun with home runs are often radio announcers.

They get to describe the moment, to spontaneously react, and to have the freedom to imprint their personal style on what they see.

They see so many home runs that several broadcasters have developed their own signature way of calling a home run. Their hometown fans identify with the signature, and it becomes a calling card for the announcer. Often the trademark phrase just popped up one day in speech and sounded good. Sometimes it could be an unconscious habit.

Some roll off the tongue more readily than others. In each case, however, the baseball fan in the city where the announcer works readily recognizes the words flowing from his mouth that label a home run a home run.

When a Seattle Mariners player would stroke a grand slam homer, their late broadcaster Dave Neihaus would say, "Get out the rye bread and mustard, grandma, 'cause it's Grand Salami Time!" That phrasing was a little bit elaborate, but no one was ever going to mistake Neihaus' call for anyone else's.

Other radio play-by-play men over the years have been more succinct. Russ Hodges went with "Bye, bye baby." Vin Scully says, "Forget it!" Phil Rizzuto proclaimed, "Holy cow!" Jack Brickhouse said, "Hey, hey!" Hawk Harrelson's choice is, "You can put it on the board. YESSSS!" Harry Caray, also known for his "Holy cow!" call also had a verbal tracking system in place: "It could be, it might be…it is. A home run!"

Rosey Rowswell in Pittsburgh had one of the best calls. "Open the window, Aunt Minnie, here it comes!" The sound of shattering glass followed, and Rowswell ruminated ruefully that Aunt Minnie hadn't made it to the window in time.

Another Pittsburgh guy, Bob Prince, said, "Kiss it goodbye."

Chris Berman, the ESPN anchorman, has been commonly imitated when using his favorite phrase. "Back, back, back, back…Gone!"

Jamie Moyer reacts after giving up a home run to Cubs outfielder Alfonso Soriano on July 15, 2010. Earlier that season, Moyer set the major league record for career home runs allowed. *(AP Images)*

For those who think such product sponsorship as labeling a score report or a visit with the opposing manager is a recent innovation, that's not so. There was a period of time, following World War II and through the 1950s and into the 1960s when even the best baseball announcers, from Mel Allen to Red Barber, were expected to announce sponsorship after every home run.

Allen would describe the on-field action this way after a home run during a Yankees game by saying: "a White Owl wallop." Allen also dealt with a different

sponsor for the same purpose: "a Ballantine Blast!" Such mixed metaphors were not considered to be unethical or unusual, just a part of doing business. Barber plugged Old Gold cigarettes after a home run by declaring the hit, "an Old Goldie."

For all of those product tie-ins and for all the natural, individual styles that went into formulating home run calls, it may be that the best of them all was Ernie Harwell's simple, "Long gone!"

The down-to-earth, the loud, and the product placement weaved in, players and fans alike eat it up. The only ones who can't stand this lively way of announcing a home run are pitchers.

IT MUST BE PITCHED TO BE HIT

Pitchers would be just as happy if home runs they gave up were ignored. They know when a home run sails out of the park and their earned run averages soar. They try to pretend it never happened. Mostly, they don't watch where it lands. Most of the time, pitchers don't watch the runner rounding the bases after a home run. They turn to home plate and signal for the umpire and catcher to give them another ball so they can get this sucker going again.

Being a pitcher who gives up a home run is probably a little bit like being an NBA player whose man beats him down the foul lane and then dunks on his head. All of the fans and highlight tapes watch your humiliation, and you have to stand around and take it.

One of the intriguing aspects about the list of pitchers who have yielded the most home runs is how successful most of them were. The byproduct of that skill in many cases was longevity. If you pitch long enough, plenty of hitters will hit home runs off of you.

Jamie Moyer's 2010 season ended early because of injury but not before he became the all-time leader in allowing home runs. The 24-season veteran southpaw passed longtime leader Robin Roberts during the summer when he permitted his 506th homer.

Although Moyer is a long shot to make the Hall of Fame, he is in good company on the list of pitchers most abused by homers. Besides Roberts, Hall of Famers

Mike Schmidt's Religion

After a 13-game cameo in 1972, Mike Schmidt broke into the majors as a full-time player in 1972 with one of the most underwhelming debuts a Hall of Famer ever mustered. He batted just .196. Yet Schmidt, a 12-time All-Star and winner of 10 Gold Gloves, distinguished himself as one of the greatest third basemen of all-time in 18 seasons with the Philadelphia Phillies and became a member of the 500-home run club. He bashed 546 homers, and although he played at a time when sluggers were in a sort of remission, he led the National League in homers a remarkable eight times.

Schmidt's league-leading marks were 36, 38, 38, 48, 31, 40, 36, and 37. The career high-water mark of 48 occurred in 1980, the year the Phillies won their first World Series. Schmidt, a three-time regular-season NL Most Valuable Player, was the MVP in the triumph over the Kansas City Royals.

"I don't think I can get into my deep, inner thoughts about hitting," Schmidt said once. "It's like talking about religion."

Ferguson Jenkins, Phil Niekro, Don Sutton, Warren Spahn, Steve Carlton, and Gaylord Perry are on the list.

"If you're around long enough, stuff like this happens," Moyer said.

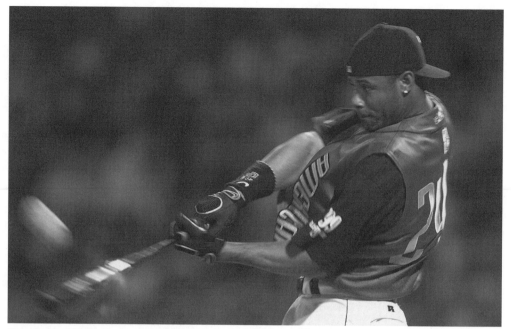

Ken Griffey Jr. hits one of his 10 home runs in the second round of the Home Run Derby during All-Star festivities in Fenway Park in 1999. Griffey won the derby for the third time.
(Stephen Jaffe/AFP/Getty Images)

Jenkins gave up 484 home runs during his 19-season career with the Philadelphia Phillies, Chicago Cubs, Texas Rangers, and Boston Red Sox. He also won 284 games.

YOU CAN'T HAVE HOME RUNS WITHOUT PITCHERS

Pitchers are not expected to hit. They are situated ninth in the batting order in the National League, and American League hurlers often go years between at-bats because of the designated hitter rule. Some pitchers bat lower than .100 and never hit a home run. Jenkins was one of the other types, a pitcher who had a fair chance to reach base.

The right-hander hit 13 career home runs. In 1971 he hit six home runs and had 20 RBIs.

"I was helping my cause," Jenkins said. "They were joking, 'We're going to move you up in the lineup.'"

Jenkins' most memorable home run was a smash in his first game as a Cub against the Dodgers and Don Sutton in 1966. He hit a homer and single that day and drove in both of the Phillies' runs in the win.

Not every pitcher has been so successful wielding a bat. Billy Pierce, a career 211-game winner primarily for the White Sox and Giants, never hit a home run in an 18-year major league career. Teammates teased him about it. However, Pierce did hit one home run while playing for Triple A Buffalo and got a special reward out of the blast, too.

"I got a case of Wheaties for it," Pierce recalled many years later.

Robin Ventura hits the 17th of 18 career grand slams for the Los Angeles Dodgers against the New York Mets on August 29, 2004. *(AP Images)*

More challenging for a pitcher than even his own feeble at-bats is mentally recovering after giving up a home run. A pitcher may be cruising along with his best stuff, just nipping the corners of the plate, when some thug with a bat spoils his day by smashing a home run into downtown Cleveland.

What the pitcher must do is swiftly recoup his swagger and focus and develop instant amnesia. If not, the next batter might take him deep, too, and the game could unravel.

"It's very tough, naturally," Pierce said of quickly regaining one's equilibrium. "The most important thing you can do is worry about the next batter. You can't live with it. You have to forget about it. It's out of your hands. You can't do anything about it."

Gaylord Perry not only surrendered 399 home runs (compared to winning 314 games), but he was never going to fight back with his own equalizing home runs. Perry might as well have gone to the plate carrying a straw as a bat. However, that was

Atlanta Braves right-hander Tony Cloninger hoists an armload of bats after hitting two grand slams and pitching the Braves to a 17–3 victory on July 3, 1966. *(AP Images)*

not immediately apparent when he was a rookie in 1962.

A veteran sportswriter was hanging out at the batting cage early in the season and spotted what he thought looked like a good swing from Perry. The writer gazed at San Francisco Giants manager Alvin Dark and said it looked as if the young pitcher might hit some home runs for him. Dark, proving to be a better judge of hitting talent, turned to the writer and said, "There'll be a man on the moon before Gaylord Perry hits a home run."

Seven years later, on July 20, 1969, as most of America sat spellbound watching on television, Neil Armstrong walked on the moon. That same day in a game he was pitching, Perry hit the first home run of his major league career. In most quarters,

Armstrong's short hike was better remembered, but Dark could have gone into business with a crystal ball.

BASEBALL'S GRANDEST HURLER

Of course, there is always the chance for pitchers' revenge by hurlers who lug more formidable lumber to the plate than Perry. Jenkins was good at extracting it, but multiply Jenkins' best day by a factor of 10 and you get Tony Cloninger.

The onetime Atlanta Braves starter and future pitching coach had a dream day against the San Francisco Giants in 1966.

On July 3 of that summer, Cloninger raised his record to 9–7 and took care of sufficient offense on his own behalf. The

Braves scored seven runs in the first inning to take most of the pressure off Cloninger right away. It was already 3–0 with the bases jammed when Cloninger's turn at bat arrived.

"I was just trying to get a hit up the middle," he said, "trying to make it a little easier for myself. I knew I hit the ball well."

Cloninger did hit the ball up the middle—over the center-field wall.

By the fourth inning, the Braves were closing in on a double-digit lead and Cloninger again came to the plate with the bases loaded. Later, Cloninger listened to a game recording and laughed when he heard the announcer saying "Cloninger is going for another grand slam."

On the face of it, the suggestion was ridiculous, but sure enough, Cloninger did it again, hitting a second grand slam in the same game. In the greatest hitting game ever by a pitcher, Cloninger had hit two home runs, amazingly both grand slams, and drove in nine runs. The Braves won 17–3, and Cloninger got the complete-game victory as well. Of all things, Cloninger's bat was shipped to the Hall of Fame to commemorate the once-in-a-lifetime achievement, one article of equipment that he never could have imagined parting with for that reason.

While the double grand slam provided a distinctive form of fame, Cloninger said he would rather be remembered for a special pitching feat.

"A no-hitter would mean more for me because I am a pitcher," Cloninger said. "I wasn't trying to hit a home run either time."

After all, it wasn't *Home Run Derby*.

(Bruce Bennett Studios/Getty Images)

CHAPTER 7

THE MOST FAMOUS HOME RUNS OF ALL TIME

450

440

430

420

410

400

390

380

370

360

350

340

330

320

310

300

290

280

270

260

"By the time I reached the dugout, my legs felt like rubber and my body was battered and bruised. There were scratches on my neck. It felt as if I had just gone 10 rounds with the heavyweight champion of the world. It was an unbelievable experience."
—Bill Mazeroski, on his home run to win Game 7 of the 1960 World Series

Bill Mazeroski lived every kid's fantasy. The Pittsburgh Pirates' Hall of Fame second baseman hit a home run in the ninth inning to win the World Series, acting out a role on the world stage that youngsters for decades pretended would be reserved for them.

In 1960, in one of the most remarkable World Series of all time, Mazeroski wrote baseball history large with a walk-off home run at Forbes Field that vanquished the New York Yankees and sent his town into delirium. For all of his ability as a slick infielder over a 17-year career, Mazeroski's name endures in the public mind a half century after the deed because of one event, one play.

Only one seven-game World Series has been ended by a home run, and it was a blast off of Mazeroski's bat that did it, giving Pittsburgh a 10–9 win. The images remain strong from that October day when World Series games were still played in the afternoon and kids hustled home from school to watch the late innings.

There is the ball leaving Mazeroski's bat like a rocket launched toward left field. There is the Yankees' Yogi Berra, positioned in left that day instead of behind the plate, his back to the field, his gaze following the trajectory of the ball. There is Mazeroski exuberantly running the bases and diving into a crowd around home plate as fans poured onto the field.

There were teenagers from the stands who leapt fences, alongside Pirate players at home plate, to greet Mazeroski.

"By the time I reached the dugout," he said, "my legs felt like rubber and my body was battered and bruised. There were scratches on my neck. It felt as if I had just gone 10 rounds with the heavyweight champion of the world. It was an unbelievable experience."

With one swing of the bat Mazeroski had morphed from player to legend. He had become a rock star besieged by shrieking fans. Neither the applause nor music has ever stopped, much to Mazeroski's continuing amazement.

Bill Mazeroski celebrates as he rounds third base after his walk-off home run in Game 7 of the 1960 World Series. *(MLB Photos via Getty Images)*

Although it is not the most famous home run call of all-time, broadcaster Chuck Thompson let free with words that defined the moment appropriately. "Back to the wall goes Berra," he said. "It is…over the fence! Home run! The Pirates win!"

Mazeroski shared the joy with his teammates, but the somewhat reticent man did not understand that what he had done was written in concrete, not merely some fleeting moment. He has lived long enough to see how people revere the hit. It just surprises him, that's all, that one blow with the bat can mean so much to so many.

"I just figured it was another home run to win a ballgame," Mazeroski said in 2010, in one of the great understatements of all time. "But here we are 50 years later, and it's bigger now than it was then. The longer and longer it went, the bigger and bigger it got."

It was a pretty big deal at the time, however.

The entire World Series had been as wacky as Abbott and Costello's "Who's On First?" routine. The Yankees were a powerhouse, stocked with big bats that could rip up a pitcher's game plan in an inning. The Yanks had Mickey Mantle, Roger Maris, Berra, and several other guys who could hit, and manager Casey Stengel loved to play tricks juggling his lineup. The Pirates were in their first World Series in 33 years. The Yankees won all of the time. They were nearing the tail end of one of their dynastic runs, but no one dared suggest that. It wouldn't be evident for another couple of years, although Stengel was on a short tether.

To reach the seventh game of the Series, the Pirates beat the Yankees 6–4, 3–2, and 5–2. But the Yankees were Sahara Desert hot, bats torching the Pirates pitchers in victories with lopsided scores of 16–3, 10–0, and 12–0. It was crazy stuff. How were the Pirates hanging in there?

Somehow, Danny Murtaugh's boys dug down for enough resilience to put up the appropriate number of clutch hits. All that mattered was putting W's on the board in some way. This Series was not going to be decided based on total runs, so a win was a win, regardless of score.

In the deciding game, the Pirates trailed 7–4 in the eighth inning before singles by Dick Groat and Roberto Clemente pulled Pittsburgh within one. Catcher Hal Smith then set the stage for Mazeroski by belting the most critical and forgotten home run in Series history. Smith ripped a three-run homer to put the Pirates ahead long before they got to Mazeroski.

It was 9–7 entering the top of the ninth, and when he went out to the field, he thought his Pirates had the game wrapped up. Not quite. The Yankees tied the score 9–9, and that was the score when Mazeroski led off the bottom of the ninth against right-hander Ralph Terry. Because he was not a big slugger, Mazeroski did not figure to end the game on his own. He thought he could start a rally with a single or get on base some way. Instead, Mazeroski feasted on a chest-high fastball.

The ball soared off his bat and cleared the brick and ivy Forbes Field fence more than 400' away.

The Pirates of 1960, with Mazeroski, Roberto Clemente, Dick Groat, Harvey Haddix, and Roy Face, were the direct descendents of the early 1950s Pirates teams that were, frankly, atrocious.

That team holds a special place in the hearts of Pittsburgh fans, especially because a half century later, the Pirates have been nearly as bad as they were in the 1950s. Although Mazeroski has been perpetually surprised by the volume of fan mail he gets seeking autographs or the number of times in a week, month, or year that he is accosted by fans who remember the homer, he does recognize its importance to them.

"It means a lot to people," Mazeroski said, "especially in Pittsburgh, where it's still a pretty popular thing. They always bring it up, and they all have a little story of where they were when it happened. They were on the school bus or walking home from school or just getting into the house after running home from school. Women tell me they remember what their mothers were cooking when it happened. I think a lot of people remember being with their fathers that day."

Pittsburgh has not let the memory slip, even for a moment, and in September 2010, a 14' bronze statue of Mazeroski running the bases, his cap waving in his right hand, was unveiled at PNC Park.

Typical of his shy nature, Mazeroski said he wished the statue depicted more of his teammates rather than just focusing on his final play of the 1960 Series.

"When I look at it," he said, "it's a statue to the 1960 World Series team. I just played a little part on that team. That's all. I just happened to get that hit at that time. If I hadn't done it, somebody would have, because we were destined to win that year."

Yankee players had to feel the same way, because they felt this one got away. Mickey Mantle was crying in the New York locker room after Mazeroski's blast, he said, because the Yankees knew they were the best team that year.

Apparently, they just could not argue against fate. Mazeroski, it turned out, was just like all of those million other kids when he was a boy. He had the same vivid imagination, picturing himself hitting a home run in the World Series.

"I imagined I hit a home run in the World Series a hundred times," Mazeroski said, "pretending I was Babe Ruth when I was a kid. Then I got to do it for real."

Some will argue that Mazeroski's home run that beat the mighty Yankees in 1960 is not the most famous home run of all time. Those people probably don't live in Pittsburgh. They probably live in New York.

THE SHOT HEARD 'ROUND THE WORLD

Bobby Thomson's "Shot Heard 'Round the World" that won the 1951 National League pennant for the New York Giants by defeating the Brooklyn Dodgers is the biggest blast. With two New York teams situated in the media capital of the world, the Giants and Dodgers were destined to get about as much coverage as the kidnapping of the Lindbergh baby.

Frank Thomas on surprise home runs for his 2005 World Series champion White Sox

Stolen base king Scott Podsednik with zero home runs during the regular season, beat the Houston Astros with a walk-off solo home run, breaking a 6-6 tie to win Game 2. And journeyman outfielder Geoff Blum hit a home run in the 14th inning to beat the Astros in Game 3.

"That's what happens in those big moments as far as getting the opportunity to do it. Unsung heroes. There were certain guys in the lineup they wouldn't throw to directly across the plate and they pitched to other guys. Scottie Pods. Good player. I like him a lot."

The preamble is part of the Thomson story, as is the broadcast call.

In an era before the National League Championship Series and division playoffs, you either won the pennant and went on to the World Series, or you went

Bobby Thomson hits the "Shot Heard 'Round the World" to win the National League pennant for the New York Giants on October 3, 1951.
(AP Images)

home for the winter. The Dodgers led the Giants by 13½ games in the NL pennant race in mid-August, and they seemingly had it wrapped up. Among the late-season Dodger recalls from the minors who were brought up to gain some seasoning for the next season was a marvelous athlete named Bill Sharman.

As the Dodgers started losing and the Giants started winning—16 in a row in all—it was all hands on deck, and a rookie like Sharman never did anything but watch. Having divided his time until then between basketball and baseball, the experience helped turn him to basketball, where Sharman became a Hall of Fame guard for the Boston Celtics and a terrifically successful coach.

Sharman watched quite a show as the Giants finished the season by winning 37 of 44 games under the direction of unpredictable manager Leo Durocher to tie the

Dodgers and set up a three-game playoff. The teams split the first two games, and on October 3, before 34,320 fans, met for the season-decider at the Polo Grounds.

In the ninth inning, Giants shortstop Al Dark singled and right fielder Don Mueller singled, bringing Thomson to the plate. Durocher, the former Dodgers manager, a fact that lent even more enmity to a bitter rivalry, was coaching at third base, but he approached Thomson, who hit 32 homers in 1951, with one simple suggestion.

"If you ever hit one, hit one now," Durocher said.

A very nervous rookie Willie Mays was on deck, hoping he would not bat. He didn't have to worry. After warming up both Ralph Branca and Carl Erskine in the bullpen, Dodger manager Chuck Dressen called upon Branca, one of his usual starters.

Thomson, a right-handed swinger, had already hit a two-run homer in the first playoff game. He took a first-pitch strike from Branca on a fastball that touched the outside corner.

Thomson did not sound like a man about to become the author of an immortal hit.

"That first pitch was a blur," he said. "Not because it was so fast, but because I was so nervous my eyeballs were vibrating."

His eyes apparently calmed down. Thomson struck the right-hander's second offering into the left-field stands. Branca was on the mound watching the ball go.

"Sink!" he ordered. "Sink! Sink!" He was imploring the ball to drop low enough for left fielder Andy Pafko to catch it, or as a worst case, play it off the wall.

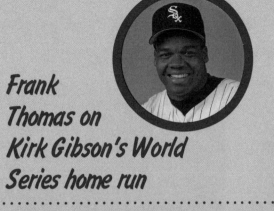

Frank Thomas on Kirk Gibson's World Series home run

"That was special. I was sure he was going to hit one after coming off the bench to pinch-hit when he could hardly walk."

The ball dropped into the third row and passed a 315' sign before landing. Thomson couldn't make it around the bases without being mobbed by fans, and he had to fight his way to the plate to step on it.

Thomson, a solid player with a good reputation, had just swatted the biggest hit of his career, a home run that would be his calling card for the rest of his life until he died at 86 in 2010 and would link him forever to Branca.

Another aspect of Thomson's hit was broadcaster Russ Hodges' handling of the moment with a call that became more famous than he was. It sounded in part, "Branca throws. There's a long fly. It's gonna be, I believe…the Giants win the pennant! The Giants win the pennant! The Giants win the pennant! The Giants win the pennant! Bobby Thomson hits into the lower deck of the left-field stands. The Giants win

Former Brooklyn Dodgers pitcher Ralph Branca, right, pretends to choke former New York Giants outfielder Bobby Thomson at an October 3, 1991, ceremony in New York marking the 40th anniversary of Thomson's home run off Branca to clinch the 1951 National League pennant. *(AP Images)*

the pennant, and they're goin' crazy! They're goin' crazy! Oh, ooh!

"I don't believe it! I don't believe it! I do not believe it! And they're picking Bobby Thomson up and carrying him off the field!"

Like Mazeroski's homer, the Thomson shot has lived on as a special baseball moment, even though the team he hit it for is now located in San Francisco and the team Branca pitched for now resides in Los Angeles. The two men, also like Mazeroski, couldn't believe that people still wanted to talk to them about the homer 50 years later.

"It's one of those things," Thomson said. "I was a lucky guy that day."

Mazeroski's home run decided a World Series. Thomson's home run decided a pennant race. On the magnitude scale, Mazeroski's home run rates higher. Neither was predictable. Both were phenomenally exciting. Both are well remembered.

For whatever reason, Ralph Branca, the pitcher on the throwing end of Thomson's homer is better recalled than the pitcher, Ralph Terry, on the throwing end of Mazeroski's.

Branca was a right-hander who won 88 games in a 12-year career and who was more than halfway through his career and most of the way through his winning by the time he allowed the Thomson blast. Branca admitted saying, "Why me?" on the wrong end of a famous play. But he said that after the game he went out to dinner with his fiancée. Her cousin, a priest, was also in

> "So many nice things have happened because I had the good fortune to hit the damn thing. Could've popped it in the air just as easily."
>
> —*Bobby Thomson, years after hitting the Shot Heard 'Round the World*

the car. The priest said, "God gave you this cross to bear because He knew your faith would be strong enough to bear it." Branca said that from that moment on he just lived with his role rather than letting it define or depress him.

The bitterness and intensity of the Giants-Dodgers New York rivalry, going head-to-head every year in pursuit of the National League pennant, contributed to the importance of Thomson's blow. Fans were distinctly divided. Few could be found who rooted for both teams, so it meant more to Giants supporters that Thomson hit the home run against the Dodgers, and it hurt Dodgers fans more that they lost in such a way to the hated Giants.

As time passed and the teams moved to California and the players retired and then began dying, Thomson and Branca got to know one another and became friends. They made many public appearances together, and inevitably they picked up stories from fans who were either inside the ballpark that day, watching on television, or listening on the radio. Two of Thomson's favorites were from fans on each side of the aisle.

A Giants fan told him he was listening to the game on the radio near Kansas City and was so overcome with excitement he suddenly he realized he was parked in a corn field without knowing how he got there. A Dodgers fan told Thomson he was working in a shoe store and was helping a female customer when the radio blared the news of the home run. He was so angry that the Dodgers lost the pennant, the man said, he threw a shoe at the wall and the high heel stuck in the plaster.

Thomson was a solid player who did something great at the right time. He was not a Hall of Famer, and he didn't make top dollar at a time when top dollar was not much more than the American average. The home run kept his name alive in baseball lore, and it provided entry into many events and invitations to activities for decades.

"The thing, that moment, has always been there," Thomson said. "It continues to amaze me, the way it's grown. I'm just so fortunate. So many nice things have happened because I had the good fortune to hit the damn thing. Could've popped it in the air just as easily."

> "It's funny. Some people remember that a lot more than I do. I remember certain parts of it, and if everybody who mentioned that to me had been to the game who said they were at the game, there'd be 800,000 people at that game, I think."
>
> —*Carlton Fisk, 25 years after his home run to win Game 6 of the 1975 World Series*

Inside, the reminders sting Branca just a little, despite being well-adjusted to the circumstances. It has been a mixed experience having the home run brought up in conversation frequently. Branca more than once likened his situation to someone who committed a crime and did his time but is never allowed to be completely free again. However, he too has been invited to many baseball functions as a result of his tie to the home run, and sportswriters have written many glowing things about him.

"We're married to each other, for better or worse," Thomson said in 2000.

Thomson, who was born in Scotland and moved to the United States with his family as a two-year-old, hit 264 home runs and knocked in 1,026 runs during his career while recording a .270 average. He retired in 1960 and began a new career as a salesman for a paper company in the New York City area.

Decades later a story came out that the Giants were stealing the pitching signs that day and relaying them to hitters. The tale dribbled out in different ways at different times, but in 1981 Branca said that a Giants player, whom he would not identify, told him about a cheating scheme that the team worked up. Branca said an electrician ran a wire from the Giants' clubhouse to the Giants' bullpen and then someone watched for the signs from the clubhouse using binoculars. A buzzer was employed, one buzz for a fastball, two for a curveball, to alert someone in the bullpen, who then relayed the pitch called to hitters. Thomson always denied he was given advance notice of what was coming.

"My gosh," Thomson said, "if I was tipped to the pitches that day, I wouldn't have taken that first pitch. It was a fastball right down the pike. The one I hit wasn't even a strike. Stealing signs is as old as baseball. I played for several clubs in my career where illegal sign stealing was practiced. I don't condone it. But it's just part of baseball."

A whole new round of sign stealing allegations surfaced in 2001 that included Giants catcher Sal Yvars saying a bench player sat in the stands with a telescope to spot the pitcher-catcher signs. Was the buzzer story true? Was this one true? Although stories have circulated, there is no proof Thomson benefited from sign stealing, and the home run lives on mostly unscathed by the conversation. However, as years passed on that score, Branca was occasionally gruff about his view about what happened. To the famous phrase uttered by Russ Hodges, Branca performed some editing. "The Giants stole the pennant," he said.

When he settled in Florida as a much older man, Thomson talked about baseball and the home run whenever anyone sought him out.

"I'm just an old guy that had a baseball career," Thomson said. "I don't take myself too seriously about stuff like this. But it always boils down to (that) I'm remembered because of the home run. So it's nice to be remembered."

When Thomson died at the age of 86 in 2010, indeed, he was remembered more vividly because of the home run.

In the early 1970s, Branca's former Brooklyn roommate, Gil Hodges, was manager of the New York Mets, and sometimes Branca threw batting practice. Naturally, he was reminded of his pitch to Thomson, but as level-headed as always, Branca said, "It's still one pitch." And in the big scheme of life, that is certainly true. "It's never haunted me," he said. Maybe the priest was right. The burden was given to a man who could handle it.

Branca, whose daughter married a baseball man, longtime manager and broadcaster Bobby Valentine, was 84 in 2010 and was still in there pitching.

> ## Broadcaster Bill White's call of Bucky Dent's 1978 home run in a one-game playoff against the Boston Red Sox
>
> "Deep to left! Yastrzemski will not get it. It's a home run! A three-run homer for Bucky Dent. Bucky Dent has just hit his fourth home run of the year, and look at that Yankees bench out to greet him."

HE WAVED THE BALL FAIR

The Fisk home run. That's all anyone has to say in Boston and people know what they're talking about.

The image brings a smile to the face of any Red Sox fan—and to many others—because it was a special home run in the World Series.

Carlton Fisk was the epitome of catcher as warrior, the armored spiritual leader of a team in charge of his pitchers, in charge of his fielders, the symbol of a coach on the field. He spent nearly equal halves of his 24-year career with the Red Sox and the Chicago White Sox and was elected to the Hall of Fame in 2000. But he was a New Englander first, growing up in New Hampshire, and when he first broke into the Red Sox lineup he was one of the region's own, a local made good.

Tape-Measure Homers

Long-bomb home runs that leave fans breathless sometimes occur in meaningless games. They just kind of happen when a slugger gets good wood on the ball and sends it floating skyward. Fans are awed over how hard hit a ball is or how far it seems to travel.

Tape measures are unfurled. Estimates are given. Precise measurements are harder to come by, but with the aid of electronic equipment, figures are now handed out with some certainty. In the end, going back through time, the longest home runs ever hit carry an air of mystique more than surety.

The following list includes home runs hit in regular-season, postseason, preseason, minor league, and Negro Leagues play. At the time they were hit someone announced that the ball had traveled "this far" off the bat.

PLAYER	YEAR	DISTANCE	LOCATION
Mickey Mantle	1951	660 feet	University of Southern California Bovard Field
Mickey Mantle	1956	643 feet	Detroit
Mickey Mantle	1963	628 feet	Yankee Stadium
Babe Ruth	1926	628 feet	Detroit
Roy Carlyle	1929	618 feet	Oakland
Neill Sheridan	1953	614 feet	Sacramento
Babe Ruth	1919	612 feet	Tampa
Mule Suttles	1929	600 feet	Havana
Dave Kingman	1979	600 feet	Wrigley Field
Frank Howard	1960	574 feet	Forbes Field
Josh Gibson	1943	565 feet	Griffith Stadium
Mickey Mantle	1954	565 feet	Griffith Stadium
Dick Allen	1973	565 feet	Comiskey Park
Mickey Mantle	1951	560 feet	Bovard Field
Ralph Kiner	1949	560 feet	Forbes Field
Norm Cash	1962	560 feet	Detroit

It was soon apparent that Fisk was much more than that as he became the glue of the team. When the underdog Red Sox advanced to the World Series to play The Big Red Machine Cincinnati Reds in 1975, Fisk was the backstop, the indispensable leader.

In a surprise to some, the Red Sox hung with the Reds of Pete Rose, Tony Perez, Joe Morgan, and Johnny Bench. On a cold night in October, in a game played at historic Fenway Park, the Red Sox sought to prolong a Series they trailed 3–2. There had been three days of rain delays leading up to the October 21 contest. Pinch-hitter Bernie Carbo kept the Red Sox alive with his own famous home run, sending the game into extra innings with a three-run homer in the bottom of the eighth.

When Fisk came to the plate in the bottom of the 12th inning, the game was tied 6–6 and after four hours of play had extended into the early morning hours of the next day. Fisk led off against Reds pitcher Pat Darcy, and when he saw a pitch he liked, the Sox catcher teed off on it, sending it high and deep to left field.

At this point, the play shifted from the merely extraordinary to the historic. The ball traveling down the left-field line seemed to be curving foul. Fisk had taken a few steps out of the batter's box down the first-base line but eyed the flight of the ball. As he ran he waved his arms in unison, almost as if he was trying to push the ball fair. His arm gestures in willing the ball straight are never to be forgotten.

Neither are his reactions after the ball struck the foul pole in left for the game-winning home run. Fisk leapt into the air and galloped around the bases with childish exuberance, clapping his hands between

The Most Famous Home Runs of All Time

1. Babe Ruth's 60th
2. Roger Maris' 61st
3. Babe Ruth's 714th
4. Mark McGwire's 70th
5. Bill Mazeroski's 1960 World Series Winner
6. Hank Aaron's 715th
7. Bobby Thomson's Shot Heard 'Round The World
8. Babe Ruth's Called Shot
9. Ted Williams' last at-bat
10. Hank Aaron's 755th
11. Barry Bonds' 762nd
12. Barry Bonds' 73rd

first and second. By the time Fisk rounded third, there were spectators on the field. He slapped a couple of hands, dodged around a couple of other fans, and jumped on home plate as his teammates surrounded it. The hit won the game for the Red Sox and extended the Series to seven games.

"It's funny," Fisk said 25 years after the blow. "Some people remember that a lot more than I do. I remember certain parts of it, and if everybody who mentioned that to me had been to the game who said they were at the game, there'd be 800,000 people at that game, I think.

"But a lot of people remember where they were for certain events in history, from Roger Maris' home run, to when JFK died,

Carlton Fisk waves the ball fair as his 12th-inning blast sails over Fenway Park's Green Monster to give the Red Sox a win in Game 6 of the 1975 World Series. *(AP Images)*

to when Nixon resigned, to that home run. A lot of things happen on specific moments. I don't ever get tired [of] it. Sometimes I feel a little embarrassed that other people are so in tune with it."

Broadcaster Dick Stockton did not busy himself with what Fisk was doing after he swung. Stockton was trying to keep his eye on the ball, and his call of the homer was very precise. "There it goes!" said Stockton, recognizing the likelihood of the ball leaving Fenway Park. "It's a long drive...if it stays fair... home run!"

If ever Fisk needs his memory refreshed all he has to do is sign onto his computer. A short video of the home run play is online. It is also fair to say that the people who remember the home run so vividly are die-hard Red Sox fans who had been through generations of support without having much to cheer.

"I don't remember much afterwards," Fisk said, "like it was in a time warp or something where everything slowed down. It was just one of those moments in the universe that was mine."

Exactly.

Despite the pandemonium on the field, after the ball struck the foul pole, it bounced back onto the field and was scooped up by Reds outfielder George Foster. It never crossed Fisk's mind to retrieve it.

"I never thought about it," he said. "I knew it came back down in play. I assumed it was just tossed into the stands."

Actually, years later, in 1999, the ball turned up at a Leland House sports memorabilia auction and sold for $113,273.

In 2005, 30 years after Fisk drove the blast that won a riveting World Series game, the Red Sox held a ceremony to name the left-field foul pole after him. The Fisk Pole is just 302' from home plate. The Red Sox chose an inter-league series game against the Reds (something not close to being on the radar screen in 1975) to make the announcement and hold a ceremony involving Fisk and the pole. It gave Fisk another opportunity to reminisce about his most famous hit.

Logically, everyone knows that Fisk didn't make the home run shot change direction, but the juxtaposition of the ball soaring and him waving is a dramatic slice of theater. And just maybe some pixie dust was involved that affected the moment. Fisk would like to think so.

"I was just wishing and hoping," he said. "Maybe by doing it, you know, you ask something of somebody with a higher power. I like to think that if I didn't wave, it would have gone foul."

On the day of the ceremony, Fisk said he wondered if he was worthy of the honor of having the foul pole named for him. For nearly a half century, Ted Williams and then Carl Yaztrezmski patrolled left field at Fenway Park, and Fisk said perhaps the pole should have been named after one of them.

The appropriateness of his name being attached to the spot in the park was apparent to all others. Williams and Yaz stood next to the pole. Fisk hit it.

"I DON'T BELIEVE WHAT I JUST SAW!"

Fisk's home run literally won a World Series game. Kirk Gibson's unlikely 1988 home run for the Los Angeles Dodgers against the Oakland Athletics not only won the Dodgers a game, but some say it

The Most Important Home Runs of All Time

1. Hank Aaron's 715th
2. Babe Ruth's 54th in 1920
3. Babe Ruth's 60th
4. Roger Maris' 61st
5. Mark McGwire's 70th
6. Bill Mazeroski's 1960 World Series winner
7. Barry Bonds' 762nd
8. Hank Aaron's 755th
9. Bobby Thomson's Shot Heard 'Round the World
10. Hack Wilson's 56th

Los Angeles Dodgers outfielder Kirk Gibson raises his arm in celebration after limping to the plate and hitting a two-run homer off of Oakland Athletics closer Dennis Eckersley in the bottom of the ninth inning to win Game 1 of the 1988 World Series. *(AP Images)*

inspired his team in such a way that it won L.A. the Series.

Gibson, the hard-nosed outfielder, was the Most Valuable Player in the National League during 1988's regular season. The Dodgers were underdogs to the powerful A's, and one reason was Oakland's superb closer, Dennis Eckersley, who had been almost untouchable that season. The Athletics won 104 games and featured sluggers Jose Canseco and Mark McGwire. The Dodgers were somewhat demoralized at the start of the Series because Gibson had a pulled a hamstring and strained a knee and could barely walk. He was scratched from the Series-opening game.

It was only late in the game while trailing the A's that Dodgers manager Tommy Lasorda turned to Gibson as a pinch-hitter—after he volunteered. Gibson had spent most of the game out of uniform. He treated his wounds with ice through the night and mostly stayed in the clubhouse instead of the dugout.

In the bottom of the ninth, Gibson hobbled awkwardly and painfully into the batter's box. It took only an instant to realize why he hadn't been playing. He couldn't run. But Lasorda wasn't looking for a stolen base or the hit-and-run. He was looking for a hit. If Gibson singled he would immediately be pulled from the game for a pinch runner. It didn't come to that, however.

There were two outs and a runner on first when Gibson came to bat. Eckersley swiftly got ahead in the count with two strikes. With a full count, Gibson swung at a breaking ball and with his powerful upper body, even if his pins were no good, he muscled the ball 360' to right.

Broadcaster Jack Buck was blown away by Gibson's moment.

"This is gonna be a home run," Buck said. "Unbelievable! A home run for Gibson! I don't believe…what I just saw. I don't believe what I just saw!"

As he ran around the bases, Gibson pumped his arms back and forth, much like a hockey player celebration after a goal. It was a grand moment in World Series history and sparked the Dodgers to a 5–4 win that day and a four-out-of-five games Series championship.

"It was a storybook ending, but it's exactly how our year was," said Gibson, who is now manager of the Arizona Diamondbacks.

It was a not-so-happy ending for A's manager Tony La Russa.

"Heartbreak," he said. "It's almost the worst of memories."

Eckersley said it took him a long time to get over Gibson's hit, and he was glad it occurred closer to the start of his bullpen career than near the end.

"If I had stopped playing then, it would have been a lot tougher," he said.

Gibson said he hit a slider. Eckersley said he threw a curve. Indisputably, Gibson hit the ball a long way.

"I took an ugly swing and The Dodger in the Sky blessed me," Gibson said. "I was stunned. We were stunned."

Stunned into action.

Gibson was so sure he would be unable to play during the game because of his leg infirmities that a couple of hours before the first pitch he told his wife to go home. She went home and walked out on history.

Year-by-Year Home Run Leaders (1970-79)

AMERICAN LEAGUE

1970	Frank Howard	44
1971	Bill Melton	33
1972	Dick Allen	37
1973	Reggie Jackson	32
1974	Dick Allen	32
1975	Reggie Jackson and George Scott	36
1976	Graig Nettles	32
1977	Jim Rice	39
1978	Jim Rice	46
1979	Gorman Thomas	45

NATIONAL LEAGUE

1970	Johnny Bench	45
1971	Willie Stargell	48
1972	Johnny Bench	40
1973	Willie Stargell	44
1974	Mike Schmidt	36
1975	Mike Schmidt	38
1976	Mike Schmidt	38
1977	George Foster	52
1978	George Foster	40
1979	Dave Kingman	48

> "I took an ugly swing and The Dodger in the Sky blessed me.
> I was stunned. We were stunned."
> —*Kirk Gibson, on his hobble-to-the-plate home run to win*
> *Game 1 of the 1988 World Series*

Gibson has no idea where the home run ball went, but he did save the bat he hit it with and kept it well-preserved in his home in a darkened room until auctioning it off for over $575,000 in November 2010. Although the bat did not shatter in a lightning storm in the way that Robert Redford's did during his last at-bat in the movie *The Natural*, his miracle hit required the retirement of the bat.

"Where the ball hit the bat," Gibson said, "it chipped a piece right out of it."

You might say that Gibson's bat was struck by lightning, too.

BLUE JAY JOE AND THE WILD THING

Bill Mazeroski's home run is the only one that ended a World Series in seven games. In 1993, Joe Carter of Toronto provided a walk-off homer to win the Series for the Blue Jays in six.

Before the New York Yankees reloaded and the Boston Red Sox ramped up, the Blue Jays had some moments of glory in the American League East. The Blue Jays were playing the Philadelphia Phillies in the Series, and Toronto led the Series 3–2. The sixth game was played before the Blue Jays' home fans.

It was looking as if there was going to be a Game Seven when Carter, a 16-year veteran outfielder with five All-Star appearances and 396 homers in his career, stepped into the batter's box. The Blue Jays were threatening with two men on, but the Phillies had their hard-throwing closer, Mitch Williams, on the mound.

A colorful player who had a kinship with Charlie Sheen's eccentric reliever in *Major League*, Williams was nicknamed "Wild Thing." The Phillies had won one World Series in their history, in 1980, and their fans were still hungry. Williams seemed likely to go down in team lore as a hero. Instead, when he fed Carter the pitch that he rocketed out of the playing field, Williams' game deteriorated and he became a pariah.

Carter belted a three-run homer and for Toronto it was game, set, match, the culmination of an 8–6 triumph.

"Touch 'em all, Joe," said broadcaster Tom Cheek. "You will never hit a bigger home run in your life."

Carter was lifted onto teammates' shoulders. It all played out the way he envisioned it in his dreams. "How many times?" he repeated when questioned. "Pick any number you want and put three dots beside it."

Toronto Blue Jays outfielder Joe Carter jubilantly rounds the bases after hitting a game-winning three-run home run in the ninth inning of Game 6 off of Philadelphia closer Mitch Williams to win the 1993 World Series.
(AP Images)

Carter did not actually see his hit land outside the yard. He lost it in the lights and after the game slipped into a camera booth to watch the instant replay.

The homer was a career-defining moment, and Carter reveled in the adulation. He got the ball back and kept it. He has a Blue Jays uniform still decorated in stale champagne. The Baseball Hall of Fame ended up with the bat that launched the homer.

Carter knew he had done something special, but he didn't expect to hear baseball fans, friends, relatives, and team officials talk about the achievement so often. It came up in conversation for years, when people first met him, when they heard his name.

"The public will not let me forget," Carter said. "But that's fine because it's something I'm proud of. I did something that gave them a big lift."

Mr. October

Reggie Jackson, a member of the 500-home run club with 563 dingers, was known as Mr. October during his playing days.

Jackson was a member of three Oakland A's World Series champion teams and was a member of two more title teams in New York with the Yankees. Loud, brash, and thought-provoking, Jackson always said what was on his mind. He announced that if he ever played in New York someone would name a candy bar after him, and he was right. The Reggie Bar did appear.

The 1973 American League Most Valuable Player was a 14-time All-Star, and his greatest playing moment consisted not of a single memorable home run but a cluster of them.

In the 1978 World Series against the Los Angeles Dodgers, Jackson hit home runs in Game 4 and Game 5. But he saved his masterpiece for Game 6. Jackson hit three straight home runs, off of three different Dodgers pitchers on three straight pitches—the first pitch of each at-bat.

BUCKY F--ING DENT

One of the most famous home runs of recent decades that did not involve a World Series was a morale-destroying, pour-fuel-on-the-fire-of-a-rivalry long shot that added to the mythology of the New York Yankees and the idea of The Curse of the Bambino for the Red Sox.

Since the Red Sox had sold Babe Ruth to the Yankees, the fortunes of the two franchises swapped. The Red Sox had been the finest team in the American League during the circuit's first two decades of existence. Everything changed for the Yankees after Ruth joined the team in 1920.

The Yankees won championships and the Red Sox forgot how to, ultimately going 86 years from 1918 to 2004 without capturing a World Series. In 1978, the Red Sox led the Yankees by 14 games in the standings on July 19. During a crazy September, the Yankees caught the Sox, and they finished the regular season tied. A one-game playoff was set for October 2 at Fenway Park.

Ron Guidry, the southpaw having his best season and on his way to a 25–3 record, started for New York. The Red Sox sent Mike Torrez to the mound. After six innings, the Red Sox led 2–0. But the Yankees exploded in the seventh.

Stepping to the plate at a crucial moment was Yankees shortstop Bucky Dent, a good fielding, hardly-ever-hitting player who seemed to possess no more power than a fourth-grader. With two men on, Dent lofted a high fly ball to left field. Carl Yazstrzemski retreated. Back Yaz went, but with the Green Monster behind him, he swiftly ran out of room. The ball

New York Yankees shortstop Bucky Dent homers off of Boston's Mike Torrez to provide the winning margin in the Yankees win in the one-game playoff to decide the American League East. *(AP Images)*

kept soaring, and it floated over the wall for a home run.

Light-hitting Dent had done it. The least likely home run threat in the Yankees' lineup came through. Pitcher Torrez couldn't believe it. The Red Sox couldn't believe it. Red Sox fans couldn't believe it. Manager Don Zimmer couldn't believe it. Not even Dent truly believed it.

"When I hit the ball I knew that I had hit it high enough to hit the wall," Dent said. "But there were shadows on the net behind the wall and I didn't see the ball land there. I didn't know I hit a home run until I saw the umpire at first signaling home run with his hand. I couldn't believe it."

Although the Red Sox fought gamely on before losing 5–4, they were dead then, losers of another pennant to the Yankees.

It is thought that Zimmer was the first one to utter the words "Bucky F——ing Dent," as evidence that a puny infielder had ruined the Sox season. "Bucky F——ing Dent" became a mantra of sorts in Boston as an expression of disgust over how the Yankees always seemed to come out ahead. It was repeated thousands of times by New England fans.

Once, years later, television reporter Jim Gray, known for asking bold questions, cornered Dent at a game as he went

> "I didn't know I hit a home run until I saw the umpire at first signaling home run with his hand. I couldn't believe it."
> —Bucky Dent on his game-winning home run in the Yankees' 1978 one-game playoff win over the Red Sox

unrecognized in Boston and hilariously asked Dent what his real middle name was.

Despite triumphing in two World Series in the 2000s, Red Sox fans still consider Bucky Dent's name to be a profanity because in their minds he picked the worst possible time to hit his most famous home run.

OTHER MEMORABLE ROUND-TRIPPERS

There have been many other home runs that decided big games.

In 1986, the Red Sox were on the brink of playoff elimination, one strike away from losing to the Angels when Dave Henderson clouted a season-saving home run off of reliever Donnie Moore. Moore committed suicide a few years later, and some said that he never got over surrendering the big homer to Henderson.

Yankees outfielder Tommy Heinrich won a 1949 World Series game for New York in the ninth inning. Dick Sisler's 10th-inning home run in 1950 clinched the pennant for the Philadelphia Phillies' Whiz Kids. Joe DiMaggio hit a 10th-inning home run that year to beat the Phils in a Series game. Just back with the

Tigers in 1945 following his military stint, Hank Greenberg slammed a homer that won the pennant for Detroit. Jimmie Foxx won a World Series game for the Philadelphia Athletics in 1930 with a ninth-inning smash. Pinch-hitter Dusty Rhodes' home run for the Giants in the 1954 World Series in Game 1 gave New York a win over the Cleveland Indians and set the stage for the upset Series victory. Unheralded Gene Tenace hit home runs in his first two at-bats to propel Oakland in the 1972 World Series.

And then there was "The Homer in the Gloamin'" by Chicago Cubs catcher Gabby Hartnett. Not only did the home run help clinch the National League pennant for the Cubs in 1938, but it was also a play shrouded in mystery, if not complete darkness.

In a tight pennant race, the Cubs, who, contrary to popular belief, have not *always* been bad and during this portion of the 20th century reached the World Series every three years, had one more win and two more losses than the fading Pittsburgh Pirates.

It was late September, with just days remaining in the season, and it was late afternoon, a half-century before Wrigley

Field added lights. The score was 5–5, Cubs at the plate in the bottom of the ninth, trying to pull out a victory before the game was halted and ordered replayed the next day. Pittsburgh was throwing Mace Brown, and Hartnett, a Hall of Fame catcher, stood in the batter's box with two strikes on him. It was all-or-nothing time, because the umps were poised to call the game after nine.

Brown fired and Hartnett connected. The ball headed for the left-field bleachers. Players lost sight of the ball in the rapidly darkening sky. Fans rushed the field. Hartnett ran the bases. The ball never came back to the infield for a tag, and he circled the bases the beneficiary of a home run that hardly anyone saw. The triumph set the Cubs apart from the Pirates, and Chicago won the pennant.

Sportswriters gave the home run its catchy name, "Homer in the Gloamin'" as an offshoot of a popular song of the time called "Roamin' in the Gloamin.'" Webster's defines *gloaming* as "twilight," or "evening dusk."

The on-site fans, players, and umpires think that Hartnett hit a home run in the evening dusk, but it was probably the least-witnessed important home run of all time.

CHAPTER 8

THE GREAT CHASES: MANTLE AND MARIS; SOSA, McGWIRE, AND GRIFFEY

450

440

430

420

410

400

390

380

370

360

350

340

330

320

310

300

290

280

270

260

They were the boys of summer in 1961, a scorching season for the home run. Roger Maris and Mickey Mantle were the Yankee twins in a spotlight so bright they needed sunglasses indoors.

They played in New York, where the glare is always brightest and the media horde always loudest. The Yankees teammates were chasing a former Bronx Bomber, the Babe.

Babe Ruth hit 60 home runs for the 1927 Yankees, and some people believed it was a record that would last forever, that it would never be approached. By 1928, combining his brute power and his singular personality, Ruth was a household name, and he had belted more than 50 home runs in a season four times. In 1920 he hit 54. In 1921 he hit 59. In 1927 he hit his 60. And in 1928 he hit 54.

Ruth dominated the statistical category in the 1920s, but by the beginning of the next decade, other sluggers appeared on the scene. It turned out that hitting 60 home runs in a season definitely seemed within the range of other sluggers.

Hack Wilson of the Chicago Cubs hit 56 home runs in 1930 for the National League record. Jimmie Foxx hit 58 homers for the 1932 Philadelphia Athletics and even had a couple of homers washed away in incomplete games. Hank Greenberg of the Tigers hit 58 in 1938.

By the time Greenberg gave chase to Ruth's record, newspapermen followed along reporting on his every swing. Even in those days Ruth's record was glamorous, and the idea that the mighty Babe could be topped was of keen interest to the readership. But it didn't happen.

THE M&M BOYS

They were two very different men, Maris and Mantle, although they were frequently discussed or written about as "The M&M Boys," as if they were brothers. Maris claimed his hometown was Fargo, North Dakota, although he was born in Minnesota. Mantle was from Oklahoma. They were children of rural America, not the bright lights of Broadway.

Mantle, the greatest switch-hitter of all time, was America's fair-haired boy, the favored son of Casey Stengel and the cornerstone of the flagship franchise of the nation's most popular sport. In 1951, he was the heir apparent not only to retiring Joe DiMaggio in center field, but also to a Yankee tradition of greatness that stretched back to Ruth. He was the dream five-tool player who became bigger than life

Roger Maris, left, and Mickey Mantle get an autographed baseball from actress Doris Day after completing a scene for the movie *That Touch of Mink*, in which Maris and Mantle played themselves. *(AP Images)*

because he played in New York. He may have been innately shy, but he adapted to the exposure by learning what to say to the media most of the time. With running mates Billy Martin and Whitey Ford, he oozed New York through his pores, a man about town who indulged a young man's desires in bars and with willing women.

He was reckless with his talent, although in a different age of reporting, no one in the mainstream media squealed on his excesses and nocturnal adventures. Mantle morphed into an athletic god, one of the most famous people in the country, and gained admiration because he was young, handsome, and an unmatched

talent. As he aged Mantle was appreciated more because he played in pain on damaged legs that he didn't complain about but which held him back from even greater performances.

Like John F. Kennedy, he was the seemingly perfect specimen, the best America could offer, a symbol of a new generation leading into the New Frontier. Americans would not learn for many years how flawed each hero was.

By 1961, Mantle was the front man of the Yankees, on his way to lifetime totals of 536 home runs, 1,509 RBIs, and 16 All-Star selections. He had won two Most Valuable Player awards and four

Roger Maris watches his record-breaking 61st home run sail over the right-field fence at Yankee Stadium on October 1, 1961. Maris broke Babe Ruth's single-season record. *(AP Images)*

home run titles, including during the 1956 season when he bashed 52. If anyone was going to challenge Babe Ruth's records, the public believed, it would be Mantle.

By comparison, Maris was the second banana, a lower-tier star but an exceptional fielder playing Ruth's old position in right. In 1960 Maris hit 39 home runs and led the American League with 112 runs batted in. Maris turned 27 in September 1961 and was younger than Mantle, going on 30 at the end of the season. By baseball definition, they were both in their prime hitting years.

Just how prime the country was about to see.

Maris was never cut out for New York. Unlike Mantle, he could not play the media game comfortably. He said what he felt and let the chips fall where they might. Sportswriters hoped he would be charming and witty and answer their questions creatively. Maris answered with his gut, told the truth, and sometimes offended. In a town that Mantle owned, Maris was an interloper. It did not come naturally to him to ingratiate himself for the sake of pleasing other people.

When he couldn't be Mantle II, Maris came out on the losing side of a popularity contest with writers and fans that should have been irrelevant to how he played on the field but wasn't. There was a conjured up rivalry between Maris and Mantle that really did not exist. They were teammates who had mutual respect, and their No. 1 goal was winning the pennant and World Series.

Maris started the season slowly. He hit one home run in April. But he picked up speed in May with 11 more. By the Fourth of July Maris had swatted 31 home runs, and Mantle was just about as hot. As the season wore on, the Yankees kept winning, and the left-handed swinging Maris and switch-hitting Mantle kept on slugging. They stayed close to one another through the hot months and into September.

A STRESSFUL SITUATION

This was one of the greatest historical chases of any baseball record ever, but what was occurring off the field was a disgrace. Maris' personality did not mesh with the writers' style. They began baiting him, hoping he would snap, so they could write that he was churlish and a whiner. There was considerable pressure on any slugger who hit home runs at a faster pace than Ruth, but the media, ostensibly a group that should be sympathetic to his pursuit, turned out to be a bigger enemy than any pitcher's best stuff.

It was not the writers' finest hour. They magnified Maris' personality quirks to make him sound like a bad guy in print. Opinion pieces appeared that suggested that Maris was not worthy of breaking Ruth's record and that if it was going to happen it should be broken by Mantle, a true Yankee through and through who was the face of the club. As time passed, Maris retreated more into a shell. At no time did the Yankees organize press conferences for him

Frank Thomas on the 1990s and 2000s Home Run Explosion

Frank Thomas hit 521 career home runs and he hit more than 40 in a season five times. His career high was 43 in 2000.

"You've got guys hitting 45 homers in a year, which is good. The ballparks got smaller. I didn't win any home run titles when I could have, but that's the way things go. I think not using drugs could have cost me a couple of home run titles. I was hitting 40, 42 consistently without drugs. You never know how many titles I could have won. I don't think people got it. They just thought that guys were getting bigger and stronger. And they were, but artificially."

before or after games or try to limit access even for a day at a time to relieve him.

Reading what the pettiest of writers said, fans began picking on Maris with insults and took sides favoring Mantle. For all of the present-day volumes of news outlets and bloggers and the like

Roger Maris poses with Sal Durante, who caught Maris's 61st home run ball in the fourth inning against the Boston Red Sox during the last game of the 1961 regular season. *(AP Images)*

that follow baseball, it is difficult to see the scenario playing out in the same way. Things peaked when Maris' family got death threats. There was little logic to such an assault on an inherently decent man whose only temerity was to do the best he could on a baseball diamond.

The stress built and built on Maris, and in the latter stages of the season he began to lose his hair. It fell out in clumps.

"It was only when Roger began losing his hair that we understood what pressure he was under," said Yankee third baseman Clete Boyer.

There were specious arguments made that somehow Mantle "deserved" the record more than Maris when reality was that no one *deserved* it, but someone had to break it. As the months passed, the two men's home run rate stayed close. Newspapers ran charts showing where Maris and Mantle stood in relation to Ruth's pace.

FRICK'S ASTERISK

And then Major League Baseball got into the act. When Ruth set the record of 60 homers in a season, the schedule was 154 games long. In 1961, the American League expanded from eight to 10 teams and the schedule expanded to 162 games. For the first time, discussions popped up suggesting that if the record was not broken in 154 games, it should be marked in the record books with an asterisk. The foolish suggestion was greeted derisively in some quarters but taken seriously in others.

At the time the commissioner of baseball was Ford Frick, a one-time sportswriter who had been a close friend of Ruth's until he died in 1948 and had even ghost-written a book for the Babe. The asterisk idea was seen as a transparent ploy by Frick to help preserve Ruth's stature. He had solicited ideas to set the records apart if it came to that and New York sportswriter Dick Young suggested the asterisk.

Worse, Frick's decision to embrace some kind of mark in the record book came in the middle of the season. It was like changing the rules of the sport after the All-Star break to alter who might win the pennant.

Much of this time, the sportswriters also wrote articles that indicated Mantle and Maris were feuding. In fact, they were sharing an apartment with another outfielder, Bob Cerv, a choice they made to leave a city hotel in order to stay out of the New York limelight.

"The only thing we argued about was who did the dishes," Mantle said years later.

One thing that made Ruth's record so difficult to break over the years was the strong way he finished the season. It was not quite as challenging for a top hitter to be "ahead of Ruth's pace" in June, July, or August. However, Ruth set a record by hitting 17 homers in September. A slugger had to either be far ahead of Ruth entering the season's final month or match him with a sizzling hot streak.

Maris came into September with 51 homers. He hit two on September 2 and his 54th on September 6. That meant he had surpassed Mantle's previous best and equaled the lowest of Ruth's four 50-plus–home run seasons. When Maris stroked his 56th homer on September 9 off of Jim "Mudcat" Grant, he seemed to have the record within reach. At this point Maris was receiving an estimated 3,000 messages a day via mail, phone calls, or through other means of communication. And that was before the age of e-mail, text messages, or cell phones.

On September 14, Mantle was at 53 home runs. To avoid the asterisk, the M&M sluggers had to break Ruth's record by September 20. That did not occur. Maris went into a mini-slump, and Mantle got hurt and didn't crack his 54th and last homer of the season for two weeks.

Attention intensified on Maris without Mantle hitting homers alongside him in the batting order. Maris said he was turned into a "freak in a sideshow" and felt he was on the verge of a nervous breakdown. Yet he still went out to hit every day. "You'll have to take it; you'll just have to," Mantle told him.

Maris did not hit a home run between September 9 and September 16,

First At-Bat Dingers

You don't have to be a Hall of Famer to hit a home run in your first at-bat. Few Hall of Famers ever did, and only a few All-Star Game participants ever did, either.

So many obscure ballplayers have hit home runs in their first at-bat that it seems as if Major League Baseball invented a category just for little-known players.

Hall of Famer Earl Averill hit a home run in his first at-bat in 1929. So did Hoyt Wilhelm in 1952, even though he was a relief pitcher who rarely came to bat.

Among the best-known players who homered in their first at-bat are: Adam Wainwright, most surprisingly because he is a pitcher; Carlos Lee; Bert Campaneris; Reggie Sanders; Gary Gaetti; Wally Moon; Chuck Tanner; Bill White; Will Clark; Jermaine Dye; and Braves 2010 rookie Jayson Heyward.

In the category of players you wish you knew more about are: Gene Stechschulte, John Hester, Joe Harrington, Luke Stuart, George Vico, and Frank Ernaga. They hit one home run but not many more.

AMERICAN LEAGUE PLAYERS WHO HIT HOME RUNS IN THEIR FIRST AT-BAT

Luke Stuart	August 8, 1921	Al Woods	April 7, 1977
Earl Averill	April 16, 1929	Dave Machemer	June 21, 1978
Ace Parker	April 30, 1937	Gary Gaetti	September 20, 1981
Gene Hasson	September 9, 1937	Andre David	June 29, 1984
Bill LeFebvre	June 10, 1938	Terry Steinbach	September 12, 1986
Hack Miller	April 23, 1944	Jay Bell	September 29, 1986
Eddie Pellagrini	April 22, 1946	Junior Felix	May 4, 1989
George Vico	April 20, 1948	Jon Nunnally	April 29, 1995
Bob Nieman	September 14, 1951	Carlos Lee	May 7, 1999
Bob Tillman	May 19, 1962	Esteban Yan	June 4, 2000
John Kennedy	September 5, 1962	Marcus Thames	June 10, 2002
Buster Narum	May 5, 1963	Miguel Olivo	September 15, 2002
Gates Brown	June 19, 1963	Andy Phillips	September 26, 2004
Bert Campaneris	June 23, 1964	Greg Dobbs	September 28, 2004
Bill Roman	September 30, 1964	Mike Napoli	May 4, 2006
Brant Alyea	September 12, 1965	Kevin Kouzmanoff	September 2, 2006
John Miller	September 11, 1966	Josh Fields	September 18, 2006
Rick Renick	July 11, 1968	Elijah Dukes	April 2, 2007
Joe Keough	August 7, 1968	Luis Montanez	August 6, 2008
Gene Lamont	September 2, 1970	Luke Hughes	April 29, 2010
Don Rose	May 24, 1972	Daniel Nava	June 12, 2010
Reggie Sanders	September 1, 1974	J.P. Arencibia	August 7, 2010
Dave McKay	August 22, 1975		

NATIONAL LEAGUE PLAYERS WHO HIT HOME RUNS IN THEIR FIRST AT-BAT

Joe Harrington	September 10, 1895	Brad Fullmer	September 2, 1997
Bill Duggleby	April 21, 1898	Marlon Anderson	September 8, 1998
Johnny Bates	April 12, 1906	Guillermo Mota	June 9, 1999
Walter Mueller	May 7, 1922	Alex Cabrera	June 26, 2000
Clise Dudley	April 27, 1929	Keith McDonald	July 4, 2000
Gordon Slade	May 24, 1930	Chris Richard	July 17, 2000
Eddie Morgan	April 14, 1936	Gene Stechschulte	April 17, 2001
Ernie Koy	April 19, 1938	Dave Mastranga	June 27, 2003
Heinie Mueller	April 19, 1938	Kaz Matsui	April 6, 2004
Clyde Vollmer	May 31, 1942	Hector Luna	April 8, 2004
Paul Gillespie	September 11, 1942	Mike Jacobs	August 21, 2005
Buddy Kerr	September 8, 1943	Jeremy Hermida	August 31, 2005
Whitey Lockman	July 5, 1945	Adam Wainwright	May 24, 2006
Dan Bankhead	August 26, 1947	Charlton Jimerson	August 4, 2006
Les Layton	May 21, 1948	Mark Worrell	June 5, 2008
Ed Sanicki	September 14, 1949	Mark Saccomanno	September 8, 2008
Ted Tappe	September 14, 1950	Jordan Schafer	April 5, 2009
Hoyt Wilhelm	April 23, 1952	Gerardo Parra	May 13, 2009
Wally Moon	April 13, 1954	John Hester	August 28, 2009
Chuck Tanner	April 12, 1955	Jason Heyward	April 5, 2010
Bill White	May 7, 1956	Starlin Castro	May 7, 2010
Frank Ernaga	May 24, 1957		
Don Leppert	June 18, 1961		
Cuno Barragan	September 1, 1961		
Benny Ayala	August 27, 1974		
John Montefusco	September 3, 1974		
Jose Sosa	July 30, 1975		
Johnnie LeMaster	September 2, 1975		
Tim Wallach	September 6, 1980		
Carmelo Martinez	August 22, 1983		
Mike Fitzgerald	September 13, 1983		
Will Clark	April 8, 1986		
Ricky Jordan	July 17, 1988		
Jose Offerman	August 19, 1990		
Dave Eiland	April 10, 1992		
Jim Bullinger	June 8, 1992		
Jay Gainer	May 14, 1993		
Mitch Lyden	June 16, 1993		
Gary Ingram	May 19, 1994		
Jermaine Dye	May 17, 1996		
Dustin Hermanson	April 16, 1997		

when he knocked his 57th out of the park off Tigers hurler Frank Lary. Maris collected his 59th homer on September 20 and then did not hit another for six days. He tied Ruth with a blast off Jack Fisher of the Baltimore Orioles on September 26, the Yankees' 159th game of the season.

PASSING RUTH

The Yankees met the Boston Red Sox at Yankee Stadium in the season's final regular-season game on October 1. The starting pitcher for Boston was Tracy Stallard, a journeyman right-hander. Stallard was a fastball pitcher, not a junk thrower, and Maris thrived on fastballs. In the fourth inning, the twain met. Stallard threw a fastball on a 2–0 count, and Maris clocked it. The ball departed for the right-field stands.

Maris had done it. He hit 61 homers in a season and broke Babe Ruth's 34-year-old single-season record.

"I was ready and connected," Maris said. "As soon as I hit it, I knew it was No. 61."

As part of his call of the play, former Yankee shortstop–turned-broadcaster Phil Rizzuto shouted, "Holy cow!"

A message on the scoreboard appeared announcing that Maris broke the record. Red Sox pitcher Bill Monbouquette said the conversation in the Boston dugout amounted to, "Jeez, he just broke Babe Ruth's record."

Jeez, indeed. For Maris it was a crowning moment he had sweated for, worked for, and even suffered for unwarrantedly. Maris received a telegram from President John F. Kennedy congratulating him. Immediately, Mantle, who was stuck in the hospital, told reporters that Maris'

accomplishment was the greatest sports feat of all time. It certainly was accomplished under the most intense microscope.

In 1967, when he retired, Mantle was asked to list his 10 greatest baseball memories, and he didn't even include the race for the record. In some obituaries when Mantle died in 1995 at the age of 63 from liver cancer, mention of the 1961 chase with Maris was virtually a footnote, summarized in a paragraph or two. The rest of his Hall of Fame career took precedence.

Maris has never come close to being elected to the Hall of Fame. He hit 275 home runs and batted .260 in 12 seasons and was a four-time All-Star while winning two MVP awards. Maris' true shining moment was hitting 61 in 1961, even if he wasn't allowed to enjoy it.

Despite all of the fanfare, no asterisk ever appeared in the record book diminishing Maris' achievement.

For the next 37 years, long after Maris' death from cancer in 1985, the single-season home run record was described as the "Roger Maris" record. Babe Ruth was not normally mentioned in the same breath.

However, if baseball fans believed that Maris' mark did not have staying power, they were seriously mistaken. Willie Mays hit 52 home runs in 1965. George Foster of the Reds hit 52 in 1977. No one else hit 50 in a season until Cecil Fielder smacked 51 in 1990 for the Detroit Tigers. Five more years passed until Albert Belle hit 50 for the Cleveland Indians. Essentially, for 35 years no player came close to challenging Maris. His record had lasted longer than Ruth's. That was a reminder of what a feat it was to hit even 50 homers in a season, never mind enter Ruth and Maris territory.

> "Because I only hit 50 home runs once, it was, in fact, an aberration. However, it was not a fluke. Nothing can be considered a fluke that takes six months to accomplish. Rather, it was a culmination of all my athleticism and baseball skills and years of training peaking simultaneously. This was my athletic opus."
>
> —Brady Anderson on his lone 50-home run season

BRADY GOES BATTY

But 1995 was the last time baseball considered the words 50 home runs and rarity in the same sentence. In 1996, the baseball landscape began to change. Brady Anderson, previously a light-hitting, leadoff center fielder for the Baltimore Orioles, stunned the sport by slamming 50 homers. It was almost unfathomable. Anderson was a workout maniac whose upper body muscle resembled Arnold Schwarzenegger's, but he never hit more than 24 home runs in a season before or after in a 15-year career.

At the time Anderson, then 33, hit his 50th home run, he was the 14th player in major league history to reach the milestone. Even the lead on the *Washington Post* game story the day after Anderson's big hit recognized the incongruity, saying, "Brady Anderson became the 14th—and perhaps the most improbable—major league player to hit 50 home runs in a year." Anderson

also hit an American League record 12 lead-off homers that season.

As the season progressed with his homer total leading the league, Anderson joked about himself. He predicted Belle would pass him (he didn't) and refused to accept the description of slugger because it carried the codicil that such a hitter was a threat to hit one out every time up.

"I try to hit it hard, get on base, and score a run," Anderson said.

In 2004, a year after Anderson left baseball, rumors about steroid use were rampant. Anderson was never specifically linked to any dirty drug test, but he also took the trouble to articulately defend his lonely 50-homer year when asked by the *Baltimore Sun.*

"Because I only hit 50 home runs once, it was, in fact, an aberration," Anderson said. "However, it was not a fluke. Nothing can be considered a fluke that takes six months to accomplish. Rather, it was a culmination of all my athleticism and

Baltimore Orioles outfielder Brady Anderson watches the ball leave his bat during an August 1996 game against the Minnesota Twins. The Orioles center fielder hit 50 home runs in 1996—the only season in his 15-year major league career that Anderson hit more than 24 home runs. *(AP Images)*

baseball skills and years of training peaking simultaneously. This was my athletic opus."

Anderson's 50-homer season has never been forgotten because of the unlikely nature of the production, but attention on it was soon eclipsed. Anderson set an Orioles team record that season, but he did not even lead the American League. A stronger-than-ever–looking Mark McGwire, who had made a big splash as a young player in 1987 by hitting 49 homers with the Oakland A's, seemed to be coming into his own. McGwire smashed 52 homers in 1996.

THE KID

The next year, Ken Griffey Jr., a prodigy with supreme raw talent who broke in with the Seattle Mariners as a 19-year-old and followed in the footsteps of his All-Star father Ken Griffey, injected himself into home run record talk. Griffey had been improving on the job steadily. He hit 45 home runs in 1993 and 40 in 111 games in 1994 before baseball went on strike. After injury setbacks, Griffey slammed 49 homers in 1996, and in 1997 he hit 56.

That was the most in the majors in a single season since Maris' stellar year.

"He's a perfect guy to do it because he's not a villain. America is comfortable with Tiger [Woods] being the best golfer. America is comfortable with [Michael] Jordan being the best basketball player. And America is comfortable with Griffey being the guy in baseball."
—*Reggie Jackson, on Ken Griffey Jr.'s chase of the single-season home run record*

Except that McGwire bested him by hitting 58 home runs during a season split between the A's and the St. Louis Cardinals. Their skyrocketing totals led to preseason discussion for the first time in many years that Maris' mark might be in jeopardy. McGwire had seemingly worked his way up to it and was the favored choice. Griffey was more of an all-around player who hit for higher average and covered ground in the outfield with enthusiasm while McGwire played first base only because he had moved over from the AL where he would have been a designated hitter.

At 6'3" and 220 pounds, Griffey was the modern equivalent of the 1950s' Hank Aaron and Willie Mays, a multitalented player who could hurt teams many ways, not just with home runs. But in the power-mad era of the late 1990s and beyond, Griffey was also part of the discussion when it came to big boomers.

Talk of a record-breaking homer year was in the air as major league teams broke from their spring training camps in 1997. Tantalizing fans were McGwire, his bulging muscles reminding observers of Popeye; the Mariners' wiry Griffey; and the rising profile of always-smiling Chicago Cub Sammy Sosa, who had hit 40 home runs the year before. By mid-season, when McGwire had been traded to the Cardinals because of salary issues, he and Sosa were playing in the National League Central Division. A couple of years later Griffey was with the Reds in the same division. It was as if that group of teams was playing a different game from the rest of the majors, fans being treated to a high-class buffet at everyday prices.

In the wake of what transpired between McGwire and Sosa in 1998 with the Second Great Home Run Chase, it is easy to overlook Griffey in the drama of 1997 and 1998. At the start of the 1997 season, Griffey's 24 home runs by the end of May represented baseball's all-time high for that point in the year. It was Griffey more than anyone else on the home run watch radar screens.

50-Home Run Club

- Except for his record 73-home run season in 2001, Barry Bonds never hit over 50 homers in a season.
- All-time career home run record-holder Hank Aaron never hit 50 or more homers in a season.
- Sammy Sosa is the only player in major league history to hit at least 60 home runs in a season three times, and he was the first Latin American player to reach 500 home runs.
- Babe Ruth hit 50 or more home runs in a season four times. So did Mark McGwire and
- Sammy Sosa. McGwire was the first player to hit 50 four years in a row.
- Hack Wilson's National League single-season record of 56 home runs in 1930 stood until 1998.
- Babe Ruth's major league record of 60 home runs in a season lasted for 34 years.
- Roger Maris' major league record of 61 home runs in a season lasted for 37 years.
- Cecil Fielder (51 home runs in 1990) and Prince Fielder (50 in 2007) are father and son.
- Of the players who hit at least 50 home runs in a season once, Barry Bonds, Babe Ruth, Willie Mays, Ken Griffey Jr., Sammy Sosa, Alex Rodriguez, Jim Thome, Mark McGwire, Mickey Mantle, and Jimmie Foxx, also are members of the 500 club.
- Hank Aaron, Frank Robinson, Harmon Killebrew, Ted Williams, Ernie Banks, and Mel Ott are among the career 500-home run sluggers who never hit 50 in a season.

SINGLE-SEASON 50-HOME RUN CLUB

Player	HR	Year	Player	HR	Year
Barry Bonds	73	2001	Alex Rodriguez	54	2007
Mark McGwire	70	1998	Jose Bautista	54	2010
Sammy Sosa	66	1998	Mickey Mantle	52	1956
Mark McGwire	65	1999	Willie Mays	52	1965
Sammy Sosa	64	2001	George Foster	52	1977
Sammy Sosa	63	1999	Mark McGwire	52	1996
Roger Maris	61	1961	Alex Rodriguez	52	2001
Babe Ruth	60	1927	Jim Thome	52	2002
Babe Ruth	59	1921	Johnny Mize	51	1947
Jimmie Foxx	58	1932	Ralph Kiner	51	1947
Hank Greenberg	58	1938	Willie Mays	51	1955
Mark McGwire	58	1997	Cecil Fielder	51	1990
Ryan Howard	58	2006	Andruw Jones	51	2005
Luis Gonzalez	57	2001	Jimmie Foxx	50	1938
Alex Rodriguez	57	2002	Albert Belle	50	1995
Hack Wilson	56	1930	Brady Anderson	50	1996
Ken Griffey Jr.	56	1997	Greg Vaughn	50	1998
Ken Griffey Jr.	56	1998	Sammy Sosa	50	2000
Babe Ruth	54	1920	Prince Fielder	50	2007
Babe Ruth	54	1928			
Ralph Kiner	54	1949			
Mickey Mantle	54	1956			
David Ortiz	54	2006			

Seattle Mariners outfielder Ken Griffey Jr. follows through on his career-high 50th home run of the season on September 7, 1997. Griffey finished the year with 56 home runs to lead the American League. *(AP Images)*

McGwire told reporters that discussion of the vulnerability of Maris' record should never really start until September because so many things can happen in a long season. But he said Griffey was better positioned to break it than anyone in 1997.

"If anyone can do it, Griffey's in a perfect spot," McGwire said. "He's in a good park to hit. He's in the middle of a great lineup. I'll be rooting for him."

Griffey had 30 home runs by the All-Star break, and "Can he do it?" stories were appearing. The issues of Babe Ruth and race were discussed. When Maris chased Ruth, some people did not want the icon surpassed. When Hank Aaron pursued Ruth's career home run record some people did not want him passed, especially by a black man. Maris was subjected to considerable abuse that made little sense. Aaron was subjected to racial abuse that made little sense.

However, a quarter of a century after his successful attainment of the career record, Aaron believed a more mature America would not harass Griffey going for 62 home runs.

"I don't think he would have as much trouble as I had," Aaron said. "Mine was altogether different. I was chasing Babe Ruth and all the ghosts that came with it."

Reggie Jackson, a lightning rod throughout his career and a member of the 500–home run club, said Griffey was popular across all races and classes and wouldn't be subjected to backward racial attitudes either.

"He's a perfect guy to do it because he's not a villain," Jackson said. "America is comfortable with Tiger [Woods] being the best golfer. America is comfortable with [Michael] Jordan being the best basketball player. And America is comfortable with Griffey being the guy in baseball."

Griffey did not break Maris' record in 1997. He finished with 56 home runs and led the American League in RBIs with 147. McGwire blasted 58 homers, with efforts split between two leagues. Although there were hints that McGwire was ready for a run at Maris in 1998, few anticipated the drama, the excitement, and the feel-good nature of the season.

CENTRAL DIVISION SLUGFEST

Baseball went on strike in August 1994, ruining what had been an exciting campaign and eliminating the World Series. Fans were turned off by the specter of billionaire owners and millionaire players feuding, and some swore off the game forever. Attendance indeed had been down or stagnant since the 1995 season.

Many times it was suggested that the electrifying emergence of Babe Ruth and his home run prowess saved baseball after the bitterness and cynicism engendered by the Black Sox Scandal. The home run chase

of 1998 was attributed with the same healing properties.

Baseball needed rejuvenating after the lingering stench of the 1994 strike. Fans had been lost. The sport needed something special to enliven the atmosphere. McGwire, Sosa, and to a lesser extent, Griffey, represented the three rings of a circus that crisscrossed the country with live shows under the big top. There were no high wire acts, no animal acts, no trapeze acts. There were home runs hit at a phenomenal rate, sometimes carrying a phenomenal distance, such as a 538' job driven through a hole in the ozone layer by McGwire that might well have had frequent flyers clinging to the seams.

Griffey, still 28 that summer, was on his way to a nearly identical season as he recorded in 1997. He once again hit 56 home runs and he knocked in 146 runs, one fewer than the year before. It was a tremendous year, but compared to the attention lavished on Sosa and McGwire as the weeks and months passed, he was a mere footnote.

Sosa had come to professional baseball wearing his dream on his sleeve. He was a shoeshine boy in the Dominican Republic who had parlayed his increasing strength into home run power and earned a multi-year, multimillion-dollar contract from the Cubs that made him the hero of his family, a star in his home country, and a wildly popular right-fielder on Chicago's North Side. He nearly always smiled, interacted with the Wrigley fans, gave a little jump as he left home plate when he was sure a deep fly ball was going yard, and he tapped his heart as an expression of love.

As the summer heated up, McGwire, a hunk of a man in excess of 250 pounds whose manhandling of his bat signaled

Sammy Sosa watches his 63rd home run of the 1998 season sail out of the yard in San Diego.
(Vince Bucci/AFP/Getty Images)

that it was a mere toothpick of a tool, was sometimes difficult to draw out. But when Sosa unexpectedly joined the hunt with all of his joy on display, it helped stimulate fan pleasure and exchange McGwire's occasionally sour demeanor for a shy smile.

The chase attracted fans more curious if Sammy or Mark hit one than whose team won what game. Fans turned the pages of newspapers seeking out box scores, clicked on radios to hear game

reports, and tuned into television sportscasts to keep on top of the home run extravaganza. Maris and Mantle were teammates, and their pursuit of Ruth's 60 played out simultaneously. No need for any scoreboard watching in that case. McGwire and Sosa traveled with their teams and produced separate news accounts. Even juicier, however, was when the Cubs and Cardinals frequently met. McGwire and Sosa were on the field at the same time as

Mark McGwire hits his 62nd home run, breaking Roger Maris' single-season record, on September 8, 1998.
(AP Images)

their teams slugged it out in pursuit of the same goal—the division title.

What a grand time it was for baseball. Ballparks were stuffed with fans wherever McGwire or Sosa traveled, and tickets for Cubs-Cardinals games attracted scalpers charging playoff prices. It became a measure of status if you could get into Wrigley Field or Busch Stadium to see McGwire or Sosa play. It was memorable icing on the cake if they hit one out of the park while you were there.

One disquieting story made the rounds during the season at the height of the chase, however. One reporter noticed a supply of creatine, a legal substance used as a dietary aid, in McGwire's locker. There was some criticism and questioning of McGwire, but more scorn seemed to be heaped upon the reporter as a snoop, even though the creatine was in plain view. The issue was dropped for the time

being, but it was a precursor to more important and scandalizing drug usage issues to come.

By the time McGwire blasted his 60th home run to match Ruth's best and to make him just the third player in major league history to smash 60 homers in a year, 700 people were requesting credentials at Busch Stadium. And that was a regular-season game.

The moment had been building for a while, a couple of years really, but when McGwire actually cracked his 60th he seemed overcome at first.

"Babe Ruth," he said. "What can you say? I mean, it is almost—you are almost speechless when people put your name alongside his name. Obviously, he was the most important sports figure in the world of that time. What is happening right now with myself and [Sammy] Sosa and [Ken] Griffey has brought baseball back on the map. If you want to say it has brought America together, it has. So be it."

During that beautiful summer of 1998, no one would contradict a baseball player's off-the-cuff philosophical comments.

Cubs-Cardinals games were nationally televised, and the cameras picked up shots of Sosa on first base chatting with McGwire as if they were old buds rather than newfound friends. Sosa brought a gracious side out of McGwire, and they uttered nothing but compliments about one another before blasting another home run in the hope of overtaking the other guy.

SIXTY-TWO AND BEYOND

McGwire hit the big blow on September 8, his 62nd home run, breaking Maris' 37-year-old record during a night game in St. Louis that ended with a Cardinals 6–3 victory over the Cubs. The record-breaking homer barely cleared the left-field wall in traveling 341' in the fourth inning. McGwire hugged his young son at home plate after rounding the bases and made a beeline for the late Maris' family sitting in a front-row box to share the moment with that clan.

McGwire seemed so overcome by the moment that he nearly failed to touch first base on his way by. His thoughts on the record, celebratory emotions running through him, it took Cardinals first-base coach Dave McKay, McGwire's regular batting-practice pitcher, to make certain McGwire stepped on the bag.

"It's unbelievable," McGwire said into a microphone set up on the field. "Thank you, St. Louis."

Year-By-Year Home Run Leaders (1980-89)

AMERICAN LEAGUE

Year	Player	HR
1980	Reggie Jackson and Ben Ogilvie	41
1981	Tony Armas, Dwight Evans, Bobby Grich, and Eddie Murray	22
1982	Reggie Jackson and Gorman Thomas	39
1983	Jim Rice	39
1984	Tony Armas	43
1985	Darrell Evans	40
1986	Jesse Barfield	40
1987	Mark McGwire	49
1988	Jose Canseco	42
1989	Fred McGriff	36

NATIONAL LEAGUE

Year	Player	HR
1980	Mike Schmidt	48
1981	Mike Schmidt	31
1982	Dave Kingman	37
1983	Mike Schmidt	40
1984	Mike Schmidt and Dale Murphy	36
1985	Dale Murphy	37
1986	Mike Schmidt	37
1987	Andre Dawson	49
1988	Darryl Stawberry	49
1989	Kevin Mitchell	47

Cubs slugger Sammy Sosa hugs Mark McGwire after McGwire hit his 62nd home run of the 1998 season off of the Cubs' Steve Trachsel. *(AP Images)*

Commissioner Bud Selig, reveling in the way baseball had been uplifted, predicted, "For generations fans will remember where they were when McGwire hit the home run."

McGwire broke the record, but the race to set a new one and win the National League home run crown for a year was still on. Sosa swiftly retaliated with two home runs of 480' each to tie McGwire at 62. They kept right on rolling through the end of the regular season.

On the last day of the season, McGwire hit two home runs to complete his year with 70 and establish a new record.

> "It's unheard of for someone to hit 70 home runs. I'm in awe of myself right now. I can't believe I did it. Can you? It's absolutely amazing. It blows me away."
>
> —*Mark McGwire, after finishing the 1998 season with 70 home runs*

McGwire seemed as amazed as baseball fans coast to coast that he had reached such a stupendous single-season number.

"It's unheard of for someone to hit 70 home runs," McGwire said. "I'm in awe of myself right now. I can't believe I did it. Can you? It's absolutely amazing. It blows me away."

Sosa powered his way to the finish line in style, as well, concluding the season with 66 home runs, the second most in history. However, Sosa had the better all-around year and led his Cubs into the playoffs, so he was awarded the National League MVP award. Sosa batted .308 and drove in 158 runs.

Sosa halfway suggested that the two sluggers might do it all over again the next season.

"You never know," Sosa said. "If you do it one time, you have the ability to do it again."

McGwire and Sosa were in the forefront of a baseball resurgence once again driven by the home run. Even pitchers like Greg Maddux and Tom Glavine, both of whom would win more than 300 games in their careers and were destined for the Hall of Fame, made a commercial spoofing the addiction to homers.

"Chicks dig the long ball," was the punch line of their TV commercial.

CHAPTER 9

HOME RUN KINGS:

HANK AARON AND BARRY BONDS

450
440
430
420
410
400
390
380
370
360
350
340
330
320
310
300
290
280
270
260

> "[Henry Aaron] was a deceptive home run hitter. It's just really hard to believe he hit as many home runs as he did. You would have thought it would have been Reggie [Jackson] or Mickey [Mantle] or Harmon [Killebrew], guys who were natural home run hitters."
>
> —*Stan Musial*

It is a reasonable bet that if you walked down any American street and asked pedestrians if they could sing a few bars of the all-time musical classic "Move Over, Babe, Here Comes Henry," that you would receive blank stares more readily than melodious singing.

How many people remember that a song was written about Hank Aaron's pursuit of Babe Ruth's career home run record? Precious few, no doubt. Even more surprising to most would be the name of the lyricist—famed baseball broadcaster Ernie Harwell, who took time out from his regular gig to pen the song in 1973.

Certainly it was one of Detroit Tigers pitcher and singer Bill Slayback's greatest hits, but it might have been a bigger hit if the Supremes, Elvis Presley, or Frank Sinatra had hitched their name to the tune. In part the lyrics go, "Move o-ver Babe, here comes Hen-ry, and he's swing-ing mean. Move o-ver Babe, Hank's hit an-oth-er; he'll break that sev-en four-teen."

Even if the song was not as big a hit as "Willie, Mickey, and the Duke," when it comes to baseball songs, never mind "Take Me Out to the Ballgame," no songster was going to produce a bigger hit than Aaron himself.

Although Babe Ruth's single-season home run record of 60 was targeted soon after he posted the number in 1927 with Jimmie Foxx and Hank Greenberg taking runs at it, there was no discussion of anyone making a serious charge at Ruth's lifetime total of 714.

Foxx retired with 534 homers. Mel Ott smashed 511 homers. Ruth's 714 was so far out on the horizon it might as well have been in another solar system. It was generally thought that the total might well last forever as the standard.

The first time baseball pundits considered the prospect of a player challenging Ruth's home run supremacy was when Willie Mays reached 600 homers. But Mays knew that he would not play long enough

Hank Aaron, then of the Milwaukee Braves, kneels in the outfield before a June, 1957 game. Aaron led the National League with 44 home runs in 1957.

(AP Images)

at a high level to break Ruth's mark. Mays retired with 660 homers.

A QUIET SUPERSTAR

Although Aaron's greatness was established early, he played in the shadow of Mays. Mays had a flashy style, and for most of the 1950s he was a star in New York, where the lights shone brightest and the television and talk show hosts spoke loudest. Aaron was based in Milwaukee and for those who considered anything but beer or cheese to be the most important thing in the world, it might as well have been a suburb of Chicago.

Also, Aaron was soft-spoken, the human equivalent of consistency. He never hit so many homers in a season that he attracted hundreds of reporters from distant precincts to watch him take a run at 60. Aaron never broke 50 homers in a year. In his most productive season Aaron stroked 47 homers in 1971 after the Braves moved to Atlanta, another comparative outpost. But he did hit at least 40 homers in a season eight times and won four National League home run crowns. Year after year Aaron piled up the home runs, whether anyone was paying much attention or not.

"He was a deceptive home run hitter," Hall of Famer Stan Musial said. "It's just really hard to believe he hit as many home runs as he did. You would have thought it would have been Reggie [Jackson] or Mickey [Mantle] or Harmon [Killebrew], guys who were natural home run hitters."

Hank Aaron's Milestone Home Runs

1.	April 23, 1954 vs. St. Louis Cardinals
100.	August 16, 1957 vs. Cincinnati Reds
200.	July 3, 1960 vs. St. Louis Cardinals
300.	April 19, 1963 vs. New York Mets
400.	April 20, 1966 vs. Philadelphia Phillies
500.	July 14, 1968 vs. San Francisco Giants
600.	April 27, 1971 vs. San Francisco Giants
700.	July 21, 1973 vs. Philadelphia Phillies
714.	April 4, 1974 vs. Cincinnati Reds
715.	April 8, 1974 vs. Los Angeles Dodgers
755.	July 20, 1976 vs. California Angels

Aaron accumulated homers in his own low-key manner. He didn't brag, and he didn't necessarily hit 500' blasts that left fans gasping. Aaron had quick, supple wrists that allowed him to get around on a ball quickly and to wait on pitches. At 6' tall and 180 pounds, he was not a massive man. He was strong but not huge, but anyone who was silly enough to underestimate him on the baseball field at any time paid a price.

FIGHTING FOR EQUALITY

Aaron was from Mobile, Alabama, a remarkable hotbed of baseball that has nurtured a disproportionate number of greats. Among those from the area are Satchel Paige, Willie McCovey, and Billy Williams, Hall of Famers all, plus Tommie Agee. Mays grew up not far away.

Aaron was born in 1934, the year before Babe Ruth retired. Unlike Ruth, he had black skin, and growing up black in Alabama in the 1930s and 1940s provided no economic advantages. Aaron was descended from slaves, and his family—including younger brother Tommie, who also became a major leaguer—lived in a house that had no windows, no electricity, and an outhouse in the backyard serving as the bathroom.

The future Hall of Fame right-fielder was a teenager when Jackie Robinson broke baseball's color line with the Brooklyn Dodgers, but the Negro Leagues were still offering the best baseball opportunities to the majority of dark-skinned Americans, even as the best players trickled into the majors one by one. Part of Aaron's professional apprenticeship was served as a member of the Indianapolis Clowns, paid at $200 a month.

When he became property of the Braves, still located in Boston, Aaron was farmed out to Wisconsin in the Northern League but was transferred to Jacksonville, Florida. Aaron helped integrate the Sally League as one of the first blacks in the old league in 1953 and encountered serious discrimination as his team traveled through the South. During this maturing process he transitioned from an error-prone shortstop to a slick-fielding outfielder.

After this brief period of being an out-of-position player, Aaron was pretty much a finished product who stepped into the majors 1954 and didn't leave for 23 years.

Aaron said one of his best attributes was patience and that he learned patience from growing up black in Alabama.

Henry Aaron watches as his 600th major league home run sails toward the left-field fence against San Francisco on April 27, 1971. *(AP Images)*

"When you wait all your life for respect and equality and a seat in the front of the bus, it's nothing to wait a little while for a slider inside," Aaron said.

Rarely has a baseball player summarized so much in such a succinct sentence.

AARON'S LONGEST

Aaron actually possessed more raw power than most believed, and once in a while it showed up. When he slugged his career 400th home run off Bo Belinsky in 1966, Aaron's blast seemed headed to Mercury without an intermediate stop. The estimate on the distance was between 535'

and 550' and came late in a game when he had also hit number 399. It was a poor night of choice for maximizing attention, as well. There were about 6,800 fans in the stands in Philadelphia.

Even Belinsky, the victim, never shy anyway, couldn't stop raving about Aaron's monster shot off him.

"It was no cheapie," Belinsky said. "It [the ball] must be lopsided. No one, but no one, ever hit one longer off me."

Aaron agreed that it was probably the longest ball he had ever hit and said that reaching 400 was a thrill. The ball was returned to him, and he was able to add it to a souvenir collection that

Willie Mays of the New York Mets and Hank Aaron of the Atlanta Braves meet at Royals Stadium in Kansas City prior to the 1973 All-Star Game.
(AP Images)

included the balls he hit for 100, 200, and 300 as well. In a scene that is difficult to imagine these days, when bullpen players heard the announcement that the home run was Aaron's 400th, they initiated a search for the ball.

Bullpen catcher Gene Oliver opened a sliding door connecting the bullpen to the stands and talked some kids into going out to find the ball.

"They found it in a parking lot half a block down the street," Oliver said. "We gave them a new ball."

In the current climate of the sports memorabilia world, the ball Aaron hit for his 400th home run would be worth perhaps hundreds of thousands of dollars.

"It was a fastball, and I was attacking," Aaron said.

"When you wait all your life for respect and equality and a seat in the front of the bus, it's nothing to wait a little while for a slider inside."

—*Henry Aaron*

CLOSING IN ON THE BABE

To be sure, located in Milwaukee or not, Aaron had a fan club of astute professionals who recognized how good he was. As the winner of two batting titles and four RBI crowns, plus a Most Valuable Player award, Aaron did not recede into the woodwork.

"Henry Aaron is the best right-handed hitter since Rogers Hornsby," said famed manager Leo Durocher, whose own playing days overlapped with "The Rajah" in the 1920s and 1930s. "He's the toughest out in the league."

In 1969, as Aaron felt his ability to turn quickly on a fastball starting to erode with age—he was 35 that season—he adjusted his batting stance. He brought his grip down lower on his bat and moved his hands closer to his body to shorten his swing. He belted 44 homers. "And for the first time I began to think about Babe Ruth."

Aaron, whose lifetime average was .305, was a 21-time All-Star selection, collected 3,771 hits, and drove in a record 2,297 runs, a record formerly owned by Ruth that he broke with less fanfare. Yet for

Frank Thomas on Hank Aaron

"Growing up in Columbus, Georgia, we used to watch the Braves all of the time. There was always some sports show that had highlights of Hank Aaron hitting home runs. They always showed the record home run and him running around the bases. That stuff was run a lot. It was exciting to see Aaron's big home run breaking Babe Ruth's record. Aaron didn't hit tape-measure home runs a lot, but he hit them consistently."

all of his great successes, including helping the Braves into two World Series, Aaron still crept up on American consciousness

Hank Aaron hits his 715th career home run on April 8, 1974, to break Babe Ruth's all-time record. *(AP Images)*

when it came to home runs. However, even before Mays retired in 1973, it was apparent that Aaron was the true front-runner to challenge Ruth as long as he stayed healthy.

In 1972, as part of a nationally syndicated question and answer newspaper feature, Aaron was asked how long it would take him to break Ruth's record of 714 homers.

"I think I have a chance to break Ruth's record," Aaron responded, "but things will have to fall my way. I have been relatively free from injuries during my career, and I would have to have the same kind of luck over the next couple of seasons."

By 1973, the national media attention focused on Aaron had exploded. He

was asked for more of his time in interviews and reporters followed every home run development of the season. At a home game in Atlanta–Fulton County Stadium, Aaron bashed his career 700th homer on July 21, 1973, and received a two-minute standing ovation.

"The press used to forget about me," Aaron said. "This year has been confusing. I'm not used to all this attention. I never said I was as good as Babe Ruth. He'll still be the best, even if I pass him. Even if I am lucky enough to hit 715 home runs, Babe Ruth will still be regarded as the greatest home run hitter who ever lived."

Oh, Henry.

Aaron's graciousness would be tested in the coming months as he closed in on

> "They drove me to it, the fans and the people that wrote all of those vicious letters to me. They were writing letters trying to tear me apart. I wanted to make people eat their words. It just showed me how much bigotry we have in this country, how many little people in this country that we have."
>
> —*Henry Aaron, on those who sent him hateful, racist letters leading up to his 715th home run*

the record. The real question in July 1973 was whether or not Aaron would be able to catch The Babe by the end of the season.

One of the most surprising facts related to Aaron's chase was a slump in Atlanta's attendance. Despite Aaron as a drawing card, despite Aaron in hard-core pursuit of one of the most cherished and famous records in the sport, as the season played out with the Braves nowhere near pennant contention, Fulton County Stadium played to near-empty houses. In late September, the Braves returned from a three-game series in Cincinnati that saw 135,000 spectators walk through the turnstiles. On the night of September 17, the Braves played at home in front of 1,362 fans. They got a treat, anyway, when Aaron ripped his 711th homer. The next day, Atlanta's attendance was 4,236.

Was Atlanta that fussy of a baseball town? Was the South still cloaked in enough prejudice to deny a black man besting a white man's record his due? The 1973 season ended perhaps a day or two too soon. Aaron clubbed 40 home runs, but his career total sat at 713, just one short of tying Ruth. He had to wait through an entire winter, spring training, and into the next April to take his next swing at the record.

DRIVEN TO OVERCOME BIGOTRY

By that time it was well-known that Aaron was being buffeted by a fierce assault of hate mail from narrow-thinking, prejudiced letter-writers who insulted him on general principles for being black and for having the temerity to try to break Ruth's home run record. No fair-thinking American could have seen that coming, but day after day in secret for months Aaron was bombarded by crude letters that revealed the stupidity of the authors more than anything else. Finally, he went public with the story, telling the world just how the minority of ignoramuses embarrassed baseball fans.

Frank Thomas on Hank Aaron's 715th home run to break Babe Ruth's record

"That was the greatest home run of all time. It was the focus of so much attention. I was living in Georgia, and they had something on every night. The death threats and everything that came with it make it the most important home run."

By May 1973, Aaron was receiving about 100 letters per day. When it became known that he was getting so much vitriol in his mailbag from racists, Aaron fans picked up their own pace of writing to encourage him.

Letters from children were mostly innocent. Some said they wished Aaron would be traded to their favorite team. One kid worried about Aaron suffering from excessive fatigue from running around the bases so much. Aaron was the first player to make $200,000 a year and had signed a three-year contract at that amount. Several of the derogatory letters talked about his being highly paid, as well as black.

Read one letter: "Hank Aaron, With all that fortune and all that fame, You're a stinking nigger just the same." The writer took the time to not only rhyme his appalling message, but he wrote the lines in the form of poetry, as well.

Read another letter: "Dear Nigar Aaron…you dirty nigar you should thank God that the white man let you play period. The white people don't owe you filthy nigars nothing."

What could possibly be going through the minds of such people?

After the 1973 season, with Aaron sitting just one homer behind Ruth, Aaron once again offered a reminder of why he was bigger than his critics. He used the hate mail as a motivator, he said.

"I decided that the best way to shut up the kind of people who wrote those letters was to have a good year," Aaron said. "The letters, I would say, inspired me."

Later, he was even firmer in that conclusion about how much the hateful letter writers helped him.

"They drove me to it," Aaron said, "the fans and the people that wrote all of those vicious letters to me. They were writing letters trying to tear me apart. I wanted to make people eat their words. It just showed me how much bigotry we have in this country, how many little people in this country that we have."

HELLO, BABE

By coming so close to Ruth's record of 714 and then having to endure a several months wait to break it, Aaron jump-started a circus. He was invited to every baseball banquet on the winter circuit. With the Braves wanting him to break the record at home—presumably fans would show up for the chance to watch that—the team

Hank Aaron waves to fans in Atlanta–Fulton County Stadium's left-field stands on the last day of the 1973 season. Aaron hit 40 home runs in 1973, ending the season with a career mark of 713, just one behind Babe Ruth's career mark. *(AP Images)*

planned to use Aaron sparingly in the 1974 season-opening road series.

Commissioner Bowie Kuhn frowned on the idea of benching Aaron in Cincinnati and in an awkward ruling ordered the Braves to play him some of the time. Aaron clouting the biggest home run of the age at the wrong time was a genuine fear for the Braves. As it was, he immediately hit the Ruth-tying home run in Cincinnati on his first swing of the season.

Happily for the Braves, they returned home for a series against the Los Angeles Dodgers with Aaron still knotted with Ruth. He was anxious to get the whole shebang over with and send home hordes of reporters checking out his life.

Aaron got his wallop over soon enough. On April 8, 1974, following a second-inning walk, Aaron came to bat in the fourth inning to face southpaw Al Downing.

Decades later, when asked about his favorite home run of his career, longtime manager Dusty Baker, who hit 242 of them over 19 seasons, chose Aaron's 715th. Baker was on deck watching. On a 1–0 pitch, Aaron laced a hard shot to left field where it cleared a fence and came down in the Braves' bullpen. Atlanta reliever Tom House speared the ball in the air. Those inhabiting the bullpen had actually contemplated a scenario where Aaron might hit the record-breaker to their hangout. They divided up

U.S. House of Representatives Resolution, July 11, 1973

"Whereas Babe Ruth attained the lifetime home run record of seven hundred and fourteen home runs while coming to bat eight thousand three hundred and ninety-nine times over a period of twenty-two major league baseball seasons; and

"Whereas this famous and longstanding record has remained beyond the reach of any other major league player since its achievement in 1935; and

"Whereas Hank Aaron of the Atlanta Braves has hit twenty-three home runs thus far in this major league baseball season bringing his lifetime total to six hundred and ninety-six home runs after coming to bat over eleven thousand times in twenty major league baseball seasons, and leaving him eighteen home runs short of Ruth's milestone; and

"Whereas the records of each of these two outstanding players of two different eras of baseball are significant and deserving of recognition; and

"Whereas today, Hank Aaron's efforts have been the target for racial slurs and insults from a small minority of individuals, it should be made clear that these utterances do not in any way reflect the feelings of the vast majority of Americans; and

"Whereas his persevering efforts in the face of near exasperating pressures have been a source of admiration and inspiration to all Americans: Now, therefore, be it

"Resolved, That the House of Representatives congratulates Hank Aaron for his accomplishments both on and off the playing field, and wishes him the greatest success in his epic attempt to surpass Babe Ruth's historic home run mark."

territory in the bullpen to each reliever and staked it out. If the ball sailed into the bullpen there was a good chance it was going to be caught on the fly, but it might be caught by any one of them. It was House's fate to be the one making the grab.

"People tell me I made a great catch," House said. "If I had stood still, the ball would have hit me in the forehead."

House, as excited as any of the 53,000-plus in the ballpark, ran the ball into Aaron at home plate during a subsequent delay to honor the slugger. Aaron had experienced a perilous journey around the bases as fans accorded him a standing ovation. Two teenagers had jumped out of the stands and ran onto the field to clap Aaron on the back and run down the third-base line with him. Aaron, who had received death threats, was worried about who they were and was relieved that they were friendlies.

Indeed, since the beginning of the season Aaron had been besieged by well-wishers and those wishing against his success. He traveled with an armed guard, rarely went out in the public, and even in a road hotel had meals brought to him by teammate Paul Casanova.

House, who gained renown as a pitching coach after his playing career, said he was so excited by the moment he actually has a blank spot in his memory between catching the ball and giving it to Aaron.

"I caught the ball," he said. "And the next thing I recall, I was at the plate."

Later, Downing was actually asked if he threw a pitch to Aaron that he knew he could hit.

"Groove it?" he said. "No, I didn't lay it in there for him. I was trying to get him to hit a sinker, going for the double play. I didn't get it down where I wanted it. People make such a big deal of the pitcher in these things. The pitcher is just a bystander. The moment belongs to Aaron."

Year-By-Year Home Run Leaders (1990-99)

AMERICAN LEAGUE

Year	Player	HR
1990	Cecil Fielder	51
1991	Cecil Fielder and Jose Canseco	44
1992	Juan Gonzalez	43
1993	Juan Gonzalez	46
1994	Ken Griffey Jr.	40
1995	Albert Belle	50
1996	Mark McGwire	52
1997	Ken Griffey Jr.	56
1998	Ken Griffey Jr.	56
1999	Ken Griffey Jr.	48

NATIONAL LEAGUE

Year	Player	HR
1990	Ryne Sandberg	40
1991	Howard Johnson	38
1992	Fred McGriff	35
1993	Barry Bonds	46
1994	Matt Williams	43
1995	Dante Bichette	40
1996	Andres Galarraga	47
1997	Larry Walker	49
1998	Mark McGwire	70
1999	Mark McGwire	65

Hank Aaron speaks at a press conference at Atlanta–Fulton County Stadium after hitting his 715th career home run. *(AP Images)*

broke Ruth's record. His wife and family had received threats, too, and he got threatening phone calls, forcing him to change his number.

"It was a sad time in my career," Aaron said. "I should have been really enjoying myself."

As much as anything beyond the sporting realm, Aaron's pursuit of Ruth's career record for home runs was a sad commentary on America in the early 1970s.

Although one of the silly questions Aaron was asked on the lead-up to breaking the record was whether or not he was going to quit as soon as he got it, Aaron played on, even returning to Milwaukee as a member of the American League Milwaukee Brewers. The town embraced him all over again in his forties, and he finished out his career mostly as a designated hitter.

When Hank Aaron's 23 seasons in the majors were complete in 1976, he had hit 755 home runs. He was more than 40 ahead of Ruth, and there seemed no one on the horizon playing at a high level of the game capable of catching up to him. The record was sure to be Aaron's for quite some time.

Unlike the ball he smacked for his 715th homer, Aaron did not get the ball from his 755th. In 1999, Richard Arndt, who in 1976 was a groundskeeper at County Stadium in Milwaukee where Aaron hit his final career home run, put it up for auction, and the ball sold for $650,000. By comparison, the ball Mark McGwire hit for his 70th home run in 1998 sold for $3 million.

At times after retirement Aaron expressed his desire to become commissioner of Major League Baseball, but instead he spent considerable time working with the Braves as an executive. When the Braves

True enough, but with such important hitting feats, the pitcher is sometimes remembered, and Downing's complicity in the action is better recalled than that of many other pitchers' throws that established hitters' fame.

Braves broadcaster Milo Hamilton had as long as Aaron did over the off-season to contemplate what he would say when Aaron inevitably broke Ruth's record. When the ball flew off Aaron's bat, Hamilton said, "There's a new home run champion of all time, and it's Henry Aaron!"

Aaron had security guards following him for nearly two and a half years until he moved from Fulton County Stadium to their new park, Turner Field, modified from its original role as the Olympic Stadium for the Summer Games in 1996, the address of the new home stadium was declared 755 Hank Aaron Drive. As he got older and slowed down, Aaron continued to receive selected honors. He was presented the Presidential Medal of Freedom, the country's highest civilian honor.

In 2007, Delta Airlines, another Atlanta institution, named a plane after Aaron. The "Hank Aaron 757" featured artwork of Aaron at the plate on its body.

"I am honored, and sometimes you know I pinch myself every now and then to see whether it is real or not," Aaron said. "I am so thrilled to have an airplane named after me. This is something I never dreamed about."

Barry Bonds high-fives teammate Junior Ortiz after one of Bonds' 24 home runs in 1988. *(AP Images)*

BONDS CASHES IN ON POWER AND SPEED

In 1998, when Mark McGwire and Sammy Sosa were conducting the chase that captivated America, their pursuit of Roger Maris' record, Barry Bonds was hitting his 400th career home run to go with over 400 steals, making him the only individual in baseball history to combine the two statistics.

The stolen base came first. The home run was hit on August 23 in Florida against the Marlins.

"I didn't want to let go of the bat," Bonds said.

Bonds, the major league record-holder with seven Most Valuable Player awards earned with the Pittsburgh Pirates and San Francisco Giants, was considered by many as the best player of his generation.

Frank Thomas' Milestone Home Runs

1.	August 28, 1990 vs. Minnesota Twins
100.	August 31, 1993 vs. New York Yankees
200.	June 9, 1996 vs. Baltimore Orioles
300.	August 7, 1999 vs. Oakland A's
400.	July 25, 2003 vs. Tampa Bay Devil Rays
500.	June 28, 2007 vs. Minnesota Twins
521.	August 9, 2008 vs. Detroit Tigers

Barry Bonds' Milestone Home Runs

1.	June 4, 1986 vs. Atlanta Braves
100.	July 12, 1990 vs. San Diego Padres
200.	July 8, 1993 vs. Philadelphia Phillies
300.	April 27, 1996 vs. vs. Florida Marlins
400.	August 23, 1998 vs. Florida Marlins
500.	April 17, 2001 vs. Los Angeles Dodgers
600.	August 9, 2002 vs. Pittsburgh Pirates
700.	September 17, 2004 vs. San Diego Padres
714.	May 20, 2006 vs. Oakland A's
715.	May 28, 2006 vs. Colorado Rockies
755.	August 4, 2007 vs. San Diego Padres
756.	August 7, 2007 vs. Washington Nationals
762.	September 5, 2007 vs. Colorado Rockies

The son of accomplished major leaguer Bobby Bonds, Barry's all-around skills most resembled those of his godfather, Willie Mays. He grew up around the Giants of an earlier generation when his father played with Mays.

"This says a lot about his ability, dedication, and all-around play," Bobby Bonds said of his son when he surpassed the twin milestones.

It was a nice beginning in the record-setting business, but no one realized that day that Barry Bonds was just getting started. Over the next several years he would erase both Mark McGwire's and Hank Aaron's names from the top of the home run lists in the record books. Pretty soon he would become the most prolific home run hitter of

all time. Like Aaron, longevity would play a role, but Bonds broke all molds, going from never hitting 50 homers in a season to setting the all-time record of 73 as he got older.

Bonds notched his 500th homer on April 17, 2001, to join the 500 club at age 36. Playing in San Francisco, Bonds at first didn't realize he got such good wood on the ball and he had a delayed reaction to its departure from the field.

"When I hit it, I couldn't believe I hit it," Bonds said. "Everything was in slow motion. Then I saw it went past those people [in right field] and I thought, 'Wow, I did it.'"

Bonds jumped up and down at the plate as fans jumped to their feet and chanted "Barry! Barry!" Afterward, Bonds was asked if he hoped to get 600 homers, and he said, "It depends on my health, but that's realistic."

What was not even discussed at that early point in the season was what Bonds was poised to accomplish in 2001. He began hitting home runs in bunches. He was at 40 by the All-Star break, and coming into the last few days of the season he was on the cusp of catching McGwire's record 70, which had been set just three years earlier.

Bonds had become the most feared slugger of his time. He had a discerning eye and accepted walks as readily as Ted Williams did. Later in the season pitchers and managers conspired to present him with ridiculous numbers of intentional walks. He began setting records for single-season totals of walks and intentional walks that year, but when pitched to he smashed the ball out of the park.

In 2001, Bonds set a major league record for walks with 177. The previous record of 170 was set by Babe Ruth in

Barry Bonds takes a cut against the Chicago Cubs in 1992, his final season in Pittsburgh.
(Ronald C. Modra/Sports Imagery/Getty Images)

1923. In 2002 Bonds broke his own record with 198 walks. And in 2004, he broke the single-season record again with 232. Bonds also had seasons that produced the ninth, 14th, and 20th most walks in a season. Managers and pitchers were so scared of his power that during one game in 2004 they participated in a play that is even rarer than an unassisted triple play. There have been only six times in baseball history when a player was intentionally walked with the bases loaded, that it was deemed more expedient to force in a run than to give the hitter a chance to do even more damage. Bonds was the fifth of those six players.

Bonds broke McGwire's record on October 5, 2001, by slugging two homers in a game against the Dodgers and then added a final one to reach 73. There were 200 reporters on hand to see him set the record.

Barely a month later Bonds was honored by the U.S. House of Representatives, which passed on voice vote a resolution lauding him for setting the record.

"For those of us who go to the Giants games, we can only say, 'Just think what he would have done if they had pitched to him,'" Rep. Nancy Pelosi said.

ARROGANCE AND RUMORS

By this point in his career, Bonds had established his greatness on the field, but

> "His arrogance is legendary. There's just been too many balls he didn't run out, too many times when he didn't run as hard as he could have after balls in the field. There's certain obligations that come with having talent for this game like he has.... I just look at the way Barry has gone about things and wish he had made things easier on himself."
>
> —*Reggie Jackson, on Barry Bonds*

was viewed in some quarters as arrogant, not friendly to teammates, and aloof toward the press. He came off as gruff and hard to get along with and then wondered why Ken Griffey Jr., as great as he was but not in Bonds' class as an award-winner, was so popular.

Reggie Jackson, whom Bonds claims as a distant cousin even though Jackson could never figure out through what family tree, said he wished Bonds had made life easier for himself rather than playing the villain all of the time.

"He swears we're related," Jackson said, "that my family's somehow related to his mother. He says it all the time. I finally decided it's fine. Hey, the guy's got all these home runs.... He's a lock for the Hall of Fame. If it makes him happy to call me a cousin, who am I to stop him? I'd feel differently, of course, if he was hitting .240. Cousin? Get lost."

Jackson described Bonds: "His arrogance is legendary. There's just been too many balls he didn't run out, too many times when he didn't run as hard as he could have after balls in the field. There's certain obligations that come with having talent for this game like he has.... I just look at the way Barry has gone about things and wish he had made things easier on himself."

Bonds never did mellow as his huge season put him on the radar screen to hunt down Ruth's 714 homers and Aaron's 755. Bonds cracked his 600th home run on August 9, 2002. He hit his 700th on September 17, 2004. But injuries limited Bonds to just five homers in 2005, leaving him stuck on 708 and with people wondering if he would be able to return to chase Ruth and Aaron.

Beyond that, whispers about steroid use were beginning to surround Bonds with comments about his bulked up body and what everyone was sure was an increased hat size. Initially reporters and fans rationalized the increase in home runs

by noting that bigger, stronger men were playing in smaller ballparks and hitting against inferior pitching. But sportswriters began to suggest that Bonds and other sluggers might be guilty of taking performance-enhancing drugs. A book had come out alleging Bonds was a clear violator.

Baseball wasn't testing for use of the substance, and all comment was speculative until the sport began phasing in a gradually enforced drug policy. Congressional hearings put some players on witness stands under oath. Suddenly, everyone who hit a lot of home runs came under suspicion, and the federal government wanted to make examples out of steroid dealers, turning the screws on players to talk.

PASSING RUTH AND CHASING AARON

This was the swirling backdrop by the time Bonds returned for the 2006 season. He passed Ruth's 714 total on May 28 when he feasted on an offering from Byung-Hyun Kim of the Colorado Rockies.

"It just cannot get any better than this," Bonds said after he homered in his home park in San Francisco. The fans toasted him and his teammates did, too, with champagne in the locker room.

There was a certain amount of relief among the celebrants as well, because it had been eight days since Bonds had hit a home run. Even his wife had gone back to

Players Intentionally Walked with the Bases Loaded

1. Abner Dalrymple, 1881
2. Nap Lajoie, 1901
3. Del Bissonette, 1928
4. Bill Nicholson, 1944
5. Barry Bonds, 1998
6. Josh Hamilton, 2008

Barry Bonds' Records for Intentional Walks

1. Most intentional walks, nine-inning game, 4
2. Most intentional walks, one season, 120
3. Most intentional walks, career, 668

her normal life and wasn't there for the big clout sending Bonds past Ruth.

"It's a great honor," Bonds said. "I have a lot of respect for Babe Ruth. Hank Aaron is to me the home run king, and I won't disrespect that ever." He was asked if he would like to be the next home run king. "Would I like to be? I'd like to win a World Series and be the home run king. I'll take both, but I'll take the World Series first. If you keep playing long enough, anything's possible."

Bonds was already 41, and he had constant knee problems. It was not clear if he could make it through entire seasons or if he would have to retire before he could

catch Aaron. The atmosphere surrounding him also seemed to heat up daily, where he was peppered with questions about potential use of performance-enhancing drugs.

In 2002, Bonds had admitted that he used protein pills and creatine, the same dietary supplement McGwire admitted using a few years earlier. The legal supplement adds to the amino acids produced by the liver and kidneys and stored in muscles to aid recovery in training. As federal investigations zeroed in on steroid dealers and trainers, including Bonds' former trainer Greg Anderson, the player repeatedly denied he took steroids.

Eventually, Bonds did testify in court and said he never knowingly took steroids even while acknowledging taking substances that experts said were steroids. By the time Bonds was closing in on Aaron's record in 2006, just about the only ballpark where he was regularly cheered was his own. The home fans in San Francisco never abandoned Bonds.

When it became apparent that Bonds was going to break the record, reporters asked Aaron if he would try to be present and just what his thoughts were. He said he would not be in the crowd whenever or wherever Bonds broke the record. Other times he joked, not even acknowledging Bonds' climb to 755 homers.

"I don't have any thoughts about Barry," Aaron said. "I don't even know how to spell his name."

A RECORD QUESTIONED

Fortunately for Bonds, he smacked his 756th career home run to pass Aaron in San Francisco, where there was no fan ambivalence about his achievement. When the ball

Barry Bonds celebrates after hitting his 756th career home run to pass Hank Aaron for first on the all-time list on August 7, 2007. *(AP Images)*

flew over the right-field fence, Bonds threw his arms into the air. Fireworks were set off. The 43,154 fans provided a standing ovation.

To the surprise of many, the Giants turned on a video board that featured a previously taped message from Aaron, who offered congratulations and praised Bonds' "skill, longevity, and determination." Aaron said, "I move over and offer my best wishes to Barry and his family on this historical achievement."

Bonds said that hearing Aaron's sentiments was important to him and that he felt in no way should his new record be viewed with suspicion because of all the drug allegations floating around.

"This record is not tainted at all," Bonds said, "at all. Period. You guys [sportswriters] can say whatever you want."

Commissioner Bud Selig, who was not in the house to watch Bonds break the record, also issued a statement. It was a mixed message if there ever was one.

"While the issues which have swirled around this record will continue to work themselves toward resolution, today is a day for congratulations on a truly remarkable achievement," Selig said.

> "I don't have any thoughts about Barry. I don't even know how to spell his name."
>
> —*Henry Aaron, as Bonds approached 755 home runs*

If anyone received a soda pop in a restaurant that lukewarm they would send it back.

The day after breaking Aaron's record, Bonds reported to the Giants' clubhouse as the recipient of a congratulatory telephone call from President George W. Bush. Bonds was still playing ball and finished the season with 762 home runs, fully intending to play again in 2008.

Yet for those who believed that all Bonds did was chortle all of the way to the bank with no worries, he actually had a myriad of woes. He had to endure continuing criticism in all news media that suggested he was a cheater for taking performance-enhancing drugs. His knee problems slowed him down. A mistress went public on him, and he and his wife divorced. A best-selling book portrayed him as a baseball pariah, disliked by his teammates and guilty of using the drugs. He was facing indictment for perjury for saying under oath he had not taken performance-

Owners of records that may never be broken in their respective sports, Barry Bonds, left, and Michael Jordan talk prior to the celebrity home run contest during All-Star Game festivities in 2003. *(AP Images)*

enhancing drugs. And although he said he didn't care, Bonds was unable to acquire the 762nd home run ball. Ultimately, the man who retrieved the ball sold it at auction for $376,612 to an anonymous buyer.

Bonds wanted to play one last season of baseball, but when his contract with the Giants was up, he was not offered a new one. One of the arguments against re-signing Bonds, besides the millions he would demand, was that he would be a distraction.

While the last home run ball got away, the Baseball Hall of Fame received the balls from Bonds' 755th and 756th homers, as well as the batting helmets he wore. Some campaigning popped up against the Hall displaying the items without putting an asterisk on them indicating that Bonds used performance-enhancing drugs.

Bonds was furious about that idea.

"I don't think you can put an asterisk in the game of baseball," Bonds said, "and I don't think that the Hall of Fame can accept an asterisk. You cannot give people the freedom, the right to alter history. You can't do it."

Anticipating his election one day, Bonds said if the Hall put an asterisk next to the items from his home run chase he would boycott the organization.

"I will never be in the Hall of Fame," he said. "Never. Barry Bonds will not be there."

No asterisks were included in the display.

Bonds' next goal as he searched for a new team was to reach 3,000 hits, something he would no doubt have done much earlier if he hadn't been walked so often.

But before the next season Bonds was under indictment on federal charges for perjury and obstruction of justice, and no team him offered a new contract. Without ever planning it or announcing it, Bonds had retired from baseball.

CHAPTER 10

STEROIDS: WAS IT ALL FAKE?

450
440
430
420
410
400
390
380
370
360
350
340
330
320
310
300
290
280
270
260

> "We need to get it over with. Get those names out there. Whoever is guilty is guilty. Whoever is not is not. Let baseball deal with it once and then move on. Every month we seem to talk about somebody and it's not a good thing. It's not healthy for the game."
>
> —*White Sox manager Ozzie Guillen*

"Wonder Boy" was the name of the bat Robert Redford used to perform miraculous feats in the movie *The Natural*, but it might has well have been Alex Rodriguez's nickname, too.

Rodriguez was the best high school player in the nation coming out of Miami in 1993, and he was still 18 years old when he took his first at-bat with the Seattle Mariners the following summer. He was a slick shortstop who—against the grain of most shortstops in major league history to that point—could also hit for average and power.

By 1996, Rodriguez was a starter and a star, in his first full season leading the American League with 141 runs scored and a .358 average. He may have been tucked away in the distant precincts of the Pacific Northwest, but there was no ignoring his talent. He also hit 36 home runs that year and he was greeted as a blessed arrival for an expansion team that had suffered in its first two decades.

Historically, shortstops have filled good-field, no-hit roles. Rodriguez was bigger at 6'3" and 225 pounds and stronger than most of his predecessors and he could bat fourth in the lineup. He was part of a new breed of shortstops who had range in the field but were not liabilities at the plate.

Rodriguez was on his way to five American League home run titles with the versatility to score runs, drive them in, and hit for a high average as well. He was a perpetual All-Star, and when he became a free agent after five full years in Seattle, the Texas Rangers made him the highest-paid player in history with an astonishing 10-year, $252 million contract that may or may not have broken the bank at Monte Carlo but certainly gave a major whack to the Rangers' treasury.

Almost instantly, Rodriguez was resented for the size of his contract, even though he continued to produce, winning three home run crowns in a row for the Rangers and pushing himself into

202

Alex Rodriguez addresses the media at the start of spring training in 2009 after admitting that he had previously tested positive for using performance-enhancing substances.
(Ron Antonelli/NY Daily News Archive via Getty Images)

the MVP discussion every year. However, his deal did hamstring the Rangers and prevent them from affording complementary players and enough pitching to compete. After three seasons, Rodriguez was shipped to the Yankees before the 2004 season.

Certain people are cut out for the bright lights of New York, and certain people are poor fits. Rodriguez was not as deft as avoiding tabloid controversies as he was in scooping up ground balls, although he handled being shifted to third base, out of shortstop Derek Jeter's path, as well as could be expected.

There were times Rodriguez seemed uncomfortable in the glare, although he tried to be accommodating, and then there were the times he became

a magnet for gossip. There was tension with his wife that went public. He was photographed with an exotic dancer coming out of a club. Eventually divorced, Rodriguez was linked with Madonna and actress Kate Hudson. For a time it seemed Rodriguez could only make news—or gossip—off the field rather than on it.

Still, the only question about his ability was whether he was the best player in the game or second to Albert Pujols. Rodriguez hit 52 home runs in 2001, 57 in 2002, and 54 in 2007. Through the 2010 season he had a streak of 13 straight seasons with at least 100 RBIs. The only knock on Rodriguez as he won three MVP awards, was that he didn't hit well enough in the playoffs. He seemed to shed that reputation in 2009 when the

Yankees won their first World Series since 2000.

During the height of the era dating back to 1998 when the first talk of performance-enhancing drugs in the sport bubbled to the surface, Rodriguez was considered an exemplar, one of the players most definitely clean.

And then in 2009 word spilled that Rodriguez had flunked a drug test. He admitted it, and that was the end of his squeaky-clean image. As he traveled around the league, fans in enemy parks started taunting him, yelling things like "Cheater!" Often their comments were sprinkled with boos.

No more was Rodriguez viewed as a pristine home run hitter who had done all of the work on his own and accomplished everything on the field without artificial aid. It was a serious blow to baseball, already on its heels from so many prior revelations that had damaged its image. One reason that the Rodriguez revelation hurt so badly was that it was assumed that he was the next player in line to inherit the mantle of all-time home run leader. It was Rodriguez, many felt, who was young enough and good enough to catch Barry Bonds and wrest the career home run record from him.

AN ERA IN QUESTION

So much of the baseball excitement that energized the nation since 1998 had been engendered by the home run, from the Mark McGwire–Sammy Sosa chase of Roger Maris to Barry Bonds breaking McGwire's single-season mark and Hank Aaron's career mark. Their long bombs had thrilled crowds. And others

like Rodriguez had hit huge numbers of homers. Was it all a fake? Was it all due to steroids? The emotion invested at the time was very real, but were the fans cheated by a spectacle that was not quite legitimate?

The genie was out of the bottle in baseball, and many rued the day. Always the sport most fastidious in its record-keeping and devotion to the purity of the sport, baseball's most sacred marks were the single-season and career home run records. Now those marks were besmirched.

On a summer's day in 1998, one of the many reporters crowded around McGwire's locker making his daily report about the home run chase, noticed a jar of creatine. The muscle-building substance was sold in stores that specialized in nutritional supplements and dietary products. With McGwire the arbiter of the nation's mood of infatuation with baseball, more abuse was heaped on the messenger than him. No one wanted to see McGwire as a Svengali.

What a time of peace, love, and happiness for the National Pastime, virtually revisiting a hippie nation as McGwire and Sammy Sosa did everything but put flowers in their hair as they ran up frequent flyer miles touring the land and engaging in endless mutual praise. They practically tripped over each other's feet with "After you, Alphonse" gestures as fans giggled in the background, spellbound by home run balls soaring and sailing.

It was a fresh lovefest with the national game, the fans reeled in from disappointment, the anger dissipated after a bitter strike that closed down the sport for a third of a season. McGwire stood tall with 70 home runs. By hitting 66, Sosa,

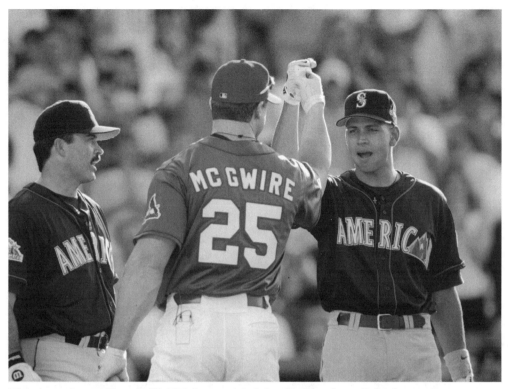

Three members of baseball's 500–home run club who have been linked to performance-enhancing substances greet one another during the 1998 All-Star Home Run Derby at Coors Field. From left are: Rafael Palmeiro, Mark McGwire, and Alex Rodriguez. *(Brian Bahr/ Getty Images)*

a comparative unknown at the season's outset, had become better known than half the people who said they wanted to become president in 2000.

Within a few years, another slugger, Jose Canseco, McGwire's former teammate on the Oakland A's who had shared the appellation "Bash Brothers" with him, was running around telling the world that 80 percent of players were on the juice. Then he proceeded to publish a book titled *Juiced*. There were skeptics when the book came out and Canseco wrote of injecting steroids into McGwire's butt, but no lawsuits were filed, the book became a best seller, and

Major League Baseball and Congress began turning the pages.

Unlike other major sports in the United States, as well as the Olympics and the Tour de France, baseball had no drug policy. There was no drug testing for *anything*, never mind performance-enhancing drugs. In reaction to the critics, management and the players' union negotiated a plan.

As the first stage of the implementation of the drug policy, players were subject to what were supposed to be anonymous drug tests that once analyzed were to be destroyed. Only after that would drug tests be taken that

205

could result in penalties. Throughout this boom time in baseball, throughout the McGwire-Sosa chase and into the early 2000s when players were ripping the cowhide off balls with their prodigious blasts, there was no rule against ingesting steroids. It was against the law, however, to buy and sell them, and federal authorities launched intensive, time-consuming investigations.

BALCO AND OTHER REVELATIONS

The bust that changed the landscape was the BALCO case.

BALCO—The Bay Area Laboratory Co-Operative—was operated by Victor Conte starting in 1984 and in 2003 was charged with providing American sports stars with performance-enhancing drugs. Many were in the track and field world. Some were in pro football. Among customers listed were baseball players Barry Bonds, Jason Giambi, Benito Santiago, Jeremy Giambi, Bobby Estalella, and Armando Rios.

It was claimed that Greg Anderson, Bonds' trainer, worked with Conte. Anderson eventually went to jail for refusing to provide any information about Bonds. In November 2007, although he repeatedly denied knowingly taking any performance-enhancing substances, Bonds was indicted based on his grand jury testimony. He said he may have used substances called "the cream" and "the clear," but if so, did not know what they were and took them on the assurance that they were not illegal materials. Several requests for extensions led to Bonds' trial being scheduled for the spring of 2011. On the same day

Bonds was indicted, Anderson was released from prison. Conte made a plea deal with authorities for illegal steroid distribution and money laundering and spent four months in prison.

As a side effect of the federal prosecution of BALCO, Major League Baseball was prevented from carrying through on its bargain with the players' union that the drug tests of 1,198 players in 2003 would be expunged. The union has been fighting for the right to regain the list and prevent its release in court ever since. Over time, dribs and drabs of information have been leaked, damaging the reputations of some players whose names were supposed to remain confidential.

At various times, with only "sources" quoted rather than infallible proof offered or Congressional appearances backfiring that harmed player images, baseball figures such as Rodriguez, McGwire, Sosa, Bonds, Roger Clemens, Andy Pettitte, Jason Giambi, 500–home run club member Rafael Palmeiro, and others have been fingered as players who probably flunked drug tests or who lied under oath about taking drugs.

The steroid morass has raised the specter that otherwise sure-fire future Hall of Famers will never be voted in and that some of the most fabulous achievers of their time might go to jail.

Facing questioning during a 2005 congressional hearing, McGwire refused to answer and famously said, "I'm not here to talk about the past." Those few words shattered McGwire's image. Retired from the game, his name began appearing on the Hall of Fame ballot, but because of suspicion that he used drugs,

> "I think if people are proven guilty to be involved with steroids, then they probably shouldn't be Hall of Famers. But until you can prove that, it's just a bunch of speculation. Because a guy's accused or kind of looks the part, that's not reason enough to assume guilt. So I think you need data. You need facts."
>
> —*Reggie Jackson*

rather than contending for induction, McGwire was stuck in the 25 percent approval area. For four years he was a virtual recluse, avoiding the limelight.

Then in the fall of 2009, it was announced that McGwire would join his old team, the St. Louis Cardinals, as a coach under his old manager, Tony La Russa. McGwire held a press conference and confessed to using drugs, although he said he did so for only a brief time and that they should not be credited with all of his achievements.

At the same congressional hearing, Palmeiro had sworn under oath that he did not take steroids. Months later, it was revealed that he had flunked a drug test. Palmeiro said if he had illegal drugs in his system he did not know how they got there. He was soon out of baseball and became another invisible figure on the American landscape. Congress debated indicting him for lying but chose not to. With 569 home runs and more than

3,000 hits, Palmeiro would otherwise be an automatic Hall of Fame selectee.

A little bit less fortunate than Palmeiro was shortstop Miguel Tejada, who was sentenced to probation for misleading Congress after pleading guilty of admitting he withheld information about an ex-teammate's use of performance-enhancing drugs.

Although only a name here and a name there were revealed, it gradually came out that there were 104 names on baseball's list for failing drug tests during the 2003 survey.

In 2009, the *New York Times* reported that Sammy Sosa's name was on that list. Sosa had also appeared before Congress with McGwire and Palmeiro and said, "To be clear, I have never taken illegal, performance-enhancing drugs. I have never injected myself or had anyone inject me with anything."

At times during his testimony Sosa cited Spanish as his first language and

Mark McGwire is sworn in on March 17, 2005, before testifying during a Capitol Hill hearing on the use of steroids in professional baseball. Seated are (from left) Sammy Sosa, Sosa's interpreter Patricia Rosell, Rafael Palmiero, and Curt Schilling. During the hearing, McGwire refused to answer several questions, saying, "I'm not here to talk about the past." *(AP Images)*

said he wasn't being entirely clear on the questions asked in English.

BASEBALL SEARCHES FOR THE TRUTH

For a time period, it seemed as if players' names were being leaked publicly one at a time, and each fresh revelation angered clean players and distorted past performances. The public started to believe everyone was guilty. Chicago White Sox manager Ozzie Guillen said he was sick of the entire situation.

"We need to get it over with," Guillen said. "Get those names out there. Whoever is guilty is guilty. Whoever is not is not. Let baseball deal with it once

and then move on. Every month we seem to talk about somebody and it's not a good thing. It's not healthy for the game."

But the problem and the history were not going to be tied up in a neat little bow so easily. Also in 2009, the *Los Angeles Times* reported that Barry Bonds had tested positive for anabolic steroids three times in the months before the 2001 season, the year he smashed his record-setting 73 home runs.

This was not a case of a newspaper picking up a leaked piece of information but the government actually releasing information. The documents were unsealed prior to a court hearing. Prosecutors seeking to move the Bonds case to trial claimed, "This is overwhelming evidence that the defendant committed perjury when he denied knowingly using steroids or ever being injected by anyone other than a doctor."

However, as Bonds' attorneys continued to appeal court rulings, they were able to diminish the charges in 2010, months before the 2011 trial date was set. One thing that was clear was that the case had finished Bonds' career before he was ready to retire. He had hoped to play somewhere in 2008 but had no opportunity. He talked of playing in 2009, but as time passed, no team expressed an interest in signing. While the case dragged on, Bonds aged into his mid-forties, and it was apparent he would never play again.

The entire steroids debate turned the baseball world topsy turvey. Cynical fans believed no one and accused all home run hitters with a broad brush. Members of the Hall of Fame who believed that the recent spate of stars were rule-breakers didn't believe they should be voted in.

Stars of the past had suffered on all-time statistical lists from the surge of recent players setting records. Reggie Jackson, who hit 563 home runs and had previously defended Bonds, felt a mix of anger at anyone who violated the rules but wanted a higher standard of proof than simple accusations in the newspapers to make sure someone was guilty.

"I think if people are proven guilty to be involved with steroids, then they probably shouldn't be Hall of Famers," Jackson said. "But until you can prove that, it's just a bunch of speculation. Because a guy's accused or kind of looks the part, that's not reason enough to assume guilt. So I think you need data. You

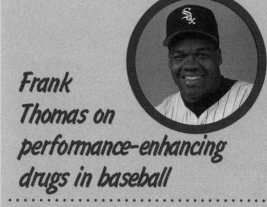

Frank Thomas on performance-enhancing drugs in baseball

"You know home runs do happen, but they don't happen every day. I think people got caught up in 'Who's going to hit a home run today?' I'm not proud of that era, but I'm proud that I achieved all that I did when all of that stuff was going on and I had a chance to dominate. I was blessed."

need facts. If you get facts, then you can brand. You can make a decision on what you're doing to do."

In some quarters, discussion turned to the dreaded asterisk of the past, the proposed mark for Roger Maris' 61 homers hit in more games than Babe Ruth played. In this instance, it was viewed as more of a scarlet letter. Everyone conceded that players hit the home runs attributed to them so they couldn't be taken back, but it was suggested that if it was proven certain players cheated, then their record should be marked with an asterisk. Jackson was a proponent of that.

"They should either asterisk it or footnote it in some way," Jackson said.

"I didn't do it to try to get an edge on anyone. I didn't do it to try to get stronger, faster, or to throw harder. I did it because I was told that it might be able to help me [get better from an injury]. That's for other people to decide. If people think I'm lying, then they should call me a cheater. Do I think I'm a cheater? I don't. God knows my heart."

—Andy Pettitte

There was a time when it was believed that only football players (primarily linemen), body builders, and professional wrestlers used steroids to build body mass. That turned out to be a naïve view. Although baseball players did not want to build the same type of muscle mass, it was clear from photographs taken of certain players as their careers progressed that they certainly had gotten bigger. That was noticeably true of McGwire, Sosa, and Bonds. Numerous snide comments were made in print about Bonds' head size increasing, not a regular part of the aging process such as an expanding waistline might be.

Suspicion surrounding baseball players taking steroids was prompted by the explosion of home run hitting in the late 1990s and early 2000s. More and more players hit more and more home runs, and the ball also seemed to travel farther when they struck it. It was suggested that some of those home runs would

have been fly-ball outs before. All of that seemed to be evidence that something was going on. What nobody really talked about was the idea of pitchers taking the same kind of performance-enhancing drugs. What for? Well, it turns out pitchers could benefit as well, and they were not likely to be entirely innocent, either.

In a sport with more subtle twists to it than a collision sport like football, the value of taking steroids was not necessarily providing muscle mass but making players stronger so they could work out harder and longer in the weight room and recover more quickly from workouts and injury. If a batter got stronger, he could hit the ball farther, and the difference between a fly-out and a home run might just be a mere 10'.

"I get angry and want to retort," Jackson said in May 2006. "But I want to be careful because I don't want people to say, 'Well, he's just another old guy complaining.' But I went from being sixth all time in 18 months to 10th. So it bothers

Victor Conte speaks to reporters during a book release party for *Steroid Nation* in New York. Conte operated BALCO—The Bay Area Laboratory Co-Operative. In 2003, BALCO facilities were searched by authorities, who discovered containers whose labels indicated steroids and growth hormones and lists of BALCO customers, including major league stars Barry Bonds, Jason Giambi, and others. *(AP Images)*

me. It doesn't affect my legacy. It doesn't affect Willie Mays' legacy as the greatest player of all time.

"There needs to be a definitive quest to find out if [drug taking] really happened. Then if it really happened, do something about it."

CONFESSIONS AND CONTROVERSY

There is a mass of confusing information out there. Some players were accused of using performance-enhancing drugs and confessed. Some players have fought like tigers against any stain on their names.

So far McGwire has been the only one of the home run heroes of recent vintage to reach the Hall of Fame ballot. Players are not eligible to be considered until five years after their retirement. McGwire had the home run numbers for election as well as the name and the perception that he had come through big time for the game itself. But when he went on the ballot, the voters squashed him like a bug. Although players who receive at least five percent of the vote stay on the ballot year by year for up to 15 years, it seems as if McGwire's credentials are going to be a hard sell unless he makes up for his taking drugs confession by curing cancer.

David Ortiz responds to questions from reporters on August 8, 2009, after it was revealed that Ortiz was one of 104 names listed as testing positive for drugs in a 2003 survey of major league players. *(AP Images)*

Sosa has steadfastly denied taking drugs and spends most of his time at home in the Dominican Republic but has said he has no doubt that he will be voted into the Hall of Fame. With 609 homers he certainly has a glittering credential to push his candidacy. It is going to be very difficult for voters to weigh the first-class deeds of players against the word that they tested positive for drug use in 2003. If there is no confession and no hard evidence to be held against a player who was supposed to be protected against the public release of his name for taking the drugs before they were officially banned, what is a voter to do besides plead a headache?

It is most challenging to evaluate clear-cut Hall of Famers who achieved phenomenal things during their careers even though they may have used performance-enhancing drugs for only a short percentage of their playing days. It was said by many that they couldn't understand why Bonds would take drugs when he had already accomplished so much. Some said he couldn't countenance the adulation heaped upon McGwire and Sosa during the 1998 home run chase that left him as an afterthought, so he bulked up and showed everyone he could break the home run record, too.

Really? Who knows? Jason Giambi, a confessed steroid user, won a Most

Valuable Player award for the Oakland A's when he was at the peak of his game. He edged out Frank Thomas, the most conspicuous anti-drug slugger of his time. Thomas won consecutive American League MVP awards in 1993 and 1994 and finished second and may well have won his third award without a bulked-up Giambi in his way in 2000.

In 2004, after Giambi signed a big-money contract with the New York Yankees, he confessed to a federal grand jury that he injected himself with performance-enhancing drugs in 2003, including testosterone and human growth hormone, and said he had experimented with them for at least two years earlier. It is difficult to know if the timetable is accurate.

Giambi's name had surfaced in the BALCO scandal, and he had been denying for months that he had used performance-enhancing drugs. Giambi told the grand jury that he obtained the drugs from Greg Anderson. Giambi testified that he approached Anderson because he knew he was Bonds' trainer and thought he must be giving helpful drugs to Bonds.

"So I started to ask him, 'Hey, what are the things you are doing with Barry?'" Giambi said. "He's an incredible player. I want to be able to work out at that age and keep playing.' And that's how the conversation first started."

Giambi was at first vilified for admitting his use of drugs. But the public storm blew over and after that he remained an accepted member of the baseball world. He took the heat, moved on, continued in the game, and was still playing in 2010. Giambi's case proved that

Sammy's Corked Bat

In 2003, before the steroids hullabaloo exploded into the public consciousness, Sammy Sosa was nailed by baseball authorities for using a corked bat and was suspended for seven games. The corked bat case, while garnering bad publicity for the Chicago Cubs right fielder, seemed like old-school hijinks compared to the newfangled drug revelations.

During a June game Sosa hit a ground ball. His bat broke, and cork was revealed to be inside. Sosa claimed that it was a bat used to entertain fans in batting practice with long home run drives and that he grabbed it accidentally. Major League Baseball officials said they believed Sosa's explanation and felt he was sincere but that he had to suffer the consequences anyway.

"At the end of the day each player must be accountable for his own equipment, complying with the rules," said Bob DuPuy, president of Major League Baseball.

the American public was forgiving. The message seemed to be that as long as a player fessed up he was welcomed back with little guilt attached to his name. This seemed particularly true for hometown fans and especially if those fans considered the player an important member of the ballclub.

Pitcher Andy Pettitte, up to that point considered one of Roger Clemens' best friends, testified under oath that he had taken performance-enhancing drugs. He would not lie before Congress, and the most he had to put up with was embarrassment. Former U.S. Senator George Mitchell was appointed to conduct an independent investigation of Major League Baseball's drug involvement, and one of the names that surfaced in his report was Pettitte's.

Pettitte admitted taking human growth hormone, although his initial admission was tentative.

"If what I did was an error in judgment on my part, I apologize," Pettitte said at first in December 2007, which was about as vague as could be and didn't satisfy anyone.

Pettitte subsequently got into true confessional mode at a press conference at spring training in 2008 a few months later.

"From the bottom of my heart, I know why I did this," Pettitte said. "I didn't do it to try to get an edge on anyone. I didn't do it to try to get stronger, faster, or to throw harder. I did it because I was told that it might be able to help me [get better from an injury]. That's for other people to decide. If people think I'm lying, then they should call me a cheater. Do I think I'm a cheater? I don't. God knows my heart."

Pettitte's confession played as well as it could. He came across as contrite even if there were a large number of doubters who wondered if his healing

motive accounted for the complete truth. His faux pas has not haunted him in the public eye. His mistake seems to be completely forgotten and is never mentioned on television when he pitches postseason games for the Yankees, which is every autumn.

In an America that bestows second chances as routinely as it brews cups of coffee, Pettitte was the beneficiary of that inclination to forgive. He skated through the narrowed eye of suspicion as cleanly as humanly possible for someone admitting he took human growth hormone.

Not everyone whose name has been released in connection with the taking of performance-enhancing drugs has been as fortunate as Pettitte. For whatever reason there seems to be a double standard, depending on the player's attitude more than what he did. Some players have been branded cheaters in the public eye, and the label has stuck as if applied with Super Glue. Others seem to be wearing Gore-Tex rain coats as protection against the storm and come through as dry as if they had stayed indoors.

THE MITCHELL REPORT

The buzz from the home run races and the steroid talk that circulated, coupled with Congressional interest in the fate of the national game, provoked Commissioner Bud Selig into forming the Mitchell Committee to investigate baseball's dirty little secret.

George Mitchell, the former senator from Maine, was appointed to head the committee, although his lack of subpoena power was an obstacle in forcing players to talk. Mitchell spearheaded a 21-month

Former Senator George Mitchell delivers remarks at the December 13, 2007, news conference in New York about Mitchell's report on the illegal use of steroids in baseball. The report lists stars Roger Clemens, Miguel Tejada, and Andy Pettitte among players linked to steroids and other performance-enhancing drugs. *(AP Images)*

investigation that resulted in the release of a 409-page report in December 2007.

The official name of the report was "Report to the Commissioner of Baseball of An Independent Investigation into the Illegal Use of Steroids and Other Performance-enhancing Substances by Players in Major League Baseball." As a catchy title it was a failure. But as an eye-catcher in content it helped illuminate the problem despite the lack of cooperation from the Major League Baseball Players Association. Still, the Mitchell Report named 89 Major League Baseball players alleged to have used steroids or drugs. No one has sued to say his name was incorrectly included.

One flaw in the compilation of information was the lack of testimony provided by active players. Jason Giambi, who had already confessed to using performance-enhancing drugs, talked to the commission. So did Frank Thomas. Thomas, who had long been outspoken against the use of drugs, volunteered to

speak. No one else did, and others invited refused to be interviewed.

The report relied heavily on comments made by Kirk Radomski, a former New York Mets clubhouse employee, and Brian McNamee, a personal trainer who worked with Pettitte and Roger Clemens, as well as other athletes. Both of those men had been cooperating with federal authorities, either voluntarily or under pressure of investigation, and supplied detailed background information to Mitchell's committee.

Although not as explicit as it would have liked to be, given the lack of cooperation from players, the Mitchell Report did issue some serious findings. It concluded that at least one player from each of the 30 major league teams was involved in alleged drug violations and that starting in 2004, after baseball's drug policy was put into effect with testing and suspensions, players switched from steroids to undetectable human growth hormone products.

Major League Baseball commissioner Bud Selig discusses the Mitchell Report during a December 13, 2007, press conference in New York. *(AP Images)*

When the report was released in December 2007, Pettitte issued his first comments. So did Clemens, a seven-time Cy Young Award–winner who extended a most extraordinary career into his forties. Clemens said, "I want to state clearly and without qualification: I did not take steroids, human growth hormone, or any other banned substances at any time in my baseball career or, in fact, my entire life."

Clemens stuck to that position even after being called to testify before a Congressional committee. His adamant stance in the face of a competing story told by McNamee resulted in his indictment in August 2010 for making false statements, perjury, and obstruction of Congress. His future seemed uncertain and even called into question his election to the Baseball Hall of Fame—which previously had been a foregone conclusion.

Among the players named in the report was Gary Sheffield, another member of the 500–home run club with 509. When federal agents searched Greg Anderson's home they found a receipt for a FedEx package connecting Sheffield with BALCO. Sheffield said he never knowingly took any banned substances. Sheffield did not seem as if he was ready to retire, but he did not have a job in baseball during the 2010 season.

When the Mitchell Report was released, chairman Mitchell said use of performance-enhancing drugs had been widespread in baseball for more than a decade and, "Everyone involved in baseball shares responsibility." The report itself said, "the illegal use of performance-enhancing substances poses a serious threat to the integrity of the game. Widespread use by players of such substances unfairly disadvantages the honest athletes who refuse to use them and raises questions about the validity of baseball records."

In the report, Mitchell singled out Thomas' cooperation, writing, "His comments were informative and helpful."

The committee sent out invitations to 500 former players, and 68 were interviewed.

To illustrate just how mixed up baseball's situation had become, players who admitted to taking performance-enhancing drugs before 2004 were not subject to sanctions because Major League Baseball had no drug policy in effect and could not retroactively punish anyone. Most players who had retired could evade even talking about the time period between the mid-1990s and 2003 because Mitchell had no subpoena power.

AN UNREADABLE RECORD BOOK

Some players came clean, saying they wanted to clear their conscience. Some players disappeared under the radar. Baseball as an organization looked forward to implementing a new policy and starting fresh with the 2004 season. Everyone was on notice that a violation would result in suspension. The biggest lingering problem, perhaps one to never be cleared up, revolved around home run records.

The single-season and career home run records are the most visible and best known in baseball. As popular as the National Football League is, almost no one speaking off the top of his head can recite

the number of yards gained by the all-time leading rusher Emmitt Smith (18,355 yards). Similarly, almost no one can recite the number of touchdown passes completed by leading thrower Brett Favre.

Just about every baseball fan knows that the single-season record for homers is 73 by Barry Bonds. Just about every baseball fan knows that Bonds holds the all-time record and that he broke Hank Aaron's record and that Aaron broke Babe Ruth's record, even if they may not be 100 percent certain that Bonds' total is 762.

What every single fan wonders about right now, however, is whether or not those records are genuine. They don't know what to believe. Under what criteria or standard would Major League Baseball ever expunge a record or list it with the dreaded asterisk? Players may admit they took performance-enhancing drugs for part of their career but not all, and it may be murky if they set a record when they were taking drugs.

One thing that seems certain from the McGwire case is that Hall of Fame voters will take into account a player's either proven or alleged history of drug taking when they cast their ballots. Like almost everyone in the baseball world, the voters have an opinion. They may be swayed by the preponderance of the evidence in a long, outstanding career, or they may believe that a blip ruins everything.

In 2006, as Bonds was closing in on Babe Ruth's total of 714 homers for second on the all-time list, some reporters sought out Julia Ruth Stevens, the Babe's then–88-year-old daughter, to ask what she thought about the sports drug controversies.

> "I personally hate controversy, but I really and truly think baseball waited too long to do something about it. It's just a shame. I'm really sad for baseball."
>
> —*Julia Ruth Stevens, Babe Ruth's daughter, in 2006*

"I personally hate controversy," she said. "But I really and truly think baseball waited too long to do something about it. It's just a shame. I'm really sad for baseball."

A-ROID

Another really sad moment for baseball occurred when it was revealed that Rodriguez had tested positive for performance-enhancing drugs and he admitted using between 2001 and 2003. The exposure and confession of Rodriguez seemed to hit especially hard because of his stature in the sport and the widespread belief that he would be the one to overtake Bonds one day. Now, even if he does, it means that someone who had admitted to the use of drugs would be the new leader.

In February 2009, Rodriguez held a press conference where he confessed. Emotional, with his voice shaking, Rodriguez admitted his mistake. He said when he signed the huge, 10-year, $250 million contract, he felt a lot of pressure to perform and wanted to do even better than he had for the Seattle Mariners.

"Back then [baseball] was a different culture," he said. "It was very loose. I was young. I was stupid. I was naïve. I wanted to prove to everyone that I was worth being one of the greatest players of all time."

He did so. And became the richest. Beyond that, when his contract was expiring with the Yankees, he signed a new one for even more money, another 10-year package weighing in at $275 million.

"I did take a banned substance," Rodriguez said. "For that, I am very sorry and deeply regretful."

Rodriguez's meet-the-press appearance followed the disclosure in *Sports Illustrated* that he was on the list of the 104 players with positive drug tests that was originally supposed to have been erased.

"To be honest, I don't know exactly what substance I was guilty of using," Rodriguez said in an unusual comment. "I was stupid for three years. I was very, very stupid."

Rodriguez said his drug taking was confined to his stay in Texas, and he apologized to Texas fans. He said he was clean since coming to New York in 2004 but haunted by what he had done.

A fan at Seattle's Safeco Field holds up a sign directed at the Yankees' Alex Rodriguez, formerly of the Mariners, during an August 2009 game. Rodriguez's use of performance-enhancing drugs was revealed earlier that year. *(AP Images)*

When the word broke that Rodriguez had taken steroids the *New York Daily News* plastered the headline "A-Roid!" across its back page. During his confession session, Rodriguez told the story that a cousin had convinced him to take the stuff. The player said his relative told him about an over-the-counter substance sold in the Dominican Republic called "boli." Rodriguez said, "It was his understanding that it would give me a dramatic energy boost and was otherwise harmless. My cousin and I, one more ignorant than the other, decided it was a good idea to start taking it. My cousin would administer it to me, but neither of us knew how to use it properly."

That was the tale Rodriguez told the world about how he got involved with performance-enhancing drugs. It was pretty much the last time he talked about his cousin, too. No telling what their relationship was after Rodriguez tested positive and went public. The cousin didn't have a forum after A-Rod threw him under a New York City Transit Authority bus.

A-ROD'S 600TH AND CHASING BONDS

In early August 2010, Rodriguez became the seventh player to hit 600 home runs. He ranked behind only Bonds, Aaron, Ruth, Willie Mays, Ken Griffey Jr., and Sammy Sosa on the all-time list, was still active, and was younger than any of the others had been when

> "To be honest, I don't know exactly what substance I was guilty of using. I was stupid for three years. I was very, very stupid."
>
> —*Alex Rodriguez*

they reached the milestone. When the season ended, Rodriguez was sitting on 613 homers, four ahead of Sosa and just 17 behind Griffey.

The 600th homer flew off Rodriguez's bat during a 5–1 victory over the Toronto Blue Jays on August 4 at Yankee Stadium. The home fans gave Rodriguez a standing ovation.

Hit off Toronto pitcher Shaun Marcum, the home run cleared the center-field wall and landed in Monument Park, where former Yankee stars are honored. A stadium security guard retrieved the ball, and it was returned to Rodriguez. Teammates met Rodriguez at home plate to congratulate him, and with the fans still screaming and applauding, Rodriguez came out of the dugout to take a curtain call.

Rodriguez hit his 600th exactly three years after hitting his 500th and he was 35 years and eight days old. Ruth was the next fastest at 36 years, 196 days. Rodriguez's wait from 599 to 600 was interminable. It took him 46 at-bats, the last 17 of them hitless, for Rodriguez to convert on the key home run.

"It was a relief just to put it past me," Rodriguez said. "There's no question

I was pressing because I wanted to get it out of the way."

Although the act of hitting the home run felt good to Rodriguez, and his reception at Yankee Stadium was as loud as the city's usual welcome to the New Year in Times Square, there was some big-picture overshadowing from the positive drug test.

"I know a lot of fans are going to have their hesitations on what it means," Rodriguez said. "But for me personally, I've played a long time and it is a big number and a special number, and I feel very good about it."

He was right that not everyone expressed uninhibited joy, and the player commonly known as "A-Rod" saw his reputation in some quarters written up as "A-Fraud."

Although the pace of Rodriguez's home run hitting has declined, even with a five-year average of 30 home runs per season he is in range of breaking Bonds' 762 mark. On the day he hit his 600th, Rodriguez was asked about the likelihood of setting a new record, but he wouldn't express thoughts on doing any such thing.

Alex Rodriguez, left, poses with Reggie Jackson at Yankee Stadium on September 22, 2010. Jackson presented Rodriguez a crystal vase in honor of Rodriguez reaching 600 home runs. *(AP Images)*

"It took me three years to the day to hit 100," Rodriguez said. "So that's not really on my radar right now. I think that's something we can revisit in two or three years and see where we're at."

Still, Rodriguez was lucky to have an agent who thought of everything, even if the prospects of things occurring were years down the road when the player signed his latest contract. As part of the contract, Rodriguez will get a $6 million bonus if he matches Mays at 660. Even if it probably won't happen in 2011 with Rodriguez needing 47 homers, it seems very likely that he will get there.

If Rodriguez hits 714 homers, tying Ruth, he will get an additional $6 million bonus. If Rodriguez hits 755 homers, tying Hank Aaron, he will get still another $6 million. If Rodriguez hits 762 homers, tying Bonds, he will cash another $6 million check. And if he breaks the record, exceeding 762, Rodriguez will be rewarded with one more $6 million bonus.

Talk about incentives in a contract.

As Rodriguez put it, though, the baseball world is years away from seeing if Alex Rodriguez will become the all-time home run king.

CHAPTER 11

TODAY'S SLUGGERS

450
440
430
420
410
400
390
380
370
360
350
340
330
320
310
300
290
280
270
260

> "Nothing fazes him, and his swing is never out of whack. There's only a handful of people I've seen who don't get into slumps."
>
> **—Larry Walker, on Albert Pujols**

Albert Pujols is the most feared hitter in baseball. He is the best hitter in baseball. And he is on a path that will take him to the Hall of Fame on a bullet train. Despite all of his accomplishments, he is not always viewed as a dominating slugger.

Wrong.

It may be that Pujols does too many things well, so he is not clumped together with the big boppers. It may be that Pujols has never hit 50 home runs in a season. Yet in any given situation when his team needs the big blow, Pujols is as likely to knock a pitch out of the park as anyone.

Other hitters may hit the ball farther. Other hitters may hit more home runs in a single season. But Pujols is like the poker player who outlasts the other card sharks who turn up three of a kind. He'll be holding a full house and the enormous pile of chips will rest in front of him on the table.

THE (NEW) MAN IN ST. LOUIS

Put simply, Pujols is The Man. He plays for the St. Louis Cardinals, whose signature player in franchise history was nicknamed The Man. But a decade into his own exceptional career, Pujols is starting to approach Stan Musial as the greatest player in team history. Musial is still front and center. Longevity alone gives him the title, but Pujols has earned the right to sit at the same table.

Jose Alberto Pujols was born January 16, 1980, in Santo Domingo in the Dominican Republic. In 10 seasons with the Cardinals he has hit 408 home runs, knocked in 1,230 runs, and batted .331. If he never took another swing, the 6'3", 230-pound, $100-million first baseman would be elected to the Hall of Fame.

Pujols' all-around excellence is rivaled in the current-day game by only Alex Rodriguez, who seems to be beginning the downward slide of his career. Pujols has led the National League in runs scored five times, hits once, doubles once, RBIs once; won a batting title; and won the 2009 and 2010 home run crowns. He has hit more than 40 home runs in a season six times, with a high of 49 in 2006. Rather than being a player who hits towering fly-ball homers, Pujols is more of a line-drive knocker.

Pujols was National League Rookie of the Year and has won the Most Valuable Player award three times. He ranks in the top five in several National League hitting categories every year and is almost always voted into the top three in the MVP race.

Pujols' high-level consistency has been stunning, said Tony La Russa, the only manager he has had in the majors.

"The only thing I ever say to him," La Russa said, "is 'Stay the same. Never change.'"

Anybody who tried to change anything about Pujols, given the results he has posted, would have to be crazy.

SURPRISE GREATNESS

Although Pujols was an instant success in the majors starting in 2001, only two years before there was no consensus among big-league teams that he was a can't-miss prospect. Even though it was granted that he could hit, scouts had trouble figuring out what position he might play. The Cardinals took Pujols in the 13th round of the 1999 amateur draft and discovered that he was a once-in-a-generation player and that he was so good he could play anywhere he wanted.

"Nothing fazes him, and his swing is never out of whack," said former

Albert Pujols listens to the national anthem with Brett Hammond, right, before a 2008 Cardinals-Marlins game in St. Louis. Hammond was one of several hundred children with Down Syndrome who got to walk around the field before the game. *(AP Images)*

teammate and batting champion Larry Walker in praise of Pujols. "There's only a handful of people I've seen who don't get into slumps."

Pujols' family was poor when he was a youngster in the Dominican Republic. He was raised mostly by his mother and a team of aunts and uncles, who instilled a positive attitude in him. Although his father, Bienvenido, was not always in the family picture, he was an influence on Albert's baseball start by sharing his passion for the game.

By the time Pujols was 16, most of his family was living in New York City. The city's crime, however, drove the family to seek new surroundings, and it moved to Independence, Missouri. The first major league game Pujols saw was played by the nearby Kansas City Royals. He maintained his own love of the sport and adjusted easily to American Legion play, the forerunner to leading his high school team to a state championship. Pujols was so good so quickly that his hitting stroke was ahead of his English speaking.

After high school he enrolled at Maple Community College in the Kansas City area. When it comes to debuts, Pujols' matched a Tony Award–winning drama on Broadway. In his first game he hit a grand-slam homer off a young pitcher named Mark Buehrle, the future Chicago White Sox All-Star, and pulled off an unassisted triple play. If his coach had given him the ball, perhaps he would have thrown a perfect game that day, too.

That little issue about what position to play Pujols at kind of disappeared as he worked his way through short stays in college, summer ball, the minors, spring training camp, and on to the Cardinals. He played shortstop, third base, outfield, and finally first base, and nobody had any complaints.

One thing Pujols fans have always admired in him is the character he has shown in the sport and off the field. He was just 18 when he met his future wife Deirdre in a Kansas City dance club. At

"You know how I want people to remember me? I don't want to be remembered as the best baseball player ever. I want to be remembered as a great guy who loved the Lord, loved to serve the community, and who gave back."

—Albert Pujols

first he lied about his age because she was 21, but he could not in good conscience keep up the charade. Deirdre was the mother of a daughter with Down syndrome and discovered most men were no longer interested in dating her when they found out. Pujols was the opposite, embracing the child, and after the marriage adopting her. Pujols has since been an active supporter of charitable events that involve Down syndrome research and fundraising special events for those affected. Pujols' wife has said publicly that he is a better man than he is a player, and for those pausing to analyze the comparison, that means Pujols would be a worthy recipient of the Presidential Medal of Freedom, a guest appearance on *Oprah*, and the honor of ringing the bell to open trading on the New York Stock Exchange. In fact, Pujols has received the Roberto Clemente Award, an honor bestowed annually on a player who combines excellence in the field with community service. Pujols started the Pujols Family Foundation for charitable work.

ANALYZING ALBERT

Way back when, Babe Ruth underwent experimental tests that tried to determine why he was such a great hitter, and scientists who examined him said he had above average eyesight, reflexes, and the like. Ruth took the test in 1921. In 2006, some human lab rats with PhDs at Washington University in St. Louis approached Pujols to see if he would be a subject in similar tests. To the best of their ability, the scientists sought to replicate the Ruth tests on Pujols. *GQ* magazine

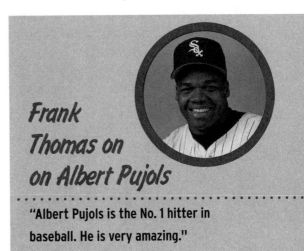

Frank Thomas on on Albert Pujols

"Albert Pujols is the No. 1 hitter in baseball. He is very amazing."

U.S. Senator Claire McCaskill, left, presents Albert Pujols and his wife, Deidra Pujols, with a copy of the congressional record recognizing five years of service by the Pujols Family Foundation. *(AP Images)*

actually came up with the idea to see how the players compared.

It was not that easy to make exact comparisons, but one number was intriguing. When Ruth performed a bat speed test, he swung a 54-ounce bat. Pujols used a 31.5-ounce bat. Ruth's swing was clocked at 75 mph, Pujols' at 86.99. On other tests, no numbers were available from Ruth's test, only the conclusion that he had tested at the equivalent of a higher percentile than the average person. The entire exercise seemed a bit half-baked, but on several of the tests the scientists decided Pujols too was above normal.

Those types of numbers never really meant anything to Pujols or to those who watched him in baseball. He knew from a young age that he could play. As soon as someone saw Pujols the first time they knew he could play.

"I don't want to sound cocky or arrogant," Pujols told *Sports Illustrated*, "but I was always great at this game."

He was certainly fully formed by the time he reached the Cardinals. As a 13th-round pick, he was not in St. Louis' immediate plans when they brought him to spring training in 2001. He had already shown he was better than any scout or general manager thought by moving through the Cardinals' minor league system at warp speed. He started in Class A in 2000 and by the end of the summer was the MVP of the Class AAA playoffs. Why was anybody surprised when he forced his way onto the Cardinals' roster the next year?

GOOD GUY, GREAT PLAYER

Ever since, Pujols has been one of the most consistent high-level players in baseball history from the start of a career. He did hit as low as .312 once, but he's also hit in the .350s twice. He had all of those 40-homer seasons but never hit less than 32 in a year. His lowest RBI total has been 103. So Pujols' worst combined season is 32 homers, 103 RBIs, and a .312 batting average—the equivalent of a dream season for many players if they could just do it once.

Albert Pujols reacts after hitting a grand slam off of Cincinnati Reds reliever David Weathers on July 3, 2009. *(AP Images)*

Even Pujols has heard whispers that he must use steroids. It is the burden all good players bear now because of what went on during the game unchecked for a decade or more. Pujols might not even know what steroids look like, but no matter, suspicion is built into achievement in baseball now.

Pujols recognizes the reality of attitude that surrounds his sport, and even if he dismisses any hints that he might be a wrongdoer he knows it is now inevitable that questions are going to be asked of

Back-to-Back 300s

White Sox slugger Paul Konerko and former White Sox outfielder Jermaine Dye did something unique in major league history. On April 13, 2009, in a game against the Detroit Tigers, they became the first teammates to hit "century" milestone home runs of at least 300 in the same game. Batting back-to-back in the White Sox batting order, Konerko and Dye hit their career 300th home runs one after the other.

"We both didn't get off to a great start," said Konerko, the Sox's designated hitter and first baseman. "It was about 15 games into the season. We were both kind of disgusted that we hadn't hit one, and we were just about at the point where we were going to start making bets to see who would do it first.

"Then Jermaine went up to the plate and hit his home run, and I was right behind him. I fell down in the count early 0–2 so I wasn't really thinking of hitting one. Then I got a pitch, and I hit it as a liner that I didn't think was out. I thought I was heading for a double. But it went out of the park. You know, when you start thinking about it, the odds [against] something like that happening in one game are pretty high. It's like two guys hitting their 500th or anything like that, but it is kind of a rarity. It's pretty amazing. All bets were off."

Frank Thomas on Ryan Howard

"He seems to be dropping off. He is a great power hitter, but he started so late."

anyone who excels. He says he has tried to live his life the right way and that he hopes he is remembered more for that than anything else.

"You know how I want people to remember me?" Pujols said. "I don't want to be remembered as the best baseball player ever. I want to be remembered as a great guy who loved the Lord, loved to serve the community, and who gave back."

In St. Louis, in what could be termed a Solomonesque ruling if it had been developed by a higher power, Pujols is known as "El Hombre." That's Spanish for "The Man." He and Stan both. Bases covered.

The biggest problem the Cardinals had is whether or not the team could keep coming up with the bucks to keep the best player in the sport in St. Louis.

HOME RUN HOWARD

Such worry might have spawned a rumor that spread like one of those

Yellowstone Park wildfires in March 2010. The Cardinals, it was reported by people citing sources, might trade Pujols to the Philadelphia Phillies for their slugger Ryan Howard.

A story from the past was recalled by the mere mention of such a possibility. Decades ago, the owner of the Boston Red Sox and the owner of the New York Yankees were said to get so drunk that they proposed and agreed on a straight-up deal of Ted Williams for Joe DiMaggio. This was based on the likelihood that the right-handed hitting DiMaggio would put more dents in the Green Monster in Fenway's left field than a 22-car accident on the Cross Bronx Expressway and that Williams, with his left-handed swing, would hit so many homers into the right-field stands at Yankee Stadium that fans would think it was hailing every day.

When they woke up the next morning, the hung-over team executives realized that the trade was impossible. Their respective constituencies would tar and feather them. So they called the deal off.

Pujols-for-Howard probably didn't even get that far, though just floating the idea intrigued some folks.

It took Phillies general manager Ruben Amaro a nanosecond to deny the rumor, even though most people would think he got the best of the deal.

"Lies," Amaro said. "That's a lie. I don't know who you're talking to, but that's a lie."

There's not a bit of wiggle room in a statement like that. However, at least the scenario seemed to confirm Howard's status as one of the best players in baseball.

On a hot night in Cincinnati during the summer of 2010, when almost all of

Wearing a throwback uniform, Ryan Howard homers during the first inning of a May 2010 game in Milwaukee. *(AP Images)*

the nights were fiery hot plus soaking wet from humidity, Ryan Howard stood in the bowels of the Great American Ball Park pushing buttons on his cell phone because he couldn't get a signal.

He walked around seeking reception and eventually made his call. Soon enough the behemoth Philadelphia Phillies first baseman, who may be the most impressive big-man slugger in baseball today, would take the field to face the Cincinnati Reds.

The game was still hours later, giving him time to talk to friends on the phone and talk baseball with sportswriters. Howard, who plays at 6'4" and 250 pounds, is big enough to play in the NFL as long as he could make tackles with Louisville Sluggers. He is past 30 now, but

when he came up to the majors as a virtual unknown to Philadelphia fans, no one grasped the sheer magnitude of his power.

THE ROOKIE ARRIVES

There are big guys who make pitchers throw cautiously, until they find out a newcomer can't hit the curveball or get around quickly enough on the fastball. Size alone does not make a slugger. Hitting home runs 500' does, and hitting them frequently does. In 2005, after some ups and downs to the minors, Howard smashed 22 home runs in 88 games. Howard could stop renting in Philly and buy a Main Line mansion. The main reason Howard even got a chance to show Rookie of the Year

Ryan Howard heads home after hitting his 100th career home run on June 27, 2007, against Cincinnati. The ball traveled 505'.
(AP Images)

Thome, a future Hall of Famer. Howard had won MVP awards at two minor-league stops and hit a combined 46 homers between Class AA Reading and Class AAA Scranton/Wilkes-Barre in 2004.

RECORD-SETTING POWER

Just to prove his what-were-you-waiting-for point to management, Howard blossomed from a half-season player to full-time war-club wielder, from a wonder-how-he-will-do guy to an All-Star, in one season. In 2006, Howard smacked 58 home runs, drove in 149, batted .313, and won the National League Most Valuable Player award in a year the voters decided not to give it to Pujols.

In 2007, Howard hit 47 homers. In 2008, he bashed 48 to lead the league again. In 2009 he clouted 45.

In 2007, Howard became the player to reach 100 homers the fastest, reaching the century mark in his 325th game, ahead of Ralph Kiner's old record of 385 games. Oh yes, the ball traveled 505'.

"It should be illegal to have that kind of power, for everyone else," said Phils outfielder Greg Dobbs.

Howard said he recognized immediately that he had hit he ball well.

"I hit it pretty good off the sweet spot and it jumped," Howard said.

Phillies manager Charlie Manuel liked the sound of the ball hitting the bat and the sight of the ball disappearing into the clouds.

"He definitely smoked that ball," Manuel said. "He has all the power in the world."

Which was sort of what Dobbs said.

stuff was an injury to Phils first baseman Jim Thome, another of the greatest sluggers of the era. Thome never got his job back with the Phillies and moved on to the Chicago White Sox.

"I was just going to try to make the most of it," Howard said of his opportunity that turned into permanent employment.

There had been indications Howard was ready for a big-time role in the big leagues even if his way was blocked by

Howard took pleasure in recounting how special the hit was and what he planned to do with the returned ball.

"It's always good to be part of history," Howard said. "I'm grateful for it. This is going up in the house. I'll give it to my parents, and I'll probably have to wrestle for it to get it back."

In 2009, Howard became the fastest player to reach 200 career home runs by smacking one in his 658th game. Kiner had the old record, hitting his 200th in his 706th career game.

"It's a nice feat," Howard said. "It's a nice record to have. I'll take it and run with it."

After getting off to such a sizzling start, the Phillies realized that Howard was going to stick around, and they made a pre-emptive move to dissuade him from seeking other contract deals. Early in the 2010 season Howard signed a five-year contract extension for $125 million. The $25-million-per-year deal runs through 2016.

Like most players, Howard remembers the first home run of his major league career. He hit it off Mets pitcher Bartolome Fortunato on September 11, 2004. Howard was an end-of-season call-up for the Phils.

"I hit it out to right-center," Howard said of his shot at Shea Stadium. "Mike Cameron was the center fielder. I wasn't sure if it was going to go because of the way he was running after the ball. I thought he might bring it back, but it landed on the batting cage out there. He scared me a little bit. It looked as if it might just clear it [the wall], but really, it went farther than that."

Year-By-Year Home Run Leaders (2000–10)

AMERICAN LEAGUE

Year	Player	HR
2000	Troy Glaus	47
2001	Alex Rodriguez	52
2002	Alex Rodriguez	57
2003	Alex Rodriguez	47
2004	Manny Ramirez	43
2005	Alex Rodriguez	48
2006	David Ortiz	54
2007	Alex Rodriguez	54
2008	Miguel Cabrera	37
2009	Carlos Peña and Mark Teixeira	39
2010	Jose Bautista	54

NATIONAL LEAGUE

Year	Player	HR
2000	Sammy Sosa	50
2001	Barry Bonds	73
2002	Sammy Sosa	49
2003	Jim Thome	47
2004	Adrian Beltre	48
2005	Andruw Jones	51
2006	Ryan Howard	58
2007	Prince Fielder	50
2008	Ryan Howard	48
2009	Albert Pujols	47
2010	Albert Pujols	42

"It felt good," Howard said. "It was one of those things where it was special because it was my first home run in the big

leagues. I got the ball back. In Shea, it was weird. There are places where no fans sit, and I hit it there. So I got the ball back."

Howard knows he was not only lucky to retrieve that ball but also to get back the ball from his 100th homer. He knows he can't count on getting the balls from his milestone homers unless something unusual happens.

"You've just got to find the good spot," Howard said. "Maybe straightaway center field where the ball takes a high bounce or something like that and comes back on the field."

The season of hitting 58 was extraordinary for Howard on several fronts. It was his first full season in the majors, and he won the home run and RBI crowns, the

MVP award, and the All-Star break Home Run Derby, to boot. Hall of Fame third baseman Mike Schmidt, who completed his career with 548 homers, held the team record going into the 2006 season with 48 homers in one year. That mark was easily eclipsed by Howard.

As the season wore on and he belted more and more homers, Howard found it difficult to get good pitches to hit. Pitchers would rather walk him than let him destroy their games with long blasts.

"Toward the latter end of the second half, when someone did pitch to me, they were very careful," Howard said. "So you have to be real selective and wait for your pitch, and if they make that mistake, you have to jump all over it."

Howard's was such a terrific year that he almost didn't know what to think about it. From being a late arrival to the lineup in 2005 and being hardly known outside of Philadelphia, his booming home runs had put him on the map, and even more important, on ESPN highlights. One minute the guy can't get a full-time job; the next he's a starter on a pennant contender, and everyone is sending him Valentines to tell him how much they love him.

"It's hard to believe that it's happening sometimes," Howard said.

THE NEW GENERATION

A comment Howard made during the season made it clear the page had turned on some other sluggers, even if they were still active and hanging in. He was asked whom he followed when he was growing up watching baseball on television, and he said the players he looked

Junior Calls it a Career

Ken Griffey Jr. retired in the middle of the 2010 season after returning to the Seattle Mariners, his first team. Griffey was not hitting well and chose to retire in his 22nd season. He ended up with 630 home runs, fifth on the all-time list.

"While I feel I am still able to make a contribution on the field and nobody in the Mariners' front office has asked me to retire, I told the Mariners when I met with them prior to the 2009 season and was invited back that I will never allow myself to become a distraction. I feel that without enough occasional starts to be sharper coming off the bench, my continued presence as a player would be an unfair distraction to my teammates and their success as a team."

Howard Lincoln, the CEO of the Mariners, expressed regret at the departure of Griffey, saying, "It's a sad day for the Mariners, our fans, for all the people in the community that have loved Ken, admired him as a tremendous baseball player and a great human being."

Griffey trails Barry Bonds, Hank Aaron, Babe Ruth, and Willie Mays on the all-time home run list. The closest active player to catching Griffey is Alex Rodriguez with 613.

up to who were his idols when he was a kid were Barry Bonds and Ken Griffey Jr. When he was a kid? Howard did eventually become friendly with Bonds and called him a mentor for advice the older player dispensed. Shades of Bonds: Howard walked five times in a nine-inning game.

Even later, when it was over, he had no ready answer for sportswriters when they asked if he had reflected on what he accomplished in 2006.

"Some day in the off-season, when I look back at this season, it will be special," Howard said. "I try to stay locked in and try to win games. One day I'll wake up and realize what happened."

MANNY NOT BEING MANNY

As the 2010 season came to an end, baseball fans might have been wondering if Manny Ramirez knew what had happened to him and if they had seen the last of him.

Ramirez, the quirky star with dreadlocks, and some recent Major League Baseball drug problems, was property of the Chicago White Sox, who picked him up as a rent-a-star to try to win the American League Central Division title. The plan fizzled, and after a tumultuous stretch it was unclear what would become of Ramirez.

A one-time RBI machine, Ramirez ended the 2010 season with 555 career home runs and 1,830 RBIs, as well as a .313 lifetime average, Hall of Fame numbers all. As recently as 2008 as he approached the end of an eight-year, $160-million contract, it appeared he would be a lock to reach 600 homers and the more rarified air of 2,000 RBIs.

But the news came out during a breach of the anonymity clause that the 12-time All-Star with the Cleveland Indians and Boston Red Sox was one of the 104 players who allegedly tested positive for performance-enhancing drugs in the 2003 survey. In addition, in 2009, Ramirez was suspended for 50 games for taking a drug commonly used by steroid users for to help restart normal testosterone production.

Ramirez has often been portrayed as an indifferent fielder who lets his concentration lapse in left field, leading to unintentionally humorous moments, and enough unexpected developments that a phrase was coined about his sometimes odd behavior: "That's just Manny being Manny." That trait was attributed to Ramirez being of a carefree nature, but more recent events in his life added a tone of seriousness.

Ramirez, who will turn 39 in the spring of 2011, can only hope for a fresh start with Tampa in a new environment and that he can put up the Manny numbers of old, or else his career will likely terminate. His reputation has taken a major hit, and his baseball future may be in tatters. Ramirez's entry into the Hall of Fame also comes into question if voters hold his drug incidents against him, as they may well.

To some, Ramirez seemed like the brother from another planet, the movie character in the peculiar picture of the same name who had his own way of doing things.

"There's a bunch of humans out here," said pitcher Julian Tavarez, a former Ramirez teammate with the Red Sox. "But to Manny, he's the only human."

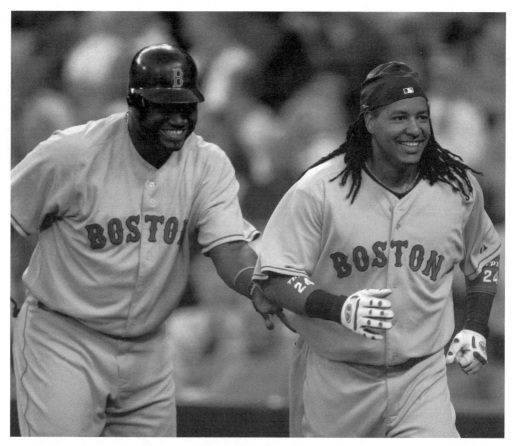

Boston teammates David Ortiz, left, and Manny Ramirez smile as they run to the dugout after scoring on a Jason Varitek double in August 2007. The two sluggers led the Red Sox to World Series titles in 2004 and 2007. (AP Images)

Until it seemed as if Ramirez lost interest in inhabiting left field at Fenway Park and provoked reliever Jonathan Papelbon into calling him "a cancer" on the team, Ramirez was quite popular in Boston. He was the kind of guy to be tolerated, offbeat nature and all, because he produced on the field. Ramirez is one of those players the comment "He could hit falling out of bed" applies to. Nothing mattered so much to Boston fans as winning a World Series for the first time since 1918, and Ramirez was a major part of the offense that led the team out of the wilderness. Heck, Moses had

to wander in the desert for only 40 years. The Red Sox were walking around aimlessly, far from their destination of a World Series trophy, for 86. Ramirez was one of the big guns on the Sox teams that won the World Series in 2004 and 2007, setting off legendary parties across New England and compelling grandsons to visit graves of long-dead grandfathers to clue them in on the box scores.

After the Red Sox won the crown in 2007, the team enjoyed its second downtown parade in three years. When the parade ended, Ramirez addressed

> "I would suggest everybody get tested, not random, everybody. You go team by team. You test everybody three, four times a year and that's about it."
>
> —*David Ortiz*

the multitudes and said, "Hey, everybody is invited to my house tonight for free drinks!" Given that he was making $20 million a year he could afford it, but it's not clear if he announced his address and how many game Bostonians showed up. But the thought was nice.

Ramirez acted quite contrite when he got nailed for the 50-game drug suspension with the Los Angeles Dodgers after the Red Sox sent him west, and this was the explanation he mustered: "Recently, I saw a physician for a personal health issue. He gave me a medication, not a steroid, which he thought was okay to give me. Unfortunately, the medication was banned under our drug policy."

It seemed like one prescription too many for Manny, and it may be one prescription too many for Hall of Fame voters. It is too soon to tell. If Ramirez can get fit and perform for Tampa Bay like the Manny of his prime to attain individual statistical numbers like 600 home runs and 2,000 RBIs, that may be enough to sufficiently reduce the backlash he may receive for failing drug tests.

BIG QUESTIONS FOR BIG PAPI

Failed drug tests or not, you hate to use formerly innocent phrases like "Ramirez's partner in crime, David Ortiz." They were indeed the Red Sox twin sluggers during the World Series glory days and Ortiz remains one of the most beloved players in team history.

Ortiz, the mammoth designated hitter, came into his own in Boston after a lower-key apprenticeship with a Minnesota Twins team that let him go in a decision that seemed to lack common sense (Can you spell Oops in Minnesotaese?). It is Ortiz, not Ted Williams, Jimmie Foxx, Mo Vaughn, Tony Conigliaro, or Manny who owns the single-season Red Sox home run record. Ortiz hit 54 homers in 2006, and the figure not only led the American League that season but also surpassed Foxx's best showing with the Sox.

"It was a great feeling," Ortiz said, "especially to do it at home in front of my fans. It was pretty fun. The people were going crazy."

Ortiz also led the American League in RBIs two years running and developed a reputation as a big-time clutch hitter, smashing walk-off homers and game-winning doubles almost routinely. In the 2004 playoffs, when the Red Sox made their unprecedented comeback from trailing the Yankees 3–0 in games, Ortiz won one game with a two-run homer and won the next game with an extra-inning single.

"To keep continually doing it, night in and night out, it's like you almost wonder, can he do it again?" said then–Red Sox teammate Doug Mientkiewicz. "And he does it. It's phenomenal."

During spring training of 2009, Ortiz, a huge man at 6'4" and something beyond his listed 230 pounds, came out with some very strong anti-drug statements.

"I would suggest everybody get tested, not random, everybody," Ortiz said. "You go team by team. You test everybody three, four times a year and that's about it." A positive test, Ortiz said, should be punished by a one-year ban from baseball. The punishment scale is currently a 50-game suspension for a first-time offender, 100-game suspension for violating the drug policy twice, and a lifetime ban with appeal provisions for a third offense.

That sounded very much like a man with nothing to fear from a stringent policy aimed at containing performance-enhancing drugs.

Imagine Ortiz's embarrassment when just a few months later, word was leaked that his was one of those 104 names listed for testing positive for drugs in the 2003 survey. There never has been clarification of what it means to be on the list and whether the evidence was incontrovertible, though it generally has been treated as such. Ortiz fought back to keep his good name by holding a press conference

Home Run Leaders, 2010

AMERICAN LEAGUE

1.	Jose Bautista	54
2.	Paul Konerko	39
3.	Miguel Cabrera	38
4.	Mark Teixeira	33
5.	David Ortiz and	
	Josh Hamilton	32
7.	Vernon Wells	31
8.	Alex Rodriguez	30

NATIONAL LEAGUE

1.	Albert Pujols	42
2.	Adam Dunn	38
3.	Joey Votto	37
4.	Carlos Gonzalez	34
5.	Dan Uggla	33
6.	Prince Fielder and	
	Mark Reynolds	32
8.	Adrian Gonzales,	
	Corey Hart, and	
	Ryan Howard	31

before a game. Ortiz insisted he never took steroids and that if he tested positive for illegal substances in his body then it was the result of something else, even though the Flintstone vitamins test has failed to fly in other contexts.

"I was definitely a little bit careless back in those days when I was buying supplements and vitamins over the counter," Ortiz said. "Legal supplements, legal

Frank Thomas on Jose Bautista

"I've got a huge question about a guy who has never hit more than 16 homers in his career and hits 54 in one year. I'm sure they tested him left and right."

vitamins over the counter. But I never buy steroids or use steroids. I never thought that buying supplements and vitamins it was going to hurt anybody's feelings."

Ortiz said that since the alleged positive test he had been screened about 15 times, including at the World Baseball Classic, and there have been no other positive readings.

So Ortiz was saying he didn't even know exactly what he was being accused of doing.

Ortiz weathered the crisis and wooed back his fan base. After a short while Red Sox fans primarily worried about Ortiz's months-long hitting slump. But he even turned that around and closed 2010 with a bang. Again, no one knows precisely how fate will treat Ortiz.

After so much bad publicity about baseball's sluggers in recent years and talk about poor pitching and lack of depth on the mound, the sport experienced a

surprising 2010 season. All of a sudden pitchers were dominating and home run hitters were in short supply. The regular season saw perfect games thrown by Roy Halladay and Dallas Braden. There were four more no-hitters, including a second one in the same season by Halladay in the playoffs.

A fan base used to seeing Mark McGwire, Sammy Sosa, Ken Griffey Jr., Alex Rodriguez, and several other power hitters swing away for 50 homers in a season was abruptly returned to the era between Hank Greenberg and Ralph Kiner. For a while it seemed possible that no one in either league would hit more than 40 home runs. Never mind throwback uniforms; this would be an example of throwback play. As it was, no one had hit 50 homers since 2007.

OUT OF THE BLUE (JAYS) SLUGGER

In the end, Pujols led the National League with 42 homers, the only one in that league to hit more than 40, and Jose Bautista of the Toronto Blue Jays emerged from virtual obscurity to produce the year's most stunning statistic. Bautista, who turned 30 right after the season, was a young player a handful of seasons removed from his rookie year. He had been a major leaguer since 2004 and had never before hit more than 16 homers.

All of a sudden he turned into the second coming of Brady Anderson. In fact, his jump from a career best of 16 homers in 2006 was lower than Anderson's second-best year. Bautista, a 6', 190-pound third baseman, clubbed 54 home runs.

Jose Bautista watches his 42ⁿᵈ home run of the year leave the park on August 27, 2010. Bautista led the American League with 54 home runs in 2010. *(AP Images)*

This was so far out of the blue that even color-blind observers became suspicious. Bautista had never driven in more than 63 runs before, and in 2010 he knocked in 124. Not so many years ago reporters following Bautista would have been perplexed but would have attributed his huge improvement to weight training, improved dieting, and a change in his swing. But the feelings among sportswriters now run more to the philosophy of "Fool me once, shame on you; fool me twice, shame on me."

Bautista is not dumb enough to think that nobody in the baseball establishment would notice the difference between his previous best home run year and his current home run year. As the home runs piled up and he broke through the once-hallowed 50–home run barrier, sportswriters did not tiptoe around the question. Bautista was asked point-blank if he had ever taken performance-enhancing drugs. He said, "No." Not that anyone expected him to answer differently, and it is not a federal crime to lie to sportswriters (who don't even put you under oath) as it is to lie to Congress after swearing on a Bible. But at least he was on record.

Bautista said he understood that fans might be a tad suspicious.

"I do," he said of understanding why. "Because of the history. It's up to guys like me and [the media] to make sure that the public gets their facts right."

In late September, when Bautista reached 50 homers, he said, "It's a big honor to be put in that elite group of

> "It's a big honor to be put in that elite group of hitters. To tell you the truth, I really haven't let it sink in yet. Right now I'm really honored and happy."
>
> —*Jose Bautista*

hitters. To tell you the truth, I really haven't let it sink in yet. Right now I'm really honored and happy."

So how did it come to pass that a player with the statistics of a middle infielder turned into a new Babe Ruth overnight? After all, Bautista hit 13 home runs in 2009. To hear the Blue Jays tell it, Bautista was a coiled spring ready to explode. In the summer of 2009, Toronto hitting coach Dwayne Murphy made Bautista stand in front of a mirror and gaze upon his swing. At the time Bautista's style was to swing wide with a looping motion, and he was easy prey for a pitcher's best stuff.

Many people with baseball expertise had missed out on the chance to grab Bautista by the bat and essentially wrap it around his brain. Bautista had played in the minors in Williamsport, Pennsylvania; Hickory, North Carolina; Lynchburg, Virginia; Bradenton, Florida; Altoona, Pennsylvania; and Indianapolis, Indiana. He had played in the majors for the Pirates, Orioles, Tampa Bay, and Kansas City before crossing the border to Canada. Apparently none of those cities had mirrors where a hitting coach could say, "Mirror, mirror, on

the wall, what is the fairest stroke of all for Jose?"

Murphy told Bautista that he needed to shorten his swing and he set about breaking bad habits. If it was that simple, then Murphy must be coach of the year on somebody's ballots.

"He's always had power," Murphy said. "He just needed a couple of tweaks."

The Dwayne Murphy Batting School will probably be opening franchises all over the nation soon.

"It's not a secret and I didn't reinvent the wheel," Bautista said as he continued to deny taking steroids and giving the credit to his Toronto tutoring.

What explanations are there for transforming a guy who was not just a 16-homer man at best, but a consistent, 16-, 15-, 13-, 12-homer man into the company of the greatest home run hitters of all time? No one believes in legal magic bullets anymore than they do Santa Claus or the Easter Bunny. So it is no wonder that the quizzes about steroids occur, as if someone is just going to suddenly blurt out a confession in such a manner. Otherwise, it is all attributable to Murphy's know-how.

Josh Hamilton homers against Baltimore on July 8, 2010. The Rangers outfielder topped 30 home runs twice in his first four major league seasons and won the 2010 American League batting title. *(AP Images)*

After the 2010 season, Bautista had 113 career home runs, just about 50 percent of them swatted in one season. He may be baseball's next great star. He may be baseball's next sad story.

HAMILTON'S REDEMPTION

Josh Hamilton can identify with that ambivalence. He has already been both. When Hamilton was drafted by the Tampa Bay Devil Rays as an 18-year-old in 1999, he was touted as a franchise-changing prospect. Hamilton received a $4 million bonus.

But rather than transform Tampa—the Rays did it through other means with other players—Hamilton descended into a hellish life of drug addiction. And not

the steroid kind but more serious street drugs that nearly cost him not only his promising career but his life. Suspended from the sport after failing screening tests, Hamilton's dramatic rise and return to the game he loves has been documented in a well-told book. It is difficult to say whether it was more surprising that Hamilton reached such a nadir in his daily existence or that he was able to overcome his problems and became an All-Star and batting champion.

Hamilton's problems included alcohol consumption and recovering from injuries suffered in a car accident. After up-and-down experiences in the minors, he was so mixed up and had violated baseball drug policies so often that he was out of

Frank Thomas on the best present-day slugger

"Right now it's Josh Hamilton. The guy's an incredible ballplayer. I watched him take batting practice. He was hitting moonshot after moonshot. I thought, 'This guy's got it.' He's a great hitter with tremendous power."

the sport entirely from 2003–05. At that point Hamilton merely longed to live a productive life, let alone fulfill his potential as a baseball player.

Tampa Bay left Hamilton off its 40-man roster, and he was picked up by the Chicago Cubs in the Rule 5 draft. The Cubs immediately swapped him to the Cincinnati Reds, and after hitting .403 in spring training as evidence of his recovery, Hamilton made his major league debut April 2, 2007, eight years after he was drafted.

It was a moment that seemed unlikely to ever arrive, but with his story explained in the newspapers, Hamilton was greeted warmly by Reds fans who gave him a standing ovation. While he waited to bat, Cubs catcher Michael Barrett said, "You deserve it, Josh. Take it all in, brother. I'm happy for you."

Despite a solid performance, the Reds traded Hamilton to the Texas Rangers at the end of the year in a deal that brought Edinson Volquez to Cincinnati. After his long and arduous journey, Hamilton emerged as a feared home run hitter and an all-around star, hitting 32 homers in 2008 and leading the leading the American League in RBIs with 130. In 2010, Hamilton won the batting title with a .359 mark.

The depth of Hamilton's addiction was revealed when he admitted to a one-day "slip" in 2009 when he drank alcohol and nearly got into worse trouble. Many times Hamilton has spoken of his struggle, and he does not pretend to be cured or no longer in need of any help. He has always sounded as if a relapse could occur.

At his worst, Hamilton described himself as "a dead man walking," so at the mercy of drugs that he blew all of his money, frequented dangerous areas, and passed out in places he didn't even know. His wife Katie played a huge role in pushing Hamilton to fight for normalcy. She always told him he would be back playing baseball and that there was a bigger plan for him on the world stage than just squandering his talent and disintegrating as a person.

"How am I here?" Hamilton said. "I can only shrug and say, 'It's a God thing.' It's the only possible explanation. Every day I'm reminded that my story is bigger than me. It never fails. Every time I go to the ballpark I talk to people who are either battling addictions themselves or are trying to help someone else who is."

Despite all of the abuse heaped upon his 6'4", 235-pound body, Hamilton

White Sox players carry Jim Thome after the designated hitter belted his 500ᵗʰ career home run—a game-winning two-run home run in the bottom of the ninth inning to beat the Los Angeles Angels—on September 16, 2007. *(Matthew Kutz/MLB Photos via Getty Images)*

has become the player that scouts envisioned when they saw him in high school. He is a three-time All-Star and in 2010 led the Rangers to the first playoff series win in the club's 50 years of existence and on into the World Series.

While Hamilton and the Rangers were still going in the playoffs, it was announced that major league players had voted for Hamilton as the *Sporting News* Player of the Year.

Hamilton got a later start than he would have ordinarily, but Jim Thome was headed into a crossroads year in

2010. The left-handed swinging star of the Cleveland Indians, Philadelphia Phillies, and Chicago White Sox was well into the 500s in career home runs and eyeing 600.

SLUGGER JIM WINDS DOWN

The 6'4", 245-pound Thome, who broke into the majors with the Indians in 1991, belted his 500ᵗʰ homer on September 16, 2007. His bottom of the ninth shot was a two-run blast that won the game for the White Sox over the Angels.

> "I've been blessed to be able to play a long time. I think baseball has done a good job cleaning up the game. At the end of the day, you just have to know you did it the right way."
>
> —*Jim Thome*

"Just can't believe it," Thome said. "I really can't. I would never have imagined doing that as a walk-off. Just amazing to see your teammates there [at home plate]. It's like a movie."

Thome's 500th homer was retrieved by a fan who lived outside of Chicago and was in the Windy City attending a convention. Thome and the White Sox traded the man a multitude of goodies for the ball. Thome promptly announced that he planned to give it to the Baseball Hall of Fame but that he wanted to make a special trip to the Hall with his father Chuck to hand-deliver it.

After snowstorms postponed their trip a couple of times, Thome and his dad finally made their trip to the Hall of Fame 11 months later, and they had a fun journey. Thome handed over the game ball to Hall vice president Ted Spencer, and rather than do so in the privacy of an office, Spencer presided over a short, public ceremony with about 100 onlookers.

"This doesn't happen to us very often," Spencer said of the Hall's acceptance of gifts. "Usually, these things come in the mail."

Thome, who grew up in Peoria, Illinois, was always a Chicago baseball fan. When he was growing up he revered the Cubs' Ernie Banks, so it felt special when he passed Banks (and Eddie Mathews at the same time) on the all-time home run list on April 24, 2008, with his 513th career four-bagger.

"I mean, Mr. Cub," Thome said. "I grew up a Cubs fan."

Banks sent Thome a congratulatory telegram.

Thome is one slugger who has never been mentioned in connection with performance-enhancing drugs, though he recognizes that he hit his homers in the middle of that era.

"I've been blessed to be able to play a long time," Thome said. "I think baseball has done a good job cleaning up the game. At the end of the day, you just have to know you did it the right way."

Also during the 2010 season, Ken Griffey Jr. retired with 630 home runs. Like Thome there has never been a hint of use of performance-enhancing drugs by Junior. Thome understands that everyone who played at the same time and hit large numbers of home runs is going to be at least partially suspect by someone.

"You can't change that," he said of the steroid era. "You can't deny that's been a part of our era. The important thing that people need to understand is that not everybody has done that. I'm not going to bash anybody. It was wrong. I think everybody understands that. If you do wrong things, you'll pay the consequences."

After a month spent with the Los Angeles Dodgers at the end of the 2009 season as his long-term contract expired, Thome went team shopping. He was turning 40 before the end of the 2010 season and he had to be a designated hitter, so that would be held against him. He wanted to win a World Series, so that eliminated some teams with no chance.

But Thome found employment and a niche with the Minnesota Twins. He clobbered 25 homers to put him at 589 career shots. In 2010 he passed Harmon Killebrew, Mark McGwire, and Frank Robinson. There is no one else between Thome and 600, and there are only Barry Bonds, Hank Aaron, Babe Ruth, Willie Mays, Griffey, Alex Rodriguez, and Sammy Sosa ahead of him. He would indeed be in special company if he reaches 600 homers.

Although the end of his career is near, Thome's good-guy personality enhances any clubhouse, and his dual purpose of winning a Series and becoming the seventh player to hit 600 home runs still motivates him to play on. He still loves playing base-

Frank Thomas on the last home run of his career, No. 521

"I didn't think it would be the last one. I'm tied with Ted Williams. That's pretty cool, but I thought it would be easy to get to 550. I wasn't thinking of retiring at all. I wanted to keep playing, but that didn't work out. So 521 turned out to be the last one."

Thomas's final home run tied him with Ted Williams and Willie McCovey in the 500 home run club, on August 9, 2008, versus Armando Galarraga of the Detroit Tigers.

ball, and he hopes his body won't let him down now that he has hit athletic old age.

"I think I'll love this game long after my body gives out, you know?" Thome said.

There's only one thing to do—keep swinging for those home runs.

Notes

31 **Why not? I had a better year than he did:** Baseball Almanac.com, Babe Ruth quotes.

32 **It's like a heavyweight fight...:** National Baseball Hall of Fame Library Archives.

33 **Maybe he'll get bored and go away:** National Baseball Hall of Fame Library and Archives, various versions of quote.

34 **I guess a lot of people think...:** Jeff Wallner, "Baseball America Celebrates the Home Run."

36 **But Mr. McGraw...:** Bob Broeg, "Mel Ott...McGraw's Pet and a Home-Run Hero," *The Sporting News*, June 12, 1971.

36 **I know, Ott...:** ibid.

36 **If I fired Mel...:** ibid.

39 **To the boy...:** "Kid Who Retrieved Babe's 700th Home Run Ball Still has $20 Bill," no publication name, National Baseball Hall of Fame Library and Archives, July 15, 1973.

39 **I'm telling you, it was the longest...:** "Babe's Homers Not Bush," Associated Press, March 28, 1974.

39 **Lord, I'd give my right arm...:** Roger Kahn, "The Real Ruth," *Baseball Digest*, October/November 1959, from *Esquire*.

39 **A holy sinner...:** ibid.

CHAPTER 3: AFTER RUTH

43 **Added pressure of being Jewish...:** *The Scribner Encyclopedia of American Lives: Volume Two*, (Farmington Hills, MI: Gale 1999), Hank Greenberg section reprint.

44–45 **There was only one Babe Ruth...:** Hank Greenberg, "How to Hit a Home Run," *Collier's*, April 22, 1939,

45 **When I say that I worshipped Babe Ruth...:** ibid.

45 **It's a funny thing about home runs...:** ibid.

45 **I didn't feel tired...:** ibid.

46 **Oh yeah?:** Stan Baumgartner. "Legs and Eyes Sound, Declares Foxx, at 37," *The Sporting News*, February 22, 1945.

46 **If I could have hit only against...:** Bob Broeg, "The Glory Days of 'Double X,'" *Sport Guide*, September 7, 1970.

47 **I'm convinced that Ralph Kiner...:** Hank Greenberg and Tim Cohane, "Hank Greenberg Says—'Ralph Kiner Will Break Babe Ruth's Home Run Record,'" *Look*, May 1948.

47 **I figured he was the greatest hitter...:** Marino Amoruso, "Ralph Kiner: During One Seven-Year Span, He was Simply the Game's Greatest Home Run Hitter!" *Sports Collectors Digest*, February 3, 1994.

47 **To beat the 60 mark...:** Hank Greenberg and Tim Cohane, "Hank Greenberg Says—'Ralph Kiner Will Break Babe Ruth's Home Run Record,'" *Look*, May 1948.

48 **Homers win more games than hits:** Les Biederman, "Homers Win More Games than Hits Says Ralph Kiner," *Sporting Life*, July 1949.

50 **Almost every threat to Ruth's record...:** ibid.

51 **Although I was playing...:** Marino Amoruso, "Ralph Kiner: During One Seven-Year Span, He was Simply the Game's Greatest Home Run Hitter!" *Sports Collectors Digest*, February 3, 1994.

51 **We finished last with you...:** Baseball-Almanac.com (Quoted various places).

52 **All I want out of life is that when I walk...:** Famousquotesandauthors.com (Quoted various places).

53 **How far away must one sit...?:** Harold Kaese, "Ted's Longest Homer Pierces Straw Hat on Head 450 Feet Away," *Boston Globe*, June 9, 1946.

54 **I could pick up his arm...:** Dan Shaughnessy, "Long Ago It Went Far Away," *Boston Globe*, June 9, 1996.

56 **I understand, naturally...:** Gerry Moore, "Ted Williams Says, 'Curb Baseball's Intentional Walk,'" *Sports Guide*, March 1941.

58 **I was gunning for the big one:** Bob Duffy, "Out With a Bang," *Boston Globe*, July 5, 2002.

CHAPTER 4: MINOR LEAGUE WHAMMERS

62 **It seemed like that ball...:** Associated Press, "Another Homer Mark Falls to Bonds," October 7, 2001.

64 **We were the best-fed...:** Richard Stevens, "N.M's Own Homer Hero Hit 72 in '54," *Albuquerque Tribune*, September 23, 1998.

65 **I told them that I could make more money...:** Associated Press, "Hit 72 in 1954: Minor league HR king Joe Bauman dead at 83," September 20, 2005.

65 **I don't really know...:** Thomas Rogers, "Sultan of a C League," *New York Times*, June 4, 1982.

65 **It didn't bother me or anything...:** Associated Press, "Another Homer Mark Falls to Bonds," October 7, 2001.

66 **I'm proud of it...:** Associated Press, "Hit 72 in 1954: Minor league HR king Joe Bauman dead at 83," September 20, 2005.

68 **After the season was over...:** Dan Daly, "Minor Hero: 'Moose' Clabaugh Hit 62 Homers—But He Wasn't a Major Figure," *Arizona Republic*, May 30, 1981.

68 **I talked to the major league scouts...:** ibid.

68 **I hit No. 62...:** ibid.

69 **I led the league in stolen jockstraps...:** Chuck McAnulla, "Bob Lennon Brushed Up Against Greatness in a Career that Included Some Major & Minor Accomplishments," *Sports Collectors Digest*, June 2, 1995.

70 **Nobody tried to tell me anything...:** Joe King, "Mize Alters Stance of Slugger Lennon," *New York World Telegram*, March 1, 1957.

70 **So I hit one off the center-field...:** Chuck McAnulla, "Bob Lennon brushed up against greatness in a career that included some Major & Minor accomplishments," *Sports Collectors Digest*, June 2, 1995.

70–71 **He was a great ballplayer...:** ibid.

71 **I said...:** ibid.

73 **Nice guy, Double X...:** "Joe Hauser: A Great Old Time Slugger," *Oldtyme Baseball News* 6, no. 5.

73 **There's nothing in baseball to compare...:** Milton Richman, "Babe Ruth of the Minors Retains Sweet Swing at 80," United Press International, July 1979.

73 **I didn't even have my eyes open yet:** ibid.

73 **I get into the box...:** ibid.

73–74 **A great man...:** ibid.

74 **I thought I was gonna hit 100...:** "Epic feats: Three players reminisce about breaking 60 barrier," National Baseball Hall of Fame Library Archives.

74 **I had those broken legs...:** "Joe Hauser: A Great Old Time Slugger," *Oldtyme Baseball News* 6, no. 5.

76 **The guy who breaks...:** Jimmy Breslin, "Dick Stuart: Pittsburgh's Problem and Baseball's Dilemma," *True*, September 1959.

76 **Sure I strike out a lot...:** Stan Hochman, "The Man Who Hit 66 Hrs," *Philadelphia Daily News*, March 14, 1962.

77 **Don't ask me why...:** Melvin Durslag, "Radatz Suggested License Plate for Stuart—It's 'E-3,'" *Los Angeles Herald-Examiner*, April 18, 1964.

77 **This is a new experience for me...:** Lester J. Biederman, "Dick Stuart 'Having A Ball' Playing Baseball in Japan," *Pittsburgh Press*, June 4, 1967.

78 **They loved Daddy over there...:** Dave Anderson, "When 'Bay-bee' Ruth Toured Japan," *New York Times*, March 26, 2000.

79 **Mr. Oh is like a god here:** David Haugh, "Oh Truly Means King," *Chicago Tribune*, July 7, 2007.

79 **I believe Oh would hit...:** Bill Lyon, "Oh Would Hit 700 HRs in U.S., Says Johnson," *The Sporting News*, January 7, 1978.

79–80 **Aaron had a short...:** ibid.

80 **How many homers he would hit...:** Joseph Durso, "Mr. Oh and Mr. Ruth," *New York Times*, August 21, 1976.

81 **The number of home runs I hit...:** Ken Marantz, "How Many Homers Could Oh Have Hit Here?" *USA TODAY Baseball Weekly*, August 6–12, 1997.

81 **Mentally, I have not been able to inspire...** Mike Tharp, "Oh Puts Bat to Rest at 40," *New York Times,* November 5, 1980.

CHAPTER 5: WILLIE MAYS AND FRIENDS

87 **Don't let this guy hit...:** James S. Hirsch, *Willie Mays: The Life, The Legend* (New York: Scribner 2010), p. 342.

87 **Man, after you get two…:** ibid., p. 342–43.

89 **For sheer power…:** "'Chance for Him to Become Top Power Hitter'—Dickey," *The Sporting News*, April 29, 1953.

89–90 **I'm glad it's over…:** Norm Miller, "Like Winning Last Game in WS: Mick," *New York Daily News*, May 15, 1967.

90 **I don't care if it was his first…:** "Mantle's No. 500 Stu's Birds, 6–5," *New York Daily News*, May 15, 1967, Dana Mozley.

90 **It was Mickey's hour…:** ibid.

91 **I have no doubt about it…:** "McLain Obliges Second Time, So Mantle Belts Homer No. 535," *Newsday*, September 20, 1968.

91 **You don't think I'd deliberately…:** ibid.

92 **God gave me the ability…:** Associated Press, "Mickey Mantle Dead at 63," August 14, 1995.

92 **He was the best player I ever saw…:** ibid.

93 **Let's play two…:** Jim Murray, "The Grand Old Game Should Be Embarrassed," *Los Angeles Times*.

93 **The riches of the game are in the thrills…:** *The Sporting News*, May 12, 1970.

93 **My winning was winning the respect…:** Qumar Zaman, "More Than 500 Reasons to Talk with Mr. Cub," *Chicago Sun-Times*, July 18, 2004.

93–94 **That's kind of what my life has always been…:** Fred Mitchell, "Fred Mitchell's Q&A," *Chicago Tribune*, April 21, 2004.

94 **It's the greatest thrill of my life…:** James Enright, "Banks in Grand Slam Record," *Chicago American*, September 20, 1955.

95 **The pitch was a fastball…:** Edgar Munzel, "Banks, on 500th, Thought of Mom and Dad," *The Sporting News*, May 30, 1970.

95 **I was thinking about my mother and dad…:** ibid.

96 **Old Man Banks hit No. 500…:** ibid.

97 **I didn't want to think…:** John Wilson, "Mathews Crashes 500-HR Club," no publication, National Baseball Hall of Fame Library Archives, July 29, 1967.

97 **I realized it was quite a milestone…:** Bob Allen and Bill Gilbert, *The 500 Home Run Club* (Champaign, Illinois: Sports Publishing Inc., 1999).

98 **I lost sight of the ball…:** Arthur Daley, "Newest Member of Five Hundred Club," *New York Times*, September 22, 1971.

99 **It was not one of my best…:** ibid.

100 **I don't like to set goals…:** Max Nichols, "A Modern Ruth? Killer Can Claim Title," *The Sporting News*, April 17, 1965.

101 **Maybe I'll hit you a couple:** Michael Mok, "Killebrew Homers His Way into Boy's Heart Forever," *New York Daily News*, May 21, 1964.

101 **Harmon's going to hit 600…:** Arno Goethel, "Killer Passes 400-Homer Milestone," *The Sporting News*, May 17, 1965.

101 **I'm glad that's over with:** Associated Press, "Killer 500th May Lead to Homer Tear—Rigney," August 12, 1971.

102 **Harmon hit home runs like…:** Tom Briere, "Baseball Hall of Fame is Final Chapter in Killebrew's Career," *Minneapolis Star and Tribune*, August 12, 1984.

102 **I always had good strength…:** ibid.

102 **My first homer was just as important…:** Associated Press, "Just Another Homer," August 29, 1963.

102 **I saw your first one…:** Bob Stevens, "Willie Wallops 500th HR; Ott's 511 Next Goal," *San Francisco Chronicle*, September 25, 1965.

102 **I just want to keep winning…:** ibid.

102 **It was a milestone in Willie's career…:** Bob Stevens, "'Milestone, But Just Another Lousy Homer to Me'—Osteen," *The Sporting News*, May 21, 1966.

102 **I wondered if I was ever going to get a hit…:** Associated Press, "No. 600 Is a Ruthian Home Run for Willie Mays," *New York Times*, September 22, 1969.

103 **I'm just glad…:** James S. Hirsch, *Willie Mays: The Life, The Legend* (New York: Scribner 2010), p. 487.

CHAPTER 6: HOME RUN DERBY AND HOME RUN POTPOURRI

106 **I've seen this fella...:** 1960 *Home Run Derby* video, episodes 16–22.

108 **It's off the wall...:** ibid.

108 **He hit one out...:** ibid.

109 **Good-bye:** ibid.

109 **It's getting to be real embarrassing...:** ibid.

112 **I guess it's pretty ridiculous...:** Gordon Eddes, "Red Sox's Nava Has Arrived," ESPN. com, June 17, 2010.

117 **I could tell during batting practice...:** Personal interview.

117 **It was a good way...:** ibid.

117 **I was not sure...:** ibid.

118 **I just got a slider...:** ibid.

118 **That's the first time...:** ibid.

120 **Everybody's always talking about...:** TheBaseballPage.com

121 **I'd prefer an owner with...:** *Chicago Sun-Times*, Mike Royko.

121 **I've pulled practical jokes...:** "Kingman Fined $3,500," *New York Times*, June 25, 1986, Associated Press.

122 **Hitting is better than sex:** *Esquire*, March 1, 1978.

122 **Better than sex?:** "Hummmm Dingers!" *The Sporting News*, July 8, 1996, Michael Knisley.

125 **If you're around long enough...:** Associated Press, "Moyer Gives Up 505th Homer to Tie Record," June 23, 2010.

125 **I don't think I can get into...:** Roger Angell, *Late Innings*, (New York: Simon & Schuster 1982).

126 **I was helping my cause...:** Personal interview.

126 **I got a case of Wheaties...:** ibid.

127 **It's very tough...:** ibid.

128 **There'll be a man on the moon...:** "Gaylord Perry," *SI Vault (Sports Illustrated)*, July 13, 2009, Elizabeth McGarr.

129 **I was just trying...:** "Grand Slam! Grand Slam!" *Newark Star-Ledger*, (no date), Pat Borzi.

129 **A no-hitter would mean more...:** "Cloninger Pitcher First, Always," *Houston Chronicle*, July 5, 1966, Dick Peebles.

CHAPTER 7: THE MOST FAMOUS HOME RUNS OF ALL TIME

132 **By the time I reached...:** Scott Pitoniak, "Mazeroski's Moment in Time," *Rochester Democrat & Chronicle*, October, 1990.

133 **I just figured it was another home run...:** Robert Dvorchak, "50 years later, Mazeroski's Home Run is Bigger than Ever," *Pittsburgh Post-Gazette*, September 6, 2010.

134 **It means a lot...:** Bob Herzog, "Maz's Moment Will Never be Over," Newsday.com, June 14, 2005.

134–35 **When I look at it...:** Robert Dvorchak, "50 Years Later, Mazeroski's Home Run is Bigger than Ever," *Pittsburgh Post-Gazette*, September 6, 2010.

135 **I imagined I hit a home run...:** Bob Herzog, "Maz's Moment Will Never be Over," Newsday.com, June 14, 2005.

137 **If you ever hit one...:** Hal Bock, "The Day Time Stood Still," Associated Press, October 2, 2001.

137 **That first pitch was a blur...:** Phil Pepe, "Whatta Shot!" *New York Post*, May 10, 1991.

137 **Sink!:** Hal Bock, "The Day Time Stood Still," Associated Press, October 2, 2001.

138 **It's one of those things...:** ibid.

139 **The thing, that moment...:** Joe Hamelin, "Thomson, Branca Share Fate, Friendship," *Riverside Inland Empire*, June 13, 2000.

140 **We're married to each other...:** John Rawitch, "The 'Shot' Heard 'Round the World,'" MLB.com, July 24, 2002.

140 **My gosh...:** Earl Gustkey, "Did Thomson Know What Was Coming?" *Los Angeles Times*, October 3, 1981.

141 **The Giants stole the pennant...:** Baxter Holmes, "Branca's solid baseball career is still defined by one inglorious moment," *Los Angeles Times*, August 24, 2010.

141 **I'm just an old guy...:** Stephen Borelli, "Years later, fame of 'shot' lives on for Bobby Thomson," *USA TODAY*, May 20, 2009.

141 **It's never haunted me…:** Kay Gilman, "The Way It Was," *New York Daily News*, October 6, 1974.

143–44 **It's funny…:** John Connolly, "Carlton Fisk Home Run Forever Frozen in Time," *Baseball Digest*, October 2001.

145 **I don't remember much afterwards…:** ibid.

145 **I never thought about it…:** ibid.

145 **I was just wishing and hoping…:** Jimmy Golen, "Red Sox Name Left-Field Pole After Fisk," Associated Press, June 14, 2005.

147 **It was a storybook ending…:** Rob Gloster, "One Moment in Mind as A's, Dodgers Meet," *Hartford Courant*, June 8, 1997.

147 **Heartbreak…:** ibid.

147 **If I had stopped playing…:** ibid.

147 **I took an ugly swing…:** ibid.

148 **Where the ball hit the bat…:** Bill Plaschke, "Revisit the Impossible," *Los Angeles Times*, June 7, 2005.

148 **How many times?:** Tom Weir, "Carter Makes History, Savors It," *USA TODAY*, October 25, 1993.

149 **The public will not…:** Mel Antonen, "Jays' Carter an Unsung Hero at Home," *USA TODAY*, January 10, 1994.

151 **When I hit the ball…:** Harvey Frommer, "Bucky Dent Home Run Game," Baseball Almanac.com.

CHAPTER 8: THE GREAT CHASES: MANTLE AND MARIS; SOSA, McGWIRE, AND GRIFFEY

160 **It was only when…:** Tom Clavin and Danny Peary, *Roger Maris: Baseball's Reluctant Hero* (New York: Touchstone Books 2010) p. 198.

161 **The only thing we argued about…:** ibid.

161 **Freak in a sideshow:** ibid.

161 **You'll have to take it…:** ibid.

164 **I was ready and connected…:** ibid.

164 **Jeez, he just broke…:** ibid.

165 **I try to hit it hard…:** Steve Jacobson, "Maturity Powers a Leadoff Hitter," *Newsday*, June 28, 1996.

165–66 **Because I only hit 50 home runs…:** Roch Kubatko, "Anderson Defends His '96 Power Trip, Says 'It Was Not a Fluke,'" *Baltimore Sun*, March 20, 2004.

169 **If anyone can do it…:** Pete Williams, "The Kid Can," *USA TODAY Baseball Weekly*, June 4–10, 1997.

170 **I don't think he would have…:** Ken Rosenthal, "Junior's Chase for Immortality," *Baltimore Sun*, May 31, 1997.

170 **He's a perfect guy to do it…:** ibid.

172 **Babe Ruth. What can you say?:** Mike Eisenbath, "McGwire Savors Feat of Joining Ruth with 60," *St. Louis Post-Dispatch*.

173 **It's unbelievable…:** Tom Weir, "Herculean Task Completed with Only Feet to Spare," *USA TODAY*, September 9, 1998.

174 **For generations fans will remember…:** ibid.

175 **It's unheard of for someone…:** Kevin Kernan, Anthony Gargano, Mara Weisman, and William Neuman, "Mac Cracks, Twin HRs Cap Historic Season," *New York Post*, September 28, 1998.

175 **You never know…:** Mike Dodd, "Sosa Helped his Team More," *USA TODAY*, November 20, 1998.

CHAPTER 9: HOME RUN KINGS: HANK AARON AND BARRY BONDS

178 **Move Over, Babe…:** Song lyrics, "Move Over, Babe (Here Comes Henry)," by Ernie Harwell and Bill Slayback, Karen Records, 1973.

179 **He was a deceptive home run hitter…:** Bob Allen and Bill Gilbert, *The 500 Home Run Club* (Champaign, Illinois: Sports Publishing Inc., 1999).

181 **When you wait all your life…:** ibid., p. 2.

181 **It was no cheapie…:** "Aaron's 400th Goes Over 500 Feet," National Baseball Hall of Fame Library Archives, United Press International.

182 **They found it on a parking lot…:** ibid.

182 **It was a fastball…:** ibid.

183 **Henry Aaron is the best right-handed hitter...:** Bob Hertzel, "Leo Durocher Says: 'Aaron Best Since Hornsby,'" *Atlanta Journal*, June 28, 1966.

183 **And for the first time...:** Bob Broeg, "Shorter Swing Keeps Aaron Hitting Homers at 39," *St. Louis Post-Dispatch*, May 29, 1973.

184 **I think I have a chance...:** "Ask Them Yourself," *Utica Observer-Dispatch, Family Weekly*, October 15, 1972.

184 **The press used to forget about me...:** Associated Press, "Aaron Joins the Babe's 700 HR Club," *New York Daily News*, July 22, 1973.

186 **Hank Aaron, With that fortune and all that fame...:** Hank Aaron and Lonnie Wheeler, *If I Had A Hammer: The Hank Aaron Story* (New York: HarperPaperbacks, 1992), p. 340.

186 **Dear Nigar Aaron...:** ibid., p. 339.

186 **I decided that the best way to shut up...:** Wayne Minshew, "Hate Mail Was Inspiration to Aaron," *The Sporting News*, November 3, 1973.

186 **They drove me to it...:** Lee Michael Katz, "Hank Aaron: He Looks Back at Some Bitter Memories; Ahead with Sights on Commissioner Job," *Los Angeles Times Syndicate*.

189 **People tell me I made a great catch...:** Jeff Miller, "Snagging a Place in History," *Dallas Morning News*, April 7, 2004.

189 **I caught the ball...:** ibid.

189 **Groove it?:** Dick Young, "Aaron's 715 Not Groovy," *New York Daily News*, April 10, 1974.

190 **It was a sad time...:** Bill Koenig, "There's a New Home Run Champion of All Time and It's Henry Aaron," *USA TODAY Baseball Weekly*, April 7–13.

191 **I am honored...:** Charles Odum, "Delta Unveils Hank Aaron 755 Aircraft," Associated Press, June 18, 2007.

191 **I didn't want to let go of the bat...:** Mark Gonzales, "Milestone of his own," *San Jose Mercury News*, August 24, 1998.

192 **This says a lot about his ability...:** ibid.

192 **When I hit it, I couldn't believe I hit it...:** Associated Press, "Bonds' 500th Homer a Game-Winner," April 17, 2001.

192 **It depends on my health...:** "500th Home Run Links Bonds with Man Who Snared Ball," *San Jose Mercury News*, April 18, 2001, Michael Martinez.

193 **For those of us...:** "House Honors Bonds," Associated Press, October 30, 2001.

194 **He swears we're related...:** Mike Lupica, "Mr. October Is Sorry Barry Plays Fall Guy," *New York Daily News*, October 3, 2001.

194 **His arrogance...:** ibid.

195 **It just cannot get...:** Gwen Knapp, "Bonds Fulfills Quest to Overtake Legend," *San Francisco Chronicle*, May 29, 2006.

196 **It's a great honor...:** John Shea, "Milestone Man: He Sets Sights on Aaron—And A Title," *San Francisco Chronicle*, May 29, 2006.

196 **I don't have any thoughts...:** Associated Press, Charles Odum, "Delta Unveils Hank Aaron 755 Aircraft," June 18, 2007.

197 **Skill, longevity and determination:** Jack Curry, "Bonds Hits No. 756 to Break Aaron's Record," *New York Times*, August 8, 2007.

197 **This record is not tainted...:** ibid.

197 **While the issues...:** ibid.

199 **I don't think you can put an asterisk....:** Associated Press, "Bonds Says He'll Boycott Hall if Record-Setting Ball has Asterisk," November 1, 2007.

199 **I will never be in the Hall of Fame...:** ibid.

CHAPTER 10: STEROIDS—WAS IT ALL FAKE?

206 **I'm not here to talk about the past:** CNN, March 18, 2005.

208 **We need to get it over with...:** "Report: Sosa Tested Positive in 2003," ESPN.com, June 16, 2009.

209 **I think if people are proven guilty...:** Jay Posner, "Jackson Wants ★ If Steroid Use is Proved," SanDiego.com, May 8, 2006.

209–10 **They should asterisk it...:** ibid.

210 **I get angry...:** ibid.

213 **So I started to ask him...:** Mark Fainaru–Wada and Lance Williams, "Giambi Admitted Taking Steroids," *San Francisco Chronicle*, December 2, 2004.

213 **At the end of the day each player...:** Hal Bodley, "Sosa's Suspension Cut to 7 Games," *USA TODAY*, June 12, 2003.

214 **If what I did was an error...:** C.J. Mahaney, "Andy Pettitte and My Confession of Sin," Sovereign Grace Ministries, February 22, 2008.

214 **From the bottom of my heart...:** ibid.

216 **I want to state clearly...:** "Clemens Fires Back, Denies Taking Steroids or HGH," Associated Press, December 18, 2007.

218 **I personally hate controversy...:** Daniel Brown, "Ruth's Daughter Feels Sad for Baseball," *San Jose Mercury News*, March 12, 2006.

218 **Back then...:** "A-Rod Admits, Regrets Use of PEDs," ESPN.com, Feburary 9, 2009.

218 **I did take a banned substance...:** ibid.

218 **To be honest...:** ibid.

219 **It was his understanding...:** Michael O'Keefe, "A-Rod Hits It Big," *New York Daily News*, November 22, 2008.

220 **It was a relief...:** Ronald Blum, "Alex Rodriguez Hits Homer No. 600 in Yankees Win," Associated Press, August 5, 2010.

220 **I know a lot of fans...:** Marc Carig, "Yankees' Alex Rodriguez Hits 600th Home Run, Acknowledges Doubts Fans Might Have," *Newark Star-Ledger*, August 4, 2010.

221 **It took me three years to the day...:** ibid.

CHAPTER 11: TODAY'S SLUGGERS

225 **The only thing I ever say to him...:** Daniel G. Habib, "El Hombre," *Sports Illustrated*, November 8, 2006.

225–26 **Nothing fazes him and his swing...:** ibid.

228 **I don't want to sound cocky...:** Joe Posnanski, "The Power to Believe," *Sports Illustrated*, March 16, 2006.

229: **We both didn't get off to a great start...:** Personal interview.

229 **Then Jermaine went up to the plate...:** ibid.

230 **You know how I want...:** Joe Posnanski, "The Power to Believe," *Sports Illustrated*, March 16, 2006.

230 **Lies. That's a lie...:** Kyle Kosteron, "Ryan Howard–Albert Pujols Supertrade Talks Denied by Phillies GM," *Chicago Sun-Times*, March 15, 2010.

232 **I was just going to try to make the most of it:** Todd Zolecki, "Phils' Howard Named NL Rookie of the Year," *Philadelphia Inquirer*, November 8, 2005.

232 **It should be illegal...:** Ken Mandel, "Howard Fastest in History to 100 Homers," MLB.com, June 28, 2007.

232 **I hit it pretty good...:** ibid.

232 **He definitely smoked...:** ibid.

233 **It's always good...:** ibid.

233 **It's a nice feat...:** "Phillies' Howard Becomes Fastest to 200 HRs," Associated Press, July 17, 2009.

233 **I hit it out to right-center:** Personal interview.

233–34 **It felt good...:** ibid.

234 **You've just got to find...:** ibid.

235 **Toward the latter end of the second half:** Jorge L. Ortiz, "Phillies' Howard Edges Cardinals' Pujols for NL MVP," *USA TODAY*, November 21, 2006.

235 **It's hard to believe...:** Rich Hofmann, "The Birth of a Slugger," *Philadelphia Daily News*, June 23, 2006.

235 **While I feel I am still able...:** "Mariners' Griffey Jr. Retires with 630 Home Runs," ESPN.com, June 3, 2010.

235 **It's a sad day for the Mariners...:** ibid.

236 **Some day in the off-season...:** Ken Mandel, "Howard Sets Club Homer Record," MLB.com, September 1, 2006,

236 **There's a bunch of humans out here...:** Mike Cole, "Top 10 Manny Ramirez Quotes," NESN.com, June 17, 2010.

238 **It was a great feeling...:** Steve Krasner, "Swinging for a Record," *Providence Journal*, September 22, 2006.

239 **To keep continually doing it...:** Tim Sullivan, "Ortiz Quickly Becoming Boston's Mr. Overtime," *San Diego Union-Tribune*, October 19, 2004.

239 **I would suggest everybody get tested...:** Peter Gammons, "Spring Training Blog," MLB.com, February, 2009.

239-40 **I was definitely a little bit careless...:** "David Ortiz Speaks to the Media About Report On 2003 Positive Test for PEDs," ESPN.com.

241 **I do....:** Bill Lankhof, "Bautista clean as they come," QMI Agency, September 23, 2010.

241-42 **It's a big honor...:** "Jose Bautista Joins Elite 50-homer Club," Associated Press, September 24, 2010.

242 **He's always had power...:** Pat Borzi, "Bautista Shortens His Swing and Sends More Balls a Longer Distance," *New York Times*, October 2, 2010.

242 **It's not a secret...:** ibid.

244 **You deserve it...:** Albert Chen, "The Super Natural," *Sports Illustrated*, May 27, 2008.

244 **A dead man walking:** Josh Hamilton and Tim McKeown, "I'm Proof that Hope is Never Lost," *ESPN The Magazine*, July 5, 2007.

244 **How am I here?:** ibid.

246 **Just can't believe it...:** September 17, 2007, "Thome Reaches 500 HR Milestone in Walk-Off Fashion," ESPN.com.

246 **This doesn't happen to us very often...:** Jim Margalus, "Thome has Hall of Fame Off Day," *Albany Times-Union*, August 29, 2008.

246 **I mean, Mr. Cub...:** Dave van Dyck, "More than Mr. Cub? It's Hard for Him to Fathom," *Chicago Tribune*, April 26, 2008.

246 **I've been blessed to be able...:** Jim Margalus, "Thome has Hall of Fame Off Day," *Albany Times-Union*, August 29, 2008.

247 **You can't change that...:** Bill Shaikin, "Dodgers slugger Jim Thome has long trip to Hall," *Los Angeles Times*, September 6, 2009.

247 **I think I'll love this game...:** Joe Posnanski, "Still Going Strong," *Sports Illustrated*, September 27, 2010.

Lew Freedman has authored more than 30 books. The award-winning journalist is currently the sports editor at *The Republic* newspaper in Columbus, Indiana. He has previously worked for the *Chicago Tribune*, the *Anchorage Daily News*, and *The Philadelphia Inquirer*.

Freedman's other Triumph Books titles are *Cubs Essential, White Sox Essential, Then Ozzie Said to Harold…The Best Chicago White Sox Stories Ever Told, The 50 Greatest Plays in Chicago Bears Football History*, and *Fergie: My Life from the Cubs to Cooperstown* with Hall of Fame pitcher Ferguson Jenkins. He lives with his wife, Debra, in Columbus, Indiana.